David Buchanan, Richmond Thatcher

An Australian Orator

Speeches: political, social, literary and theological, delivered in the Parliament of

New South Wales, and on the public platform

David Buchanan, Richmond Thatcher

An Australian Orator
Speeches: political, social, literary and theological, delivered in the Parliament of New South Wales, and on the public platform

ISBN/EAN: 9783337071882

Printed in Europe, USA, Canada, Australia, Japan

Cover: Foto ©Suzi / pixelio.de

More available books at **www.hansebooks.com**

AN AUSTRALIAN ORATOR

SPEECHES, POLITICAL, SOCIAL, LITERARY AND
THEOLOGICAL, DELIVERED IN THE PARLIAMENT
OF NEW SOUTH WALES, AND ON THE PUBLIC
PLATFORM

BY

DAVID BUCHANAN

*Of the Middle Temple, Barrister at Law, Member of the Parliament of New
South Wales for the last Twenty-five Years*

EDITED BY

RICHMOND THATCHER

OF SYDNEY NEW SOUTH WALES

LONDON
REMINGTON AND CO PUBLISHERS
HENRIETTA STREET COVENT GARDEN
1886

To A. B.

THIS SMALL VOLUME IS DEDICATED BY

THE AUTHOR IN TESTIMONY OF A REGARD THAT WILL DIE

WITH HIM, AND WHICH ANY LANGUAGE HE

COULD USE WOULD FAIL TO EXPRESS.

SYDNEY, 1ST MAY, 1886.

PREFACE.

A FEW of the following speeches were published in Sydney, New South Wales, where they were delivered, most of them in the Parliament of the country. They were very favourably received in Australia, both by Press and people, and sold rapidly. The small volume then published is now considerably enlarged by the addition of several speeches, delivered since the date of the publication referred to, and is now published in London simply to satisfy an apparent curiosity which, in England, has grown of late, and which seems greatly to concern itself with all that pertains to the young, vigorous, wealthy, and rapidly progressing colonies of Australia.

Our country is not a hundred years old, that is, since its discovery and foundation by Englishmen. Our present Constitution and free Parliament have only been in existence since 1857, not thirty years. We have had some very eminent and able men in that Parliament, and, under those circumstances,

B

it may be interesting to the English reader to
have some means of judging of our Parliamentary
talk. I have therefore collected a number of Mr.
David Buchanan's ablest deliverances for publication in London. Mr. Buchanan has long been
a conspicuous figure in the public life of Australia.
He has been a member of the Parliament of New
South Wales for over a quarter of a century. He
has introduced and passed several important
measures, and he has always enjoyed the reputation of being a sterling, independent, out-spoken
Liberal, as those who may honour this little volume
with a glance will soon find out. No better idea
of Australian political life, action, and thought
could be attained than by a careful perusal of Mr.
Buchanan's terse, incisive, vigorous utterances.
All over Australia Mr. Buchanan has long enjoyed
the reputation of being an eloquent speaker, both
at the Bar and in the Senate. It may be that the
more fastidious English taste will not altogether
relish some of the more forcible of his effusions,
but they were relished by the keen, active,
energetic people of Australia, and are now
offered to the candid consideration of the English
public as a fair average sample of the public
political speech of New South Wales. The
Editor asks no favour in the consideration of
those speeches. He only asks that they may be
judged by their merits and with the fairness of
Englishmen.

RICHMOND THATCHER,

Randwick, New South Wales,
    26th March, 1886.

CAPITAL PUNISHMENT.

[On the 25th January, 1861, Sir Henry (then Mr.) Parkes moved the second reading of a Bill to abolish capital punishment, on which occasion Mr. Buchanan delivered the following speech :—]

MR. EWART's annual motion in the House of Commons to effect the purpose of this Bill has long rendered me familiar with all the arguments used to support the principle of the Bill now before the House, and which I trust will be thrown out by a decisive majority. The honourable member for East Sydney, Mr. Parkes, has not added anything new or original in the shape of argument to what we have already known as being continually put forth by the upholders of his views. Indeed, we could well afford to leave the honourable member unanswered, so little has he said that in any way calls for argumentative reply. The subject of prison discipline, or the proper and just dealing with prisoners, is one of large importance—all the more important when we reflect upon the strange notions that are abroad in reference to their treatment, and the

spurious diseased sympathy which seems to set in
in favour of great criminals, and of which the
Bill now before the House seems to be an emanation. I am afraid we are going so far with our
superfine philanthropy and heaven-born benevolence that we run a strong chance of losing all
distinction between the virtuous and the vicious,
the criminal and the upright honest man. There
are in all towns of the world, and in this town as
well, a large body of very poor struggling honest
people, who have remained honest amidst all
manner of squalid misery, battling with hardships
and privations in a life or death struggle for bare
existence. These people have endured all those
hardships and sufferings patiently and bravely,
and have preserved their integrity surrounded by
many temptations. They are poor and wretched,
but honest, and are sustained mainly by hope in
bearing up against the hardships of their lot.
Now this is the soil by cultivating which a
healthy philanthropy might reap a rich and
tangible harvest. No more wholesome, healthy,
or holy feeling than that of sympathy here.
Sympathy and active aid from philanthropy in
this quarter would be a blessed spectacle in
harmony with righteousness and truth, and
elevating and inspiring all concerned with the
purest feeling of religion. This is the proper
quarter for the exercise of a just and rational
philanthropy. When philanthropy and benevolence are spurious, as well as diseased, they
play strange pranks, and often most wofully
mistake the road. A jail, I always understood,
was a place of punishment, but the danger we
have to guard against is to see that it is not
transformed into a place of easy, comfortable,

quiet recreation and repose, entirely at the instance of the aforesaid diseased and spurious philanthropy. No man can be said to be possessed of a healthy moral feeling who does not hate the criminal scoundrel who compels you to confine him in a jail. There can be no love of the good and virtuous without a corresponding hate of the vicious and criminal; and the nature where this hatred does not exist is an unwholesome nature, diseased to the extent of almost rottenness. When prisoners are all properly classified in a jail, with a view to discipline and their own advantage, a uniform spirit of stern, sharp severity should pervade the place. They should be made to feel constantly that they are in a place of punishment, and that society detests them and their crimes until by repentance or reformation a better opinion or feeling is justified. The time was when the jail was a terror to evildoers; but poor, sickly, tottering philanthropy has pretty well shorn the place of all its terrors. What poor man lives so well or is so well cared for as the inmates of our jails? Are the honest poor housed as well, kept so clean, or fed so well, with doctors to attend them when ill, and clergymen to supply their spiritual wants? Well, then, I say that it is a blind, ignorant, diseased, and benighted sympathy that only feels an interest in a man when his detestable villany makes him the inmate of a prison. I maintain, and have always maintained, that every act of kindness by which things are made soft and comfortable for these prisoners in our jails is a wrong done to the poor honest man, who, outside, is contending with hardship and want to preserve his integrity, as well as his existence. Philanthropy, in these

days, is perpetrating no end of mischief in rendering it almost impossible to rule the ruffianism of
our prisons, teaching them by every means in its
power that their crimes have enlisted its love and
interest instead of its deepest and most authentic
hatred. All intermeddling, at the instance of
philanthropy, with the government of our prisons,
should be stopped forthwith. Even visitors should
not be allowed there, and the prisoners should
never see a face but those of their jailers, and be
taught to understand that both they and their
crimes are hated by every true honest man, which
cannot be altered but by their own repentance and
resolute purpose to amend. This question of
prison discipline is one that will have to be looked
into one of these days, not in the way of making
it more comfortable for prisoners, but in shaping
things so that the bare mention of the word jail
will never be heard by our scoundrel class without
a shudder. I trust honourable members, in consideration of the importance of this part of the
subject, will pardon me following it up a little
farther before considering what I believe to be the
advantage of the death punishment. I have said
that it is the duty of every healthy wholesome
nature to hate the criminal scoundrel who compels
you to lock him up in prison. There are two
principles existing here patent enough to all of us,
good and evil. There can be no love of both—the
love of the one necessitates the hatred of the other,
and how any man can say that he hates evil and
loves the doer of it is one of those problems
entirely beyond my comprehension. Let me put
a case to bring the truth of this matter vividly and
clearly before honourable members. A poor patient,
faithful, loving wife and mother finds the reward

of all her anxious kindness and devotion in brutal
ill-usage at the hands of her scoundrel husband.
She has borne this for years without murmur, but
it ends in the ruffian kicking and trampling the
life out of her. Does the Christian religion
encourage love for a detestable wretch of this
kind ? The Bill before the House, if passed into
law, which I trust it never will be, would save
him from the only punishment equal to his deserts ;
. but will any man answer me and say that that
man is in a healthy state, morally, whose soul
does not blaze into fiery and divine hatred of such
a ruffian. I am sick to death of this weak,
effeminate mixing up of right and wrong, good
and bad, and pretending to see no difference
between them, but to have the same feelings of
love, pity, and sympathy for the criminal that
are entertained by all good men for the struggling,
devoted poor but honest man. Who can say what
may happen in these days if the philanthropy that
staggers about like a drunken lunatic gets the
upper hand, and is allowed to do as it likes inside
our jails. Most pernicious is that ignorance and
mawkish cant that is perpetually getting up an
agitation to save some detestable criminal from
his appropriate punishment. If this sickly system
of spurious benevolence in the treatment of our
prisoners is continued we will very soon be
admonished to change our tactics. I do not
wish to shut the door against a prisoner's reformation, I rather wish to open every door that
could lead to so desirable a result. But no man
need imagine that he can commit crime with
impunity ; and when he finds, in a prison shorn
of every attraction, the iron entering his soul,
he must read this as a lesson which the sooner he

learns the better will it be for himself, if not
learned it will necessitate the administering of
a still more drastic dose. The Bible is a book
where true and correct guidance, in almost every
state of circumstances, is sure to be found. I
need not say that its teaching is entirely opposed
to the maudlin philanthropy I have been speaking
of as well as to the principles of the Bill now
before the House. There is a passage in it that I
have often thought over in reference to the right
feeling to be entertained towards criminals; it is
this: "Let him who doeth evil be afraid, for the
magistrate beareth not the sword in vain, but is
God's minister on earth, a revenger executing
wrath against those who do evil." What a commentary is this upon the broken-winded philanthropy and lamentable love that pretends to live
in some hearts for great criminals. A revenger
executing wrath is a very different character from
your platform orator pouring forth diseased mis-
placed sympathy on behalf of the objects of that
wrath. Remark also, that it is not pity or
sympathy that is executed, but wrath, deep
heaven-born hatred of crime and its perpetrators,
hanging over the seat of justice a drawn sword,
as the emblem of the work done. Holding these
views in reference to crime and criminals, honourable members may imagine with how much
detestation I contemplate the proposal before
the House involved in the Bill introduced by the
honourable member for East Sydney. That Bill
is the sort of climax or outcome of all that wretched
philanthropy I have been exposing and which
aims at making things smooth and comfortable
for the worst of all criminals—the murderer. To
abolish capital punishment while you leave capital
crime rampant is certainly not the most approved

method of going to work. This Bill begins at the wrong end. The best and surest method of abolishing capital punishment would be to try and abolish capital crime, but to begin by abolishing the punishment while murder stalks abroad, I am sure will not meet with the approval of this Assembly. It has been alleged, I think, by the honourable gentleman who introduced this Bill, that imprisonment for life is a more terrible punishment than death. Well, in reply to this, I assert that there is not a feeling, principle, or instinct of humanity that does not give the lie to this statement. All animal life, from man downwards, prove, every minute of time, how infinite is their estimate of the value of life, and what prodigious superhuman efforts of courage, endurance, and desperate daring they will make to save it. But I will enforce my argument by an illustration that may bring the matter rather sharply home to the honourable member for East Sydney, the introducer of the Bill now under discussion. Suppose the honourable gentleman, through a combination of mischances, found himself in the position of being sentenced to imprisonment for life, and was actually so sentenced, I ask him what would be his thoughts and feelings on receiving some such communication as the following: "Her Majesty having carefully considered your case, and from some of the facts and circumstances attending it, of a mitigatory character, Her Majesty has been graciously pleased to extend to you the royal prerogative of mercy, so that instead of being imprisoned for life, your original sentence, you will, by way of mercy and mitigation, suffer the secondary penalty, and be taken out to-morrow morning and hanged by the neck until you are dead." (Loud laughter and cheers.) In the face of this I wonder if the honourable member would still hold that imprisonment for life was a more terrible punishment than death. But as far as I am concerned I do not desire to inflict a severer punishment than death on the murderer; if imprisonment for life is a severer punishment I am quite content to abide by the lighter punishment of death, leaving to my opponents the odium and cruelty of advocating what they assert is a severer and heavier punishment, namely, imprisonment for life. There is also a stupid phrase often used in the discussion of this subject, and used, I believe, in this debate, "That you can't put a man to a worse use than to hang him." I quite agree with this, but at the same time I declare that you can't put a murderer to a better use than to hang him, nay more, that you are bound by every principle of religion, justice, and right to hang him, and if you allow any maudlin sentimental cant to prevent you performing this, your plain duty, the society in which you live will be the sufferer; besides, has anyone ever tried to measure the danger of accumulating in a jail all our desperate murderers, men whom you can't punish any further, and who would be constantly increasing on your hands, and whose safe custody would form the most perplexing and difficult problem of the day, because, mark you, this congregation of murderers would form a body of men driven to absolute desperation, ready to murder a warder, or anyone who came near them, with as little compunction as they would light their pipes. Macbeth says:—

> I am in blood
> Stepped in so far, that should I wade no more,
> Returning were as tedious as go o'er.

So will it be with this continually increasing gang of desperadoes, forming a danger to the State that the supporters of this Bill would do well to ponder deeply before they advance another inch on the road they are going. It has been advanced as an argument during this debate that in Tuscany they have abolished the punishment of death, and that now, under imprisonment for life, murder is much less frequent than when the death punishment prevailed. If this is so, it must arise from accidental circumstances and nothing more, and will have no permanency. If those who have used this argument don't agree with this view, they will be forced to the adoption of the only view left them, namely, that the Tuscany murderers may be imagined saying to themselves something like this: "Well, it's no use committing murder now, because we can't enjoy the luxury of being hanged. As long as they hanged us for it we had some inducement to commit murder, but now that they have abolished hanging and substituted imprisonment for life, we have not the slightest inclination to commit murder." I put it to the House whether this is not a fair inference from the argument and the way it has been used? Statistics of this description are not to be relied upon as bearing out the conclusions that people generally put upon them. But no matter what statistics prove or disprove, as long as I have my senses about me, I will never part with the punishment of death for the murderer—the most formidable and destructive weapon we can stike him with. There are two crimes—rape and murder—thoroughly deserving of death, and, in the interests of society, I trust that this House will never part with the effective and most richly-deserved punishment for these

offences. The punishment of death, whatever
people may say to the contrary, is the most dreadful of all punishments. It annihilates hope, the
grand sustainer of humanity. There is no despair
so black that hope, with its thousand suggestions,
will not cheer and lighten; no dungeon so dreary
that the rays of hope will not penetrate; no chains
so heavy that hope will not ease and dissipate.
Yes; hope springs eternal, and gilds and illumi-
nates with brightness the hardest lot that man
can be consigned to, but to take a man in the full
vigour of youthful manly health and strength, and,
at a given signal, strangle the life out of him, is a
punishment compared to which all others dwindle
to nothing. In the interests of good government
and of the safety of society, I trust that the
punishment of death, in certain cases, may be
retained, and that the Bill before the House may
be thrown out as a serious danger to the State.

[The Bill was thrown out by a large majority.]

DIVORCE BILL.

[IN the year 1870, Mr. Buchanan moved the second reading of the Divorce Bill. The following is an abridged report of his speech:—]

MR. SPEAKER,—In moving that this Bill be now read a second time, I hope hon. members will come to the consideration of it with minds untrammelled by prejudice or bigotry of any kind. This is a question, the importance of which cannot be magnified ; it is a question removed far above the atmosphere of party, therefore I trust this House will deal with it in the interests of truth, and the happiness and well-being of the people of this country. In introducing this Bill, I am introducing no new principle. The principle of divorce has been acted upon for two hundred years in the mother country, and other countries, such as America, Victoria, Canada, &c., have adopted it with advantages to themselves of the most undeniable character. Hon. members are of course well aware that in Catholic times divorce was not allowed, the Church of Rome holding marriage to

be a sacrament and indissoluble on any ground
whatever; but notwithstanding this there were
such things as dispensations granted in those
times. The indissolubility of marriage, as declared
by the Church of Rome, was found to be attended
with so much inconvenience that a loophole of
escape was very soon found. The Church still
adhered to the sacramental dogma and the indissolubility of the tie, but it evaded it by declaring
the marriage invalid, and therefore null and void.
The marriages that the Church of Rome thus
declared invalid were so declared, not from
any wrong done by either of the parties, for,
however flagrant that wrong might have been,
it must have been borne in patience, as the
Church could afford no relief on that ground, but
some miserable, wretched pretext was bolstered
up, and, upon the payment of a sum of money, the
marriage was declared null as having been invalid
from the beginning. The grounds of such appli-
cations were generally a remote consanguinity,
and hon. members will see how easily they could
have been obtained when I tell them that one
marriage was declared invalid on the ground that
the husband had stood godfather to a daughter of
his wife's third cousin. The fact of the matter is
that this declaring of marriages invalid by the
Church of Rome was done without reference to
the justice or injustice involved, but simply to increase the revenue of the Church so that the priesthood might wallow in all that luxury and licentiousness which has characterised them in all ages
and in all countries. The revenues from this
source were at one time nearly as great as from
the sale of indulgences, which indulgences when
obtained—and they can only be obtained by pay-

ment—the person who is so favoured may commit any sin, no matter how monstrous, if not with the express approval of the Church, at all events without any of its censures. I have no hesitation in saying that in any given year there have been more marriages declared invalid by the Romish Church than there have been divorces granted by all the Divorce Courts in the world in the same time, with this difference, that the Divorce Courts have acted legally, and on proof of guilt, while the Romish Church has acted from no higher motive than a grovelling desire to enrich her coffers, and hesitates not to perpetrate rank injustice as well as deep sin, that the priesthood may be clothed in purple and fine linen, and live in rank and idle luxuriance. From all my reading and investigation of this subject I am persuaded that this indissolubility of the marriage tie is a device of the Romish Church originated and maintained for no other purpose than extortion and the systematic fleecing of the poor helpless victims who fall so easy a prey to their priestly tyrants. Well, then, upon all this ignorance and degradation arose the sun of the Reformation, and with its piercing rays dispelled all those dense fogs of superstition which had so long enervated and obfuscated the minds of men. The reformers were earnest, truth-loving, Bible-reading men, and one of their first acts was to knock the Romish dogma on the head as to the indissolubility of marriage. They appointed several of the most eminent of their number to confer on this subject, and it would be difficult to find in any age or State so noble a band of men of genius and learning as drew up the document known as the *Reformatio legum*, the deliverance of this eminent body. In that document it is laid

down that marriage is a civil contract, dissoluble
on the ground of adultery, and all Protestant
churches have ever since held this opinion, and
although it was only enacted as the law of England
so lately as 1857, still it was the practice in England ever since the Reformation, and divorces were
constantly granted every year by special Act of
Parliament, while in Scotland it was the law of
the land, grantable on application to the Supreme
Court. The process in England was so expensive
that it could only be taken advantage of by the
rich, and in consequence of this the present divorce
law was introduced by the House of Lords, ten of
the Bishops voting for it, and most ably supported
by Lords Lyndhurst, Cranworth, Campbell, &c.
On its coming to the House of Commons it was
carried by over two to one. This Act has now
been in operation in England for twelve years with
marked advantage to the interests of the people.
It has been in operation in Scotland since the time
of the Reformation, and we have the testimony of
such able jurists as Lord Stair and Mr. Erskine
that it has worked most beneficially, and promoted the moral welfare of the people in a large
degree. But whatever may be the result and
working of that law, one truth is plain, that not a
single solitary voice has been raised, either in
Scotland or England, asking for its repeal. Is
there an hon. member in this House who for a
moment supposes that this Act would be allowed
to stand a single day in the mother country, if the
experience of it had been evil? It stands there
now unchallenged by a single man, and at every
sitting of the Court affords relief in cases where to
withhold relief would be to perpetuate cruel wrong,
and to force persons into the commission of sin,

which they would avoid if the law allowed them.
I have not referred to the Scriptural justification
of this measure, simply because it is so plainly and
clearly in favour of granting divorce on the ground
of adultery, that I did not deem it necessary. I
am satisfied that every unprejudiced mind will
agree with me that our Saviour admitted that
marriage might be dissolved on the ground of
adultery, when He said, "Whosoever putteth
away his wife, saving for fornication," &c. I
think this is a most clear admission on the part of
our Saviour that a man might dissolve his marriage on the ground of adultery, and it is a view of
the subject which the whole bench of bishops co-
incided with when the matter was under discussion
in the House of Lords; at all events I would have
been the last man on earth to have brought in this
measure unless I believed it was in accordance
with the teachings of the Bible, clearly laid down
in several parts of the Word of God. Well, then,
I come to the measure immediately under discussion, and in reference to it I candidly admit that
it differs from the English Act, but in a manner
which should all the more recommend it to hon.
gentlemen. The English Act gives the man the
right to dissolve his marriage on the ground of the
wife's adultery, but it does not deal out the same
justice to the woman. She cannot dissolve the
marriage on the ground of the husband's adultery;
he must accompany the adultery with cruelty,
desertion, or some other crime. Well, I say I
detest this injustice, and have blotted out the
wrong from the Bill I have had the honour of
introducing to this Parliament, and which is now
under discussion. The whole spirit of the English
law is most unfair in its dealing with woman, and

the lowest possible ideas are at the bottom of refusing to give her equal rights with men in this matter of divorce. Let hon. members take any view of the matter they like. Let them take the Scriptural view, which I submit is the only view they should take, and will any man dare to say that, in the eyes of God, the crime of the man is less than the crime of the woman, or that God would measure out one penalty for the woman and a less penalty for the man? Surely not. Well, then, if they assume that marriage is a civil contract, which I admit it is, and nothing more, are not both parties equally bound by it? and should not the same consequences follow a breach by either party? Surely the most common and everyday principles of justice, if allowed fair play, would settle this matter triumphantly in favour of the Bill. But I may be told, and I have no doubt will be told, that the wife's adultery is attended by more serious consequences than the man's, inasmuch as it may introduce spurious offspring into the family. I meet this with the answer, may not the man's adultery introduce spurious offspring into some other family? The miserable selfishness of such a view as this, subordinating as it does the high morality and unerring justice of God to a low human selfish fear, is, in the last degree, degrading to the advocates of such a principle. I say to the members of this House, let us, as a Parliament, lead the way in an attempt to elevate woman to an exact equality with man in the eye of the law, a thing which British law has never yet done, but on the contrary, in all its dealings with woman, has treated her with an injustice which is founded on feudal barbarism and that wretched vassalage, the spirit of which animates

certain orders in England to this day. I look upon
the change I have made in the English Act, by
which equal justice is done to the woman, as the
best part of the Bill I have laid before this Parliament. It was most warmly supported by many
of England's ablest prelates, and Lord Lyndhurst
delivered a most striking and remarkable speech
in favour of it, voting and protesting against the
third reading of the Bill, because this very equality,
which is in the thirteenth clause of the Act now
before hon. members, was not incorporated in the
English Act. I therefore trust that a sense of
justice will prompt hon. members to adhere to the
thirteenth clause as it stands — that they will
stamp with the seal of their condemnation the sin
of the man equally with the sin of the woman—
that they will palliate in no degree the sin of the
man, but visit it with the same consequences that
they are prepared to mete out to that of the
woman—and in doing this they will act in accordance with God's justice, which is the only rule
and guide to direct us in this matter. The thirteenth clause involves the whole Bill, and on this
clause it must stand or fall. I have one word to
say to the Roman Catholic members; and first let
me say a word or two as to their much-talked-of
petitions against the Bill. Hon. members know
very well the worth of these petitions, and how
they are 'got up. They simply embody the
opinions of the priests, and the mode by which
they are originated and completed affords an
admirable illustration of priestcraft in all its
debasing, enslaving tyranny. When the Roman
Catholic priests require a show of petitions for any
purpose a draft is prepared at head-quarters and
issued to all the churches in the country—then,

by a most vehement beating of the drum-eccle-
siastic, the poor deluded followers of Romanism
are commanded to sign it. Every nefarious trick
is resorted to—a table is erected at the church
doors, and all and sundry are enrolled, including
hundreds of children whose names are taken down
for them. If any one dares refuse to sign the
petition he is instantly subjected to a withering
fire from the spiritual artillery of the Church, and
is branded and scouted for daring to think for
himself.   Let hon. members look at the petitions
already received—they will find most of the names
written in the same handwriting.   I am not surprised at this, because popery was never distinguished for enlightening its followers ; but I am
informed, by eye-witnesses, that whole schools of
children have had their names attached to these
petitions by command of the priests.   Does this
not show what an unscrupulous body these priests
are, and how they hesitate not to insult this Parliament by sending petitions, signed by hundreds
of children, meaning us to believe that they eman-
ated from men and women? But thank God there
are men in this House who are prepared to take
these priests in their own craftiness and expose
their nefarious, scheming devices on all occasions.
I say boldly these popish petitions are worth
nothing.   They, as far as they are signed by
adults, emanate from poor, deluded, priest-ridden
slaves who have basely surrendered their thoughts,
their minds, their independence into the hands of
men who live by deluding them, and whose system
is built upon the ruins of human liberty, the wilful
and systematic falsification of God's Word, and
the degradation and utter debasement of human
nature itself.   I tell those priests that the less

they cross our path the better—the more they
come in collision with us the more disastrous will
it be for them and their system, and I am sure
the House asks no more humiliating spectacle—
humiliating as exposing most thoroughly the
unscrupulous acts of popery—than an inspec-
tion of those very popish petitions now lying
on the table. Now then let me say a word or
two to the Roman Catholic members of this
House. According to their own statements they
cannot possibly be affected by this Bill—they
cannot take advantage of it. I therefore think
if they acted rightly they would not vote at all.
The Protestants can take advantage of the Bill,
and if the Roman Catholic members vote against
it, what is it but an insolent attempt to thrust their
dogmas, which we Protestants repudiate and despise, down our throats? They will try by their
votes on this occasion to compel all the Protestants in the community to be bound by the dogma
that marriage is a sacrament and indissoluble. It
would be vain to hope for independent action from
a set of men who are driven by their priests like
sheep, and who have basely surrendered their
thoughts into the keeping of men equally feeble,
ignorant and fallible. Under such circumstances,
the representatives of the Roman priesthood, for
they are not representatives of the people, will be
found to a man voting against this Bill. I care
not for this—I believe the independence and intelligence of the House will guide it to a correct
conclusion. I will never for a moment believe
that this Parliament, composed of educated gentlemen from all parts of the country, will affirm
the monstrous doctrine that a woman may scandalously break her marriage vow and cover her

husband with dishonour, and that the law should allow the injured man no relief or redress. I will never believe that this Parliament will allow one of the parties to a marriage contract to trample the contract and all his or her obligations under foot, while it still holds it binding on the other. I cannot for a moment suppose that this Parliament will so stultify itself as to allow cruel wrong to exist without the application of a remedy. Is it for the interests of morality or public policy that a marriage contract should be maintained when the very soul has been knocked out of it by the adultery of one of the parties to it? Will hon. members of this House say that all these cruel wrongs that have desolated and laid waste many a previously happy home are to be aggravated and inflamed by the cruelty and injustice of the law? That a woman who has basely betrayed her husband, and in open day is living a life of infamy before his very face, is still to be allowed to bear his name, and while she has laughed the contract to scorn, the law is to hold it binding upon him during her life? Let hon. members only bring the very commonest sense to bear on this subject, and they will soon see the necessity as well as justice of this measure. I know there will be a great deal of sentimental trash talked about the danger of passing such a Bill as this. I can almost already hear the rush of that fearful tide of misrepresentation which is sure to set in when such a measure as the one we are now discussing comes on the carpet. I have no doubt we will have fearful pictures of the immorality which this Bill, as if by the wand of an enchanter, is to call into existence, the moment it is made law. My comfort is that it has always been so, that no reform was ever yet introduced to the world without a chorus of misgivings and abundant predictions of all manner of evil. But confident and full of hope, I press on this measure as one demanding the most prompt and decisive action on the part of hon. members. It is a measure which one of England's most eminent prelates has described as having purified the moral atmosphere of English society. It is a measure which will tend to heal all those festering sores and wounds which are slowly but surely eating their way to the very vitals of society. It is a measure which will be hailed by many a man and woman in this country as affording them relief from a sense of cruel degradation and great moral wrong. In one word, this is a measure which, while it leaves the pure and holy institution ·of marriage resting securely and safely upon the immovable foundation of human necessity, opens up an avenue of escape from the burden of a contract which, through the misconduct of one or other of the parties, has become vitiated and corrupt, a fruitful source of wretchedness and moral debasement. This measure only steps in after the marriage vow has been broken, dishonoured, and trampled upon, and aims, in the interests of virtue, at the dissolution of a tie, the existence of which is gall and wormwood to the injured party. It will afford an opportunity of putting an end to a most unhappy and unholy alliance from which every germ of peace, love, purity, and honour has departed. It will enable a man or woman to break and for ever dissolve a dissolute and disreputable connection, the bare thought of which wrings their hearts with anguish, and crimsons their cheeks with shame. It will rekindle hope in hearts

already plunged in despair, and will open up a new
world and brighter prospects to the victims of the
cruellest and saddest of all domestic calamities.
Hon. members will therefore, do well to pause in
the deepest earnestness ere they reject a measure
of this character, so pure and so philanthropic in
its aims and objects; but, whatever may be the
fate of this Bill, whether it is rejected or passed,
its opponents will have some difficulty in denying
the justice, righteousness, and truth of the principle on which it is founded.

[Mr. Buchanan sat down amid loud cheers from
both sides of the House, and on a division the
Bill was carried by 30 to 10. The Upper House
rejected the Bill, but Mr. Buchanan introduced it
again and again, until he ultimately carried it,
and it became law.]

GOLD FIELDS BILL.

[ON February 12th, 1873, Sir George Innis, Solicitor-General, moved the second reading of the Mining Bill, when Mr. Buchanan delivered the following speech :—]

MR. SPEAKER,—Sir, in rising to address myself to the measure now under discussion, I think I may safely assert that in anything I have to say on this important question I will speak the sentiments of my constituents. They may not agree with me in every detail, but in the strong condemnation that I will deliver of all the main features of the Bill, I believe I will express the exact sentiments and opinions of the intelligent miners of the West. I appear here as the representative of the largest constituency in the country. By a return laid upon this table some time ago the electors of the Western Gold Fields were numbered at 20,000, nearly double that of East Sydney, and greater than East and West Sydney combined, which constituencies are represented in this House by no less than eight members. There are as many as twelve representatives of the people in this House who do not represent as many electors as the Western

Gold Fields electorate contains. I, therefore, having the honour to represent a constituency so large and so important, am entitled to the respectful attention of the members of this House ; above all, I am entitled to their respectful attention when I speak on an occasion like the present, when the subject matter under discussion comes so completely home to the business and bosoms of my constituents. There is one thing that I have been much struck with during this debate —that is, the want of interest shown by hon. members in this great and deeply interesting, as well as important subject. During the entire speech of the hon. member for the Southern Gold Fields it seemed almost impossible to keep a quorum together, and I am positive that the attendance during his whole speech would not average twenty members. Well, I ask, is not this scandalous? And yet, notwithstanding this, and in spite of the fact that scarcely a member has read the Bill, we will find them voting for it simply because it is introduced under the wings of a Government, whereas, had it been introduced by a private member these very gentlemen who will now vote for .it, to please those in power, would have trampled it under foot as an outrage upon every principle of justice and right. This is not very flattering to the honour and character of this House, but it is true, nevertheless. I ask those gentlemen who have not read the Bill to read it before they vote, and if they won't or can't read it for themselves, let them, in God's name, have the common sense and decency to come in and listen to those who have read it and studied it also. It grieves me to see a number of hon. members— young men, too—continually nestling behind the

Colonial Secretary, surrendering their right of thought into his hands, and following him in every direction, and wherever he goes, without reference to conviction or the sanctity of individual opinion. Surely those youths would act a more spirited part if they confronted authority rather than slink behind it. If they appreciated and understood their position as representatives of the people, they would see at a glance the degradation they are steeped in by allowing any Government to count upon them at all times, and to look upon them as little better than voting machines, who dare not exercise the right of thought or of independent action. Would that I could inspire them with the independence and nobility of purpose which would prompt them to act rather as a curb and restraint upon authority than as one of the main sources of its strength. All power, instead of being supported by independent members, should be jealously watched, and no opportunity lost to restrain it and keep it within bounds. But what hope is there for a country where the young men distinguish their advent to public life by an inglorious, ignoble surrender of all spirit and all independence, and become wretched tools and flunkeys serving and waiting upon authority. I am fully alive to the fact that no reading of this Bill will do such members any good. When the division comes it will not be the injustice or justice of what they are voting for that will agitate them, but their whole anxieties will be absorbed in their desire to know where the members of the Government are sitting, and in their eagerness to place themselves behind them. Can we, therefore, hope for anything like justice from a House like this? Can we expect that the claims

of the gold miners will be regarded when the
whole business of a representative of the people
seems to be the support of a Government? But
hopeless as the task is, it is my duty, and I will
resolutely perform it, of showing this Mining Bill
in all its naked deformity—I will point out
atrocities in this measure that will shock the
sense of justice of all who listen to me, and before
I have done I will make it appear so ill-digested,
ill-considered, arbitrary, and oppressive a piece of
legislation that, if intelligence and independence
were characteristic of this Assembly, it would be
unhesitatingly and resolutely trampled in the dust
as an insult to the entire body of the miners, and an
infamous outrage upon all that we have hitherto
regarded as the equal rights of all men, and the
just and equitable principles of human government. This may be thought the language of
extravagance and exaggeration, but it can only be
so thought by those who have not read the Bill.
Apart altogether from the fearful wrongs that are
scattered through the Bill, from beginning to end
it is drawn by a mere legal pedant. From first to
last it is burdened and choked up with floods of that
barbarous legal jargon that seems to have been
invented for no other purpose than rendering confusion worse confounded. There are whole series
of clauses that no miner could possibly act upon
without having a skilful lawyer constantly at his
elbow. Its wordy, complicated, and involved
character, is perplexing in the extreme, and if
the country is visited by so dire a calamity as the
passage of this Act, I say, Mr. Speaker, that the
toiling, hard-working, patient gold miners would
be justified in rising up in open war against it,
rather than suffer its infamous enactments to sink

them to despair. Let hon. members, instead of
deserting their duty, only take the Bill up and
read it for themselves. If they are honest they
are bound to do so before they vote ; and if they
vote for the Bill, as I doubt not many will do without doing so, then the country may well view with
alarm the danger to which it is exposed by the
presence of such men in its Parliament. If hon.
members won't listen to gentlemen who have studied
this measure, and who will make good all they have
said against it, I ask them will they listen to the
miners themselves on the subject? Need I say that
I believe they will not. The miners have spoken
out in several petitions, and, in the name of justice,
I ask the members of this Assembly to listen to
them. There is a petition from Gulgong signed
by over 3,000 men. It condemns the Bill as a
whole for many and divers reasons. Hon. members
meet me with the assertion that they wish to pass
it. They conclude with a prayer that their views
may be embodied in the Act, but if their views
were carried into effect this Act would be so
mutilated and destroyed that nothing would remain of it. To carry out the views of the petitioners a new Act would be required. Let any
one follow me through this petition, and then say
whether the petition is not against the Act *in toto*,
and whether it would not be utterly impossible to
embody the views of the petitioners in the Act
without, by the very process, creating a new Act
altogether. The petition asks that the miners
should have the right of framing their own regulations. Grant this, which I assert you should do,
and you cut out a large slice of the Bill. They
then object to a number of the clauses ; to the
construction of the Warden's Court. They pray

that the duties of Warden be excised from the
Bill, thereby demolishing, at one fell swoop, dozens
of the clauses. They object to the Mining Appeal
Court as "productive of ruinous delay and excessive cost." That all the clauses relating to the
conditions of occupation, the registration, or the
forfeiture of any claim be omitted. They condemn
all the clauses relating to leases, and all the clauses
as to mining on private property. After this who
will say that these petitioners wish the Bill passed ?
Here is a whole army of the most formidable and
fatal objections to every principle of the Bill, and
yet, because the petitioners in their courtesy merely
ask that their views be adopted, their petition is
actually quoted as being favourable to the Bill.
Where would the Bill be, I ask, if the views of
those petitioners were adopted? It would be out
of existence; a blessed relief to all concerned.
This petition from Gulgong is a most able document; with every sentiment and principle there
laid down I most cordially agree. Those petitioners
are entitled to the most respectful consideration of
this House, and it would have been well for the
unhappy author of this measure, the honourable
and learned Solicitor-General, if some of those
petitioners had been by his side when he drew this
unique and marvellous literary curiosity, the Mining Bill of 1873. Let us, therefore, hear no more
about those intelligent petitioners being in favour
of the second reading of the Bill. We all know
that the right and proper parliamentary action is,
when we are opposed to the principle of a Bill, to
vote against the second reading, and undoubtedly
this would have been the recommendation of the Gulgong petitioners had they not thought that it was
perhaps the more courteous proceeding merely to ask

that their views be embodied in the Bill. I assert, sir, that it would be difficult to imagine a more sweeping condemnation of any measure than that which breathes from every line of the Gulgong petition. Let the Solicitor-General and the Government only have faith in what they see. The Solicitor-General seems to have a strong objection to place the power of drawing regulations in the hands of the miners, but only let the House grant them this one advantage and a very short time will suffice to prove the efficacy of the reform. I trust the House will listen to the voice of the miners, so clear and intelligent in its expression, and I do trust hon. gentlemen will read carefully the different petitions from the various gold fields, and show at least some deference to the wishes of those who are so seriously concerned. I will now, sir, proceed to justify all the strong language I have applied to this Bill. I will go over it *seriatim,* and deal with important and unimportant objections as they occur, although I believe I will encounter few of the latter description. I have used very emphatic strong language in condemnation of this Bill, but as I go on hon. members will see the necessity for such language. I have said that it was an outrage against justice —a piece of rank treason against every known principle of right—a black and damnable insult thrown in the face of liberty, and a most atrocious and studied wrong inflicted upon a most laborious and worthy class of the community. I ask the House to judge between me and the proofs of this which I will now˙ produce. I feel almost disheartened at the prodigious nature of the task I have imposed upon myself in exposing the innumerable wrongs of this Bill of 173 clauses, and

I first call attention to clause 4 which, under the pretence of providing for the preservation of existing interests, perpetrates the absurdity of having two laws affecting mining interests—while it is perfectly right to preserve existing interests, surely a statesman would have managed matters so that one law would have ruled all. As it is, there are at present in existence about 4,000 leases, and the holders of those leases are to hold them on different terms, and by a different law, from the present. The consequence will be endless difficulties and disputes. Leases will be issued under the proposed law, and the miners, finding many people holding land on different terms, and having different laws affecting them, will come in collision with them, and disputes and litigation will be the order of the day. Well then I say that a statesman, in view of all this complication and trouble, would have so arranged matters that, while both laws would be assimilated, all existing interests would be preserved. Clause 7, providing for a Minister for Mines, I object to. I do not believe it would be of any advantage to the miner; while, politically, it is open to very serious objection. What is wanted is the appointment of a shrewd, intelligent, practical man as secretary to the mining department, with full charge, under the Minister of Lands. His duties would be to take charge of all mining matters, and to be ready at a moment's notice with all papers and information on all matters connected with the department. Such an officer, with no other duty to perform, would soon bring our mining affairs into order and regularity. I object to the power of the Executive being strengthened in this House by the appointment of another Minister. We have seven Ministers

in this House, and if the House of Commons had
the same proportion they would have upwards of
seventy Ministers of the Crown there—an enormity
which, of course, would never be tolerated. The
influence of those seven Ministers on the members
of this House is already too great without increasing it. The Executive power in this House should
be cut down rather than increased. The appointment of one or two more Ministers would enable a
Government to carry everything, and completely
paralyze the efforts of the independent and genuine
members of the House. On these high constitutional grounds I oppose the appointment of another
Minister. I would not grudge the expense if I
thought such an appointment would advance the
interests of the miner; that expense would be no
trifle with an under-secretary and staff of clerks,
officers, servants, &c. The next clause, 8, provides
for schools, museums, and the appointment of a host
of professors, teachers, readers, &c., which is sheer
absurdity if it is meant to benefit the gold miner
by all this. I have no objection to your having as
much of it as you like in the Sydney University,
the proper place for it, but introducing such ideas
in a Mining Bill is in my view in the highest
degree utopian. Hon. members will observe that
the Warden mentioned in the Bill is a person endowed with enormous powers—powers that it
would be almost dangerous to entrust in the hands
of an angel from Heaven—and in clause 11 his
power commences; he is there empowered to pro-
claim an entire area within a radius of two miles, a
gold field upon it being so reported by a person
claiming to have made such a discovery. This
may be all very right, but I surely don't require to
tell hon. members that it is a large power to be

entrusted to a Warden, and might be worked
tremendously to further nefarious purposes.
Clause 13 provides for the appointment of Wardens, and heaps up expenses by the appointment
of a numerous staff of highly-paid officials. The
proviso enacts that no Warden shall hold any
interest in any claim or mineral lease. Very good,
but why limit it to the Warden? why not place
the Mining Minister, the Appeal Court Judges
under the same restriction? Clause 17 provides
for what is called Consolidated Miners' Rights,
which means that one man may take out miners'
rights for fifty or a hundred, or, for the matter of
that, five hundred men. This principle is intended
to strike a blow at the independence of the miner.
It destroys his individuality and makes him something like the serf of the monopolies which employ
him. Let the gold miner always maintain his
independence and his character as a gold miner.
This Bill, I say, all through favours monopoly and
the great capitalists, and deals most harshly with
the individual miner. In the next clause, 18,
sub-section 1, there is a notable piece of injustice.
Speaking of taking up land, it says—" and such
quantities, dimensions, and boundaries shall be
determined at *or after* the time of taking such possession, and be subject *to alteration and adjustment
from time to time."* Hon. members will see that
there is here no finality : what is your land to-day
may be altered to-morrow; there is no fixity of
tenure. It is liable to change at any time, and
uncertainty is the atmosphere that looms over
the unhappy miner by this sorry enactment.
Clause 20 seems to me abstruse nonsense, like so
many others in this masterpiece of mining legislation. Clause 22 enacts that no man shall do this,

that, and the other unless he has a miner's right.
Why, he has no *locus standi* unless he has a
miner's right, and therefore this clause is like so
many others, mere surplusage. Clause 24 heaps
up expense upon the miners and all the residents
on the gold fields, and this pervades the whole
Bill. Wherever there is a chance of taking money
out of the miner's pocket, this Bill does it. A
business license, by this clause, is £5; by the present Act, I believe, it is only £1. Clause 29 confers a most dangerous power upon the Minister—
that of reserving any land he likes, on a newly-
discovered gold field, from mining, residence, or
business purposes. A corrupt Minister might
reserve the best portion of a gold field and divide
it among his friends, which the next clause (30)
enables him to do. That this power would be
abused, who is there that listens to me can for a
moment doubt? but, whether or not, no such power
shall ever, by my vote, be placed in the hands of
any man. Then we come to clauses 34 and 35,
which deal in the most arbitrary manner with the
business people. A man puts up a store, at great
expense, on the gold fields, and just as he is about
to realize something like a fair return for all his
labour and risk, the Government propose to sell his
land. The advantage this Act gives the owner is,
that he will get it if he is the highest bidder, with
the value of his improvements deducted. But
suppose he is unable to raise means to put himself
in the position of the highest bidder—what then?
Why, he is turned out, and a stranger steps in to
enjoy the business he has made, the connection he
has established, and the entire advantages of the
position. A more gratuitous or senseless wrong
was never imagined or inflicted. Clause 36 is im-

portant, as embodying the very principle for which
the diggers contend as to mining on private property. By this clause the diggers may go on private property to cut a race, on giving the owner
compensation for the damage done. What more do
they want in asking to mine on private property ?
If it is right to allow miners to go on private property to cut a race, on giving compensation to the
owner, must it not be equally right to allow miners
to go on private property to sink a shaft on giving
the owner compensation. The Solicitor-General
affects horror at the idea of invading private property for mining purposes, but he has enacted it
in this (36) clause, although, perhaps, he is not
aware of it, which is his position in reference to
many of the clauses of this Bill. I have spoken of
the enormous power of the Warden under this
Bill; by clause 38, sub-section 6, he has the power
to suspend this sub-section for a period of two
months. The hon. member for the Southern Gold
Fields says it is so at present; that may be, but it
is, nevertheless, an enormous power, and a power
liable to the very gravest abuse. Sub-section 9
of this clause lays an embargo upon all the water
in the country. It says no license shall be granted
for the use or diversion of any water which may
be required for public purposes. Why, I would
like to see the Solicitor-General dip his finger into
that piece of water in New South Wales that may
not be required for public purposes. Therefore
hon. members will see what desolation this power
would create were it enforced. Clause 44 comes
down on the pockets of the miners again at the
rate of not less than 5s. nor more than 20s. per
sluice head per annum. The miners pay nothing I
understand at present. In the following clauses

the author of the Act uses terms such as—"Act of Council now or hereafter to be in force," which satisfies me that he acted without thought or consideration in framing this Bill—or, as the Gulgong petitioners say, "artlessly copied from other Acts of other countries, what has no meaning or application here." What Act of Council can ever be in force hereafter in this country? I can't understand what the learned gentleman means by "Act of Council," and I am certain the solution is as I have already stated. Clause 50 admits of a monstrous state of things under it; prospecting leases may be issued of 640 acres, distant more than three miles from the nearest gold field; and if the ground so leased turns out payable, then fifty acres is given to the prospector. Had this clause been in operation when the Home Rule was discovered, that gold field might have been in the sole possession of a dozen people; but our comprehensive Solicitor-General never thought of this. All these clauses are against the miner, and in favour of monopoly; and indeed, so far does this Bill go in this path, that I believe if it is enacted without amendment it will lead to serious disturbance all over the gold fields. If hon. gentlemen will turn to clause 60 they will see that the Warden is endowed with a jurisdiction denied to the Courts of Petty Sessions, or to the District Courts. In fact he has unlimited jurisdiction, and can decide on matters involving from pounds to millions. He is a marvellous person, this Warden, as I shall show as I proceed. By the clause I am considering, namely, clause 60, in any dispute all gold that has been taken from the claim must be lodged in the hands of the Warden until the dispute is

settled. Under this clause, on some of the rich
Hill End claims, if they happened to be contested,
it might be that the Warden might get £100,000
lodged with him. Was ever man so trusted?
Surely the miners would require some guarantee
for their money before they parted with it in this
way. But there is nothing for it; this law compels them to part with it in the manner described.
All the clauses from 60 to 70 are so involved that
it would be dangerous for any miner to act upon
them without the advice of a skilful lawyer.
Clause 71 purposes to grant leases even if the
applicant shall not have complied with the regulations. Will this not open the door to litigation
and all manner of disputes? What advantage
has the man who has complied with the regulations if he could have gained his object without
such compliance? What an evident want of
thought and consideration this proves in the
drawer of the Bill. Clause 77 provides, in cases
of ejectment, that the Attorney-General appears
in the Warden's Court as one of the parties.
What a precious chance a poor miner would have
with the Attorney-General his opponent and the
Warden the judge—the Warden who is the mere
creature of the Government, and who would
tremble for his office if he dared to decide against
the Attorney-General. I now come to the consideration of the Bill under that section headed,
"The Administration of Justice," which literally
bristles with wrongs of the grossest character.
Clause 88 enacts that there shall be no appeal
from the Warden unless the sum exceeds £30.
Now I ask why is the miner to be deprived of
rights enjoyed by the rest of the community?
All the people have the right of appeal from

Courts of Petty Sessions from £10, and I cannot understand why the gold miner is to be subjected to an injustice from which all the rest of the community are exempt. Clause 92 confers more power on the Warden, and Clause 96 heaps expense on the miner by giving the Warden the power of sending for scientific witnesses in the shape of mining engineers, surveyors, accountants, experts and other scientific persons, all of which tremendous expense is thrown upon the miner who loses. Clause 97 is a clause remarkable for its injustice—it enacts that a person, if unwilling to take an oath, may make an affirmation, but it puts this great power in the hands of the Warden at the same time: "It shall be lawful for the Warden, upon being satisfied of the sincerity of such objection." Well, here the whole thing rests with the whim or caprice of the Warden, who may be an insolent, ignorant puppy for aught we know, and who has the power here of saying to any man, "I am not satisfied of your sincerity, and, therefore, if you decline to take an oath I will send you to prison for contempt." I characterise this, and denounce it, as a piece of destestable tyranny, and a scandalous insult to the whole mining community. A little further down another piece of flaming injustice is to be met with. The clause provides for trial by Warden and three assessors, and if two of the assessors are of one opinion and the Warden and one assessor are of another, the Warden carries the point. What is this but the grossest injustice? It may be that the two assessors are men of supreme intelligence, and have arrived at the correct conclusion; and it may be that the other assessor and the Warden are a couple of block-

heads, and so stupidity and injustice would
triumph over intelligence and right. Under the
provisions of the Act, intituled, Special Powers
and Duties of Warden, it is enacted that on the
decision by a Warden's Court, it shall be lawful
for the Warden to "order that any gold or
auriferous earth in the possession, and being the
property of the party by whom payment of any
sum in respect of any such debt, damages, or
costs, as last aforesaid shall be ordered," &c. I
should like to know how the Warden is to ascertain the value of auriferous earth. I point out
this merely as showing the slipshod way in which
the Bill is drawn. Clause 110 gives a tremendous
power to the Warden—namely, of granting an
injunction without notice to the other side. How
this power will be abused, and great injustice
wrought, I require not to point out. Clause 111
provides that the Warden may order gold in dispute to be placed in the hands of any person.
This gold may be of any value, and the Warden
may order it to be placed in the hands of anyone.
One would think that this clause was actually
drawn for the express purpose of enabling a dishonest Warden to plunder the gold-miners. How
beautiful is the idea of not ordering the gold to
be placed in his own hands ; if he disappeared
suspicion would be raised, but the gold being in
the hands of any person, that person may have
decamped while the Warden is preparing leisurely
to follow him. Then again, clause 113 gives the
Warden power to imprison for disobedience of an
order, and this without previous notice or summons to the person disobeying. What fantastic
tricks would those Wardens not play with powers
of this description placed in their hands. Clause

115 is a detestable piece of grinding tyranny.
It enacts that any order of commitment may be
made *ex parte,* that is, on hearing one side only,
so that a digger may be working quite innocently,
conscious of having committed no wrong, while
someone is making a charge against him behind
his back. The first intimation the poor digger
hears of it is his arrest on Warden's warrant, and
in gaol he will be left to wonder what on earth he
could have been guilty of. This is a treat pro-
vided for the respectable miners of New South
Wales by our sapient Solicitor-General. The
next part of this wretched measure I would draw
hon. members' attention to is the Appeal Court,
namely, the District Courts. I protest against this
as involving ruinous delay and excessive cost.
The judges of the District Courts are overworked
as it is, and the time between the sittings of such
Courts is too long. The unfortunate miner would
find all his works suspended for three or four
months in the event of an appeal; he and all his
witnesses would require to travel to the town
where the Court met, and the expense there
would be serious indeed, and then they might
find that the District Court judge could not
undertake their case, and so it would be put off
till next sittings. What is wanted is a mining
judge to visit the gold fields once a fortnight, or
once a month, for the purpose of hearing appeals,
and so transact the business promptly and expe-
ditiously. I find in this clause there is a provision for an appeal to the Supreme Court only
when the sum exceeds £500. Why should this
be? All the rest of the people have the right of
appeal from the District Court to the Supreme
Court on sums under £200; but the gold miner is

here again treated differently, and deprived of
rights enjoyed by all the rest of the community.
There is also another wrong inflicted on the miner
in this clause; he is deprived of the right of
appeal to the Privy Council. How valuable this
right is let hon. members ask the many parties
who are now enjoying property which they would
never have had but for this great right of appeal
to the Privy Council; and if there is one section
of the community more than another who should
have this right it is the gold miner. Questions
involving large sums will often arise on the gold
fields, and I for one will never be a party to
the removal of any of the safeguards by which
right and justice are secured. Above all, I
will never be a party to the removal of so
formidable a barrier against wrong as the right
of appeal to Her Majesty in Council. Under the
division of the Bill headed "Mining Assessors,"
there are some startling enactments. In clause 1,
hon. members will see that, although the Warden
sits as a judge and also as a juryman, he has the
sole power of making up the jury list, and may
strike off anyone who "in the opinion of the
Warden is not a person of good repute." So that
the Warden, if he has any little game to play,
may kock off whoever he chooses from the jury
list by omnipotently saying, " I, the Warden, am of
opinion that So-and-So is not a person of good
repute." Was there ever such infernal folly enacted
in this world before? Does this childish Solicitor-
General, or this childish and foolish Assembly,
think that the gold miners will stand anything?
True it is they are an orderly, patient, respectable
body of men, but beware how you goad them to
despair. Have a care that your tyranny and

insult may not become unbearable. This Bill
seems to have been conceived in every imaginable
folly and absurdity. Clause 140 provides that if
an assessor is once sworn he should never be
sworn again. This puts me in mind of the
celebrated Dr. Franklin's remark to his father
when he was assisting him to take in twelve
months' provisions, " Had you not father, as well
say grace now for the whole twelve months'
supply and save trouble saying it at each meal? "
Why, again, are the miners to be treated
differently from the rest of the community? If it
is thought a guarantee that truth will be spoken
through the administration of an oath, why take
away the guarantee from the miners? In clause
146 the Warden may be expected to commit grave
blunders, through the extravagant powers committed to his hands. If he is of opinion that a
witness is prevaricating, he may send him to gaol
for two months; or if any one shall, in the
opinion of the Warden, in any way misbehave in
Court, or be guilty of any contempt whatever, he
or she shall receive two months' imprisoment. It
is easily to be seen that, by this clause, a silly
Warden—and the probabilities are ten to one that
the Wardens will be silly people—might send an
honest, truthful digger to prison for two months
through mistaking his rough honesty for impertinence. Then we come to penalties and forfeitures,
and in clause 151 a £10 fine is inflicted for selling
a box of matches without a business license. By
clause 152, employing any unauthorised person—
that is a man without a miner's right—to take a
letter to the post office mulcts you in a £10 fine.
A carrier who has no miner's right, merely
camping on a gold field, is liable by this clause to

a fine of £10. Clause 153 revives the old intolerable nuisance of hunting diggers for their
miner's rights, and can only lead to vexation and
annoyance without serving any good purpose.
Clause 158 inflicts a penalty of six months'
imprisonment on any man who, having lost his
case before a Warden's Court, shall assault, or
threaten to assault, the successful party. No
allowance is here made for the distress of a man
who finds himself the victim of an adverse
decision; and if, in his anger, he should let slip
the words to his opponent, "I'll punch your
head," six months in prison is his fate. So hon.
gentlemen will see that this measure goes on
piling wrong on wrong and injustice on injustice
—without remorse or dread—on the head of the
unfortunate miner. Clause 161 gives a power to
the Warden which, if hon. members could only
comprehend, it would make their blood curdle.
The Warden may forfeit the claim. Now, I do
not go into the grounds on which this forfeiture
may be executed—I utterly repudiate and deny the
right of any man to such a power. I would not
give it to the Supreme Court constituted by all
the judges; to take a man's claim from him,
which might turn out to be worth thousands,
because he had not complied with the terms and
conditions of any lien or mortgage, is an unexampled and unheard-of piece of reckless ignorant
cruelty and tyranny. But, nevertheless, it will be
enacted by this House because it is composed of
members who don't represent the people, but
come here to support a Government, through
thick and thin, for reasons best known to themselves. The next and last section of the Bill I
have to consider is the mining on private property,

which I look upon as a mere insult to the miner.
Why did not the Solicitor-General take the manly
course, and tell us he was afraid to deal with this
subject? But whether he does so or not it will not
be this wretched abortion that he has drawn that
will satisfy anyone. The views of the miner are
the right to mine on private land on giving fair
compensation, and the right of no man to hinder
him—unless this is conceded him those clauses
might as well be struck out. I have now gone
over this entire Bill, and I ask hon. members to
say whether or not they approve of it. I have
shown defects in it of such a character that those
who have listened to me cannot plead ignorance if
they vote for them. I cannot expect that the
bulk of hon. members of this House will read the
Bill, and I have no hope that they would understand it if they did read it. I therefore ask them
to listen to those who have read it, and be guided
by them in this one instance. This is a serious
question, and if hon. members will not listen to
me, in the name of honour I ask them to listen
to the army of miners who have petitioned against
the Bill. If you are dead and insensible to this
paramount duty of the office you hold, go on and
perpetrate injustice upon injustice until a day of
reckoning comes, when the eyes of many members
of this House will be opened to the fact that there
are other duties for a true and honest representative of the people than a systematic, crawling,
servile support of a Government. I oppose this
measure as in every way bad. I oppose it as
having been conceived in ignorance and shallowness, the uniform accompaniments of presumption.
It is a measure that will fall like a millstone upon
the energies of the gold miner, paralysing his

efforts and retarding his progress. Above all, it is a measure so hateful in its injustice and so foul in its wrong, that it strikes at the very foundation of all the miner's hopes of peace for the future. I therefore oppose it with an intense inveterate determination of purpose. If an ignorant and misguided Assembly, turning a deaf ear to the prayers of these petitioners, persist in the support of a measure which they have, confessedly, never read, let the memory of this fearful wrong stamp itself indelibly upon the character of this Parliament. Let it be known far and wide that I have been told in the course of this address that only three members have read the Bill—and let it be further known that scarcely twenty members could be kept together during the course of the discussion, and that, in all probability, barely a quorum will divide on the measure; and then let the country judge of this Parliament and the fitness of its members to perform their important functions. Whatever derangement or injury is visited upon this great interest by the passage of this infamous Act, I, at least, stand clear of all responsibility, and to make assurance of this doubly sure, I beg to move—"That the order of the day be discharged with a view to the introduction of a measure more concise and intelligible, less complicated and involved, and better calculated to promote the prosperity and advancement of the great mining interests of this country."

[The amendment was lost by 22 to 2, and the second reading of the Bill carried by 20 to 2. The Parliament is composed of 73 members. The Bill never got beyond the second reading, the Government having withdrawn it.]

REPRESENTATIVE RIFLEMEN.

[MR. DANOAR having moved that £1000 should be voted to send riflemen to Philadelphia, Mr. Buchanan opposed the vote in the following speech :—]

MR. SPEAKER,—I was not in the House when this proposal to spend a £1000 of the people's money for such a purpose was first brought forward, and the more I have thought on the subject since, the more I am satisfied that this expenditure cannot be characterised in any other way than as a most profligate expenditure. (Hear, hear.) When I reflect that the people of the interior have to contend with bad roads, bad bridges, or no bridges, that they, in many places, have no end of difficulty in bringing their produce to market through the roads being almost impassable, I can easily imagine how great a help the expenditure of even this £1000 would be to many of them. (Cheers.) At all events, will any candid member of this House say we are justified in spending this money, in the way proposed, while the settlers in many parts of the interior are struggling with

every sort of drawback and downdrag through
the want of money to improve and ameliorate the
difficulties of their position. I say we are not
acting true to our duty if we expend this money
in the most preposterous and absurd piece of
folly that ever entered into the heart or mind to
conceive, while there is a single district where it
might be spent with advantage and benefit to the
inhabitants. We propose to expend £1000 on the
sheerest absurdity, while petitions constantly flow
in upon us to grant such sums, and even smaller
sums, for roads, bridges, courthouses, and
numerous other wants of the people which
cannot be neglected without leaving the poor
people to struggle as best they may with
difficulties that are well-nigh overpowering.
(Cheers.) And yet we have the Government
looking on at this iniquitous proposal with a
complacency which shows how little they have
the prosperity and progress of the people of the
interior at heart. Why the Government would
have allowed the matter to pass as a formal
motion, and now instead of offering it their most
strenuous opposition, they are going to vote for it
and support it. I have no hesitation in saying
that the Government are acting in this matter
with an indifference to the people's rights, and
with a reckless disregard of all principle and
duty, which stamps them as unfit for their places.
What right have they to vote this money of the
people's away for this extravagantly ridiculous
purpose, while they know so well that numbers of
the people in many districts have been asking,
and asking in vain, for such a sum to be expended
in useful and necessary works, which would be of
unspeakable advantage to the districts in ques-

tion? Will anyone say that the £1000 which is
to be expended in sending some idle people across
the ocean to shoot at a mark in Philadelphia,
could not be more advantageously and better
expended on many a bad road in the country?
Well then, if this is true, how dare the members
of this House vote any such a sum for so idle and
profligate a purpose? How can members who
vote for this detestable and unprincipled folly
face their constituents of the interior who, in
many cases, can hardly bring their produce to
market without danger to their lives and property?
Do the members who are about to vote for this
£1000 not think they would be more faithfully
performing their duty to those who sent them
here by refusing to do this wrong, for wrong it is,
while there is a single district in the country that
would be bettered by having the advantage of
this vote. I shall oppose the iniquity at every
possible stage, believing that the expenditure is
a most unprincipled expenditure, without a
shadow of justification, and lowering and degrading to us as a representative body. Whoever heard of such a proposal as this being
mooted in the House of Commons? The people of
England I believe, send riflemen to Philadelphia,
and other places, but did anyone ever hear of any
member of the House of Commons proposing to
take the money for such a purpose out of the
public purse? The member who made such a
proposal would be scouted, and both he and his
motion unhesitatingly trampled under foot. In
England, the section of the people who indulge in
this sort of fun have to pay for it, and the British
Parliament has never yet been degraded by such a
proposal as we are now discussing. I am utterly

E

at a loss to account for the large amount of
support this proposition is receiving, and can only
account for it by the fact that it is brought forward by a very rich man, and in saying this I am
not paying a very high compliment to the
character of this Assembly. Nevertheless, it
seems to me strictly true. Suppose the member
for Wollombi, or myself, or the member for the
Upper Hunter, had brought forward this motion,
do honourable members think we would have been
supported by a single vote besides our own? The
proposition would have been hurled out of the
House with indignation; but because it was
brought forward by a wealthy individual, hence
all this unanimity which is an indirect worship of
the golden calf, and infinitely contemptible to the
members so acting. The Government, which
should be, as all members are bound to be, the
vigilant, watchful guardians of the public purse,
have egregiously failed in their duty in this
matter; they have abandoned their duty, I
believe, for no higher purpose than to conciliate
a vote or two, but the people will judge between
them and me, and I very much mistake the
character and intelligence of those people if they
fail not to visit with the severest condemnation
the expenditure of this large sum of money on
mere idleness, which could be otherwise spent for
the benefit and advantage of the people. We are
told forsooth that this expenditure will improve
our riflemen in some miraculous way; that it will
do the colony no end of indescribable good; that
it will bring us into notice, and so forth. Is not
this the merest puerility, and the most contemptible childishness? Even suppose it did
make all our riflemen first-rate shots, I cannot

imagine this to be any great advantage in war.
There is no occasion for this great nicety of aim.
It matters little, in war, whether a soldier strike
the enemy on the head or on the foot, so that he
strike him at all. What is the difference if a
soldier aims at a certain man and only succeeds
in hitting one a yard from the man he aimed at?
(Great laughter.) The service rendered is quite
the same. Is a man not equally destroyed if you
send a ball through his bowels, instead of through
his heart, which you aimed at? (Laughter.) No
doubt this would be considered bad shooting, but
could the very best shooting be more effective?
If I am opposed to all the gentlemen opposite me,
and in attempting to destroy them, fire a shot at
the member for New England, who is immediately
in front of me, which shot misses him, but knocks
over the Premier (roars of laughter), that is bad
shooting, but still for the purpose of war it is
most effective, and what is more, the best and
most accurate shooting could not be more effective. In the hurry-scurry, hubbub, and carnage
of war men do not take deliberate aim; they have
a general direction to fire low, and many a shot is
fired on mere speculation, in the hope of hitting
somebody, there being no merit at all in hitting
anybody in particular. The great purpose of all
the firing in a battle being to kill, it is surely
exactly the same thing if a man in firing at No.
1 misses him, and kills No. 2. (Laughter.) The
conclusion from this reasoning is therefore that
accuracy of aim is of no advantage to the soldier,
and never can be as long as you have to fire
at numbers, where the most aimless rifleman,
firing without precision, and at random, is almost
certain to kill his man, which is all that the best

shot in the regiment can do. But surely there is
a far better training for soldiers than this rifle
shooting. The endurance of great fatigue has
always been held to be a high attribute of the
soldier. Let our men march out to Parramatta
and back two or three days in the week in full
accoutrements ; let them camp out in all sorts of
weather, march thirty miles without food or
drink, and lie down in the mud for a bed, this is
the training for soldiers, and a little of it would
do more to make an effective army than practising
at rifle butts day and night. Some honourable
members, by way of joke I suppose, talk of a
team of lawyers being sent out. Well, who can
doubt but that this would be a far nobler and
grander purpose? Rightly or wrongly there can be
no doubt of this, that no human being has in any
age of the world gained a renown so universal as
the Philadelphia lawyer. Even in our childhood,
when anything smart or clever was done, our very
nurse would compare us to a Philadelphia lawyer.
Whenever we are brought in contact with a proposition utterly insoluble, we are generally told it
would puzzle a Philadelphia lawyer. The reputation of these Philadelphia lawyers is therefore
as universal as it is apparently well founded.
What a transcendently glorious enterprise would
it not therefore be to send forth a team to compete
with them in a race on the wide ocean of legal
lore. Surely this mere shooting at a mark sinks
out of sight in comparison to the grandeur of
such a competition. Our ordinary lawyers here
are by no means everyday personages; they are
not to be considered as a parcel of legal monks
cloistered in cells, poring over musty statutes;
no, they are men largely conversant with the

world and its affairs, thoroughly imbued with all
ancient and modern learning; men whose everyday avocations require the exercise of the most
unerring sagacity, the most marvellous shrewd-
ness, and the most miraculous common-sense,
combined with an accuracy, activity, and industry
which are the only sure passport to a successful
professional career. Well, then, why not send such
a team to test the prowess of the far-famed and
renowned Philadelphia lawyers? In such a cause
there is glory to be gained. Imagine, in the event
of victory crowning our efforts, what a halo of
renown will surround our name; we will for ever
afterwards be known as the nation that plucked
the laurels from the brows of the great lawyers of
Philadelphia, and our fame and name will reach
to every nook and corner of the habitable globe.
A glory of this character would be worth paying
for, but the pitiful and wretched proposal of dis-
tinguishing ourselves as marksmen—mere marksmen, as if we could neither read nor write—is too
contemptible for serious consideration. But without any further fun or folly, let the members of
this House look to what they are doing before
they consent to throw away a thousand pounds of
the people's money in any such mad proposal as
that now before the House. It is a wasteful,
extravagant, unprincipled robbery which cannot
be justified, and a cruel wrong to the best interests
of the people of this country. I will oppose it to
the death, and if I stand alone it shall never pass
without an effort at its obstruction on my part.

THE DRAMA.

[ON Wednesday, June 11th, a public dinner was given to Mr. Creswick, the celebrated actor; the Hon. Geoffrey Eager occupied the chair, supported by several Ministers of the Crown, Members of Parliament, &c. The toast of "The Drama" was entrusted to Mr. Buchanan, who proposed it in the following speech. The *Sydney Mail*, in copying the speech into that paper, says : " The speech of Mr. Buchanan at the dinner given to Mr. Creswick, of which a condensed report appears in another part of this issue, partook so much of the character of a literary essay that we make a place for it here" :—]

MR. CHAIRMAN AND GENTLEMEN,—The toast that I have now the honour to propose is that of "The Drama." The toast is one that I would like to do some sort of justice to if I could. It is one that I could have wished had fallen to someone more capable of dealing with so great a theme. I am anxious to do justice to it, and, knowing my own great deficiencies, I venture on the subject in something approaching to a spirit of sheer desperation. I believe that mankind were born with a love of the drama implanted deeply in their nature, and when I see a man who professes to dislike or discountenance the drama, I believe firmly he is

acting against his natural feeling or inclination in
deference to some erroneous principle or mistaken
delusion, which makes a victim of him to his own
detriment, and in large deduction of his innocent
enjoyment and recreation. As long as human
nature remained as it was the drama would always
be supported. The people of the world would
always like to see the world brought before them
on the boards of a theatre, and the peculiarities of
humanity hit off in some well-conceived, cleverly-
constructed drama. As long as men and women
are agitated by hopes and fears, swayed by
stormy passions, stimulated by love and hate, and
have hearts brimful of both laughter and tears, the
drama will always retain its hold upon the people
as a most attractive source of amusement and instruction. Nay, whatever may be said to the
contrary, there was no useful or moral lesson that
could not be taught from the boards of a theatre,
and the stage need stand second to no school as a
powerful moral and intellectual instructor. And
how could it possibly be otherwise, when we
reflect upon the intellectual character of the men
who have written for the stage? Their very names
were household words, cherished and embalmed in
millions of hearts as the great leaders and throned
monarchs in the realms of thought. I do not
speak of foreign dramatists, but confine myself to
our English writers, and when I mention such
names as Shakespeare, Jonson, Addison, Samuel
Johnson, Goldsmith, Massinger, Sheridan, Byron,
Scott, Knowles, and Bulwer, surely there is no
room to wonder that their immortal productions
should captivate the general ear, and raise the
theatre high in popular estimation as a school of
instruction, moral and intellectual, second to none.

If anyone dissented from this view, let me ask him what school, or what pulpit if you like, was ever illuminated by fire so pure and bright as flamed from the genius of those men? I will go further and ask, as has been asked before, What sermon, from any pulpit in the world, ever more powerfully or eloquently enforced the command : "Thou shalt do no murder," than the representation of Macbeth? How fruitful is that magnificent play in its moral lessons and the grandeur of its moral teachings! How frightfully false and deceptive does Macbeth find his rash and reckless philosophy, " I am in blood stepped in so far that, should I wade no more, returning were as tedious as go o'er ; " and again, " Things bad begun make strong themselves by ill." What a painful commentary upon this, and what a picture of desolation and woe and sharp-biting never-ceasing remorse is offered to our contemplation in the guilty pair, unable to rest night or day, or even to eat without fear :—

Ere we will eat our meal in fear, and sleep
In the affliction of those terrible dreams that shake us nightly.

Well might Macbeth add :—

O, full of scorpions is my mind, dear wife!

Bad and wicked as we know them both to be, we cannot help feeling compassion for them as we see them tossed about on such a raging sea of torment and misery, with no help, no hope ; left a prey to the stinging remorse of their own poisonous thoughts, with no consolation but this :—

Better be with the dead
Whom we, to gain our place, have sent to peace,
Than on the torture of the mind to lie in restless ecstasy.

It is a terrible picture, carrying with it a terrible lesson, and in the hands of great actors transforms the theatre into a school of the highest moral teaching, where the best of us may derive instruction not easily found elsewhere. I hope you will not misunderstand me. I am not here undervaluing the pulpit—I am merely insisting that the stage should get its due. It has always seemed to me a mystery that certain people should absent themselves from the theatre, even when the works of the great masters whose names I have already mentioned were on the carpet, on the ground of religious principle. I need not tell you that thousands of the most sincerely religious people, in all countries, think it no sin to patronise a play, and I lose all patience when I hear people say that it is wrong to go and see a play, when I know it is full of wisdom and truth, and could not but operate in the most healthy way upon all spectators. Those people who acted thus might think themselves pious, but in reality they were only bilious; their religion, such as it was, proceeding more from the disordered state of their stomachs than the purity of their hearts. I am sure it would be difficult to find in any part of New South Wales any place where anything approaching to so high a moral and intellectual entertainment was served up for public gratification as that which interested and enlightened the crowds assembling nightly for the last five months at the Victoria Theatre under the magic of Mr. Creswick's great dramatic genius illustrating the grand and immortal productions of Shakespeare. This long engagement of Mr. Creswick's has not only been a great success, but it has done much for the education of the people in disclosing to them many of the beauties of

Shakespeare hitherto unnoticed, and familiarising them with a genius so commanding and exalted that all classes bend under its fascinations, proudly acknowledging the pre-eminence and power of the unrivalled poet. How few, if any, remain insensible to the irresistible fascination of Shakespeare. There is no ignorance so dense that the rays of his powerful genius do not penetrate, carrying even to the most benighted a pleasure and a comfort they cannot account for. But surely that man is not to be envied who fails to discover a deep and profound meaning in the stormful agonies and mournfully pathetic wailings of Lear; whose heart does not vibrate in deepest sympathy with poor Othello, as he sees him with fatally erroneous guidance, launched out on that stormy sea of doubt and darkness, where he sinks and perishes, dragging down with him the sweetest innocent that ever man's imagination pictured; or whose wisdom and power of thought is not increased and stimulated by the deep, far-reaching philosophy of Hamlet; or who could not extract a moral, and a striking one, from contemplating that burning hell of remorse and bitterness that poisons the life and lays waste the peace and happiness of Macbeth, wringing from him, in the depth of his desolation and despair, the painfully pathetic confession —" Macbeth shall sleep no more."

But it is not alone in painting those dark pictures of human nature in its extremity that Shakespeare is renowned. Never was there a more fascinating, fantastic, light, aerial being than the great poet, full of wild, grotesque fun, unrivalled wit, overflowing humour, and a dialogue matchless in its epigrammatic force, and characterised by an eloquence, philosophy, and wisdom

that we might search all other literature for in
vain. No one was ever blessed with the poetic
faculty in a higher degree. Do you ask for an
illustration? Take his description of a moonlight
scene in one line —

How sweet the moonlight sleeps on yonder bank.

Could anything be imagined more vivid? That
one line calls up, as if by magic, the quiet, soft,
dreamy stillness of a moonlight night with the
force of reality. Again, take another illustration,
literally among thousands —

Night's candles are burnt out, and jocund day
Stands tiptoe on the misty mountain tops.

Was not that a marvellous description of daybreak?
On reading it one almost felt the sweet, fresh morning air playing about his temples. Nothing, indeed, could be more graphic or poetic. Every
great moral purpose Shakespeare served by the
power and beauty of his everlasting dramas. Did
any combination of temperance societies ever serve
the cause as Shakespeare had done in exhibiting
Cassio as a drunkard, the sport and laughing-stock
of his comrades, " unlacing his reputation for the
name of a night brawler." Or had they ever
such texts to preach from as Shakespeare had given
them? "Oh, that men should put an enemy in
their mouths to steal away their brains ; " "Every
inordinate cup is unblessed, and its ingredient a
devil." Well, this was the great author whose
magnificent genius Mr. Creswick had been illustrating with unrivalled power at the Victoria
Theatre, to the edification and delight of thousands
of the people. The drama could never die while
humanity retained its ordinary everyday intelli-

gence. So long as the theatre was lighted up by
the genius of our great dramatists, it would prove
itself a never-failing source of enlightenment, instruction, and pure innocent delight, attractive
alike to high and low, rich and poor, and often-
times affording solace and comfort to those who,
turning aside from the cares and anxieties of the
world, had found pleasure and satisfaction in the
contemplation of the great masterpieces of our
noble dramatic literature.

[This speech was much applauded throughout,
and at its close.]

MITRED MOUNTEBANKS.

[MITRED Mountebanks and Lay and Surpliced Lunacy in contention with sound reason and common sense, being a reply to the opinions of Archbishop Vaughan and Mr. Dalley on the question of public education. This address was delivered in the Temperance Hall, where an immense audience assembled, many being unable to get in.]

MR. CHAIRMAN AND GENTLEMEN,—I daresay you will have observed that when Mr. Dalley or Archbishop Vaughan have anything to say in public they receive marked attention from the press— (hear, hear)—the leading journal, on a late occasion, awarding Mr. Dalley no less than nine columns of space, while Archbishop Vaughan is sometimes treated to thirteen columns. Now, I think that few will be disposed to deny that this is an attention and consideration out of all proportion to the value of their utterances. (Loud cheers.) I think this is the way it is done : those gentlemen deliberately write out all they have to say long before the night of meeting, and the probability is that their speeches are in print before they are delivered. (Laughter.) I do not expect

any such attention from the press, simply because
I have neither time nor inclination to supply the
manuscript; but I will at least have the satisfaction of conclusively proving, in the estimation of
this overcrowded meeting, that there has nothing
so feeble, nothing so shallow and fallacious fallen
from any speaker or writer in the history of this
controversy than what has fallen from Archbishop
Vaughan and Mr. Dalley. (Loud cheers.) Not
only this, but I believe I am correct when I say
that this meeting will not separate without passing
a resolution that not another farthing of the money
of the State shall be spent for the support of
Denominational schools. (Loud and prolonged
cheering.) Mr. Dalley had, no doubt, the reputation of being a man of considerable accomplishments. I do not deny the justice of this opinion,
although my view of the matter is much more
moderate than that which seems to prevail—
(hear, hear)—and I always carry with me the
thought of the mental disability or defect which
must accompany the man who seriously believes in
such a creed as that of Rome. (Loud cheers.) I
use the word seriously, because thousands of people
merely pretend to believe in it, and one-half of its
adherents are too ignorant to have any rational
belief at all. (Cheers and laughter.) The man
who seriously believed in the monstrosities of such
a creed was beyond the pale of reason, and must
be left to the full enjoyment of his miserable
delusion. (Loud laughter.) Mr. Dalley, I remember, not many months back, was on our side
on this great question. (Hear, hear, and cheers.)
He was a member of a Government that struck a
heavy blow at Denominationalism, and I know of no
more melancholy picture than the sight of such a

man allowing himself to be made a tool and
instrument of a benighted priestcraft (loud cheers),
and advocating on a public platform as truth
what he has so frequently exposed and denounced
as the most absurd error. (Prolonged cheering.)
Mr. Dalley is now acting under the shadow of a
dark and dangerous superstition. He has apparently surrendered himself, body and soul, into the
hands of a gang of ignorant priests. Let us,
therefore, this night, with all solemnity, erase his
name from the roll of the army of progress.
(Loud cheers.) He has lashed the putrid festering
dead body of Popery to him, and, thus accoutred,
let him drift on towards that eternity to which we
are all hastening, deriving what consolation he
may from its dead, rotten carcase. (Great cheering.) Mr. Dalley opened his address with a
miserable, unmanly whine about the ill-treatment
and insults the poor Roman Catholics were receiving. I suppose he referred to the sharp criticism
of their religious and political views. Now whatever is offered to human belief for its acceptance
is, that moment, subject to the ordeal of the
severest criticism, and, if necessary, the most
powerful exposure and denunciation ; and just in
proportion as a man is wedded to the truth, in the
same proportion is he bound to come forward in
fierce antagonism to every form of falsehood.
Well, then, we are asked to believe in the dogmas
of Rome. We are told they are true. Knowing
them to be as false as hell, where they apparently
originated, we are bound, by our respect for, and
love of truth, to come forward, on all occasions,
and expose this monstrous system by every fair
and just means. (Prolonged cheering.) Insulting
the poor Roman Catholics forsooth ! Does Mr.

Dalley forget who began this sort of thing? (Loud cheers.) Is he oblivious to the fact that Archbishop Vaughan denounced our most excellent public schools "as seed plots of immorality, infidelity, and lawlessness?" Does Mr. Dalley imagine that the ladies and gentlemen who send their children to those schools, which Mr. Dalley so lately eulogised, do not feel cruelly insulted by the language of Archbishop Vaughan? Since Archbishop Vaughan has opened this controversy with lying abuse of our Public School System— let him look to it—he may expect no quarter after this. Living in such a miserable glass house as he does, let him not be surprised if it is shivered to atoms. But the amusing part of Mr. Dalley's address is that no sooner than he has uttered his whine about the ill-usage of the poor Roman Catholics, he straightway commences to sneer at those gentlemen who have appeared on Sydney platforms advocating the opposite side, and never did Mr. Dalley commit a greater mistake than in this. Unfortunately for Mr. Dalley's sneers the Sydney platform speakers have been men eminent for their high intellectual attainments. Dr. Kelynack and the Rev. Mr. Jefferies will rank higher than either Mr. Dalley or Archbishop Vaughan, or both put together, in the possession of a keen intellectual insight and great mental depth and strength. Dr. Kelynack's deliverance, in point of eloquence, thoughtfulness, argumentative force, and remarkable felicity of expression, was far and away superior to anything that has ever fallen from Dr. Vaughan, and I would not insult Dr. Kelynack by comparing it to the wishy-washy platitudes of Mr. Dalley's nine columns. Mr. Jefferies' fine scholarly disquisition, so full of truth and common-sense, might be used as a text-book to educate Mr. Dalley and Archbishop Vaughan. (Great cheers.) Yet those are the men that Mr. Dalley, with boundless flippancy and presumption, attempts to sneer at. The only other gentleman that appeared on the Sydney platform was the Rev. Pastor Allen, an honest, truth-loving man, who, in point of refinement and culture, was, surely, infinitely superior to the Father Gilhoolies and Father Mulcahys of the other side—(roars of laughter)—Mr. Dalley's enlightened spiritual guides—to say nothing of the elegant and highly classical-looking and polished Paddy Quinn, the Bathurst Bishop. (Prolonged shouts of laughter.) If many of Mr. Dalley's spiritual guides could write their own names it was as much as they were equal to, and yet Mr. Dalley, surrounded as he is by the lowest type of ignorant Irish priests, and used by them as their mouthpiece and tool, has the short-sighted insolence to affect to sneer at such men as Dr. Kelynack and Mr. Jefferies. Another remarkable feature in this extraordinary address of Mr. Dalley was his reference to toleration. How dare any Papist take such a word in his mouth ! (Loud cheers.) Mr. Dalley belongs to a Church that is the most intolerant organization in existence—(hear, hear)—an organization which, when it is in the majority, prohibits all other worship but its own. All Protestant worship was suppressed in Catholic countries, and Protestants were not even allowed to bury their dead within the towns of Catholic countries ; and yet Mr. Dalley, with an insensibility and ignorance of the character and history of the political organization which he belongs to—miscalled a Church—dares prate about toleration. Suppose this

F

country was a dependency of a Catholic power, that our Government were all Roman Catholics, and that out of seventy-three representatives of the people, comprising our Parliament, that only eight or nine were Protestants, what sort of toleration might we then expect? (Long continued cheering.) Why, our free worship of God, according to our deliberate belief, would be put down by violence, and the nauseous fables and lies of Rome would be thrust upon us, calling forth, on our part, resistance to the death. (Great cheering.) Glancing at Mr. Dalley's utterances a little further, there was nothing in his whole speech I was more absolutely shocked and horrified at than his eulogy of the detestable Jesuits. Mr. Dalley, after sounding the praises of the Jesuits in the language of extravagance, says that they have blessed every portion of the earth where they have been. Jesuitism had become an English word, and what did it mean? Fraud, deception, double-dealing, and lying (loud cheers); and not only so, but the Jesuits had adopted a system of what they called morals, by which every crime in the calendar, from murder downwards, might be extenuated, and the commission of it defended as a virtue. They had earned the detestation of Europe, and Roman Catholic Governments had expelled them from Roman Catholic capitals. They were repeatedly expelled from Rome, France, Austria, and Spain, not by Protestants but by Roman Catholics, who could not endure their gross immoralities nor their destructive teachings so ruinous to all human rectitude and virtue. Their treasonous designs against the good government of states, and their hateful and hellish teachings, had raised humanity against them, and forced them to skulk about

wherever they went in disguise, and yet Mr. Dalley
comes before a Sydney audience, in this enlightened era, to eulogise the Jesuits and their
principles, and to tell his hearers that this
detestable crew had blessed every spot of earth
where they had been. The Jesuits were hated
among men, even among Roman Catholic men.
Their principles are the most pernicious ever
imagined even in hell's darkest corner, and the
people may imagine the extent of Mr. Dalley's
blindness and the depth of his delusion, standing,
as he does, in the infamous position of the eulogist
of such men. In speaking of the Jesuits as I have
done I have merely spoken the opinion of
enlightened Europe. They had been destroyed
in England, and would never get a footing there
again. (Loud cheering.) In case anyone was
so foolish as to imagine for a moment that I had
exaggerated in speaking of the Jesuits, I will
support my position by the opinion of two very
great men, one of them possessed of the most
distinguished and powerful intellect at present
living, and the other the purest public man in
Europe—I refer to Thomas Carlyle and General
Garibaldi. (Prolonged cheering and great enthusiasm.) General Garibaldi was a very different
man from Mr. Dalley (great laughter); he had
seen Popery in all its hateful deformity, he was
born and bred in its midst; he looked on it as the
downdrag of his country and the degradation of his
countrymen; he saw, under the rule of the priest,
the people growing up in ignorance, crime going
about unpunished; the priests halving the spoil
with the criminal; he saw open and undisguised
immorality rampant, and beggary, and thieving,
as the most direct product of Romish priestcraft.

Listen to what he says, then, of Mr. Dalley's favourites—the Jesuits. What he says is in a letter addressed to myself, and is as follows:—

" Capera, 16th March, 1870.

"MY DEAR BUCHANAN,

"The principal obstacle to human progress is the Romish priest, and those who think civilization will destroy him easily are mistaken. An impure emanation of evil in the human family, he is like that herb that spreads the more you apparently destroy it. Look at the Jesuits, hated, insulted, trampled upon, and expelled from every city in Europe; they are at present the absolute masters of the Pope and his imbeciles, and in France they are all powerful. It is a pity that a generous people like the Irish should fail to see that the Romish priest is the main cause of their abasement, their misery, and their degradation.

"I trust you will not suffer the presence of this human reptile in your beautiful and virgin country; and if any-one says there must be liberty to all, answer him that you will not give liberty to vipers, assassins, and crocodiles—and the Jesuit priest is worse than any or all these.

" Yours, ever sincerely,
"G. GARIBALDI."

So speaks the illustrious Garibaldi, a man who saw his country ruined and cursed by Popery, and devoted himself to its exposure and denunciation during the whole of his brave and glorious life. (Loud cheers.) I will now read to you what the renowned Thomas Carlyle says of those accursed Jesuits. Carlyle is a man whose genius stands unequalled, at present, in the world's history. With a tithe of it you could make a score of such minds as your Newmans, Mannings, and Vaughans; he is a man whose splendid and powerful intellect is as much admired in France,

Germany, and America, as in England, and he is not a greater ornament to literature than he is a friend to truth. One cannot read the magnificent writings of Thomas Carlyle without being struck with their eternal truthfulness. I believe he would die sooner than write what was not true— a great philosopher and patriot, no literary man has conferred such services on the human race; he will therefore be listened to with the utmost deference and respect, and this is what he says on the subject :—

" So it may be said these current, and now happily moribund times of ours are worthy to be called, in loose language, the age of Jesuitism—an epoch whose Palinurus is the wretched mortal known among men as Ignatius Loyola. For some two centuries the genius of mankind has been dominated by the gospel of Ignatius, perhaps the strangest, and certainly the most fatal, ever preached hitherto under the sun. To me this Loyola seems historically definable as the poison fountain from which those rivers of falsehood and bitterness that now sub-merge the world have flowed. Under this thrice Stygian gospel of Jesuitism the Papist has this long while sat ; a doctrine of devils I do think, if ever there was one, and are now, ever since 1789, with endless misery and astonishment, confusedly awakening out of the same, uncertain whether towards swift agony of social death, or towards slow martyrdom of recovery into spiritual and social life. Jesuitism and its many Popish supporters who have believed the falsehood of it; universal prevalence from pole to pole of such a doctrine of devils ; reverent faith in the dead human formulas, and somnolent contempt of the divine ever living facts ; who will deliver us from the body of this death, a living criminal (as in the old Roman days) with a corpse lashed fast to him. What wretch could have deserved such a doom ? Jesuitism, centuries ago, gave satisfaction to the devil's

advocate, the Pope, and other parties interested. Its
founder was canonized, named saint, and raised duly into
heaven, officially so-called ; whereupon with many he
passes ever since for a kind of god. Alas! the admiration of mankind goes a strange road in these times. A
poor man, in our day, has many gods foisted on him, and
big voices bid him worship or be damned in a menacing
and confusing manner. What shall he do? By far the
greater part of those gods, canonized by the Pope, are .
mere dumb sticks and stones, and, occasionally, beatified
prize oxen ; nay, some of them who have articulate
faculty are devils instead of gods. If Ignatius, worshipped
by millions as a kind of god, is, in eternal fact, a kind of
devil, or enemy of whatsoever is god-like in man's
existence, surely it is pressingly expedient that men were
made aware of it—that men, with whatever earnestness is
yet in them, laid it awfully to heart. Of Jesuitism, then,
I must take leave to say, there can this be recorded, that
probably it has done more mischief on the earth than all
else put together. A scandalous mortal, O brethren of
mankind, who live by truth and not by falsity, I call its
founder. Frantic mortal, wilt thou at the bidding of any
Pope war against Almighty God? Is there no inspiration then but a Romish one, with big revenues, loud
liturgies, and red stockings? Quench not among us, I
advise thee, the monitions of that thrice sacred gospel,
holier than all gospels which dwells in each man direct
from the maker of him, the knowledge of right and wrong.
The principles of Jesuitism are hateful, and even hellish.
To cherish pious thoughts and assiduously keep your eye
directed to a heaven that is not real, will that yield divine
life to you or hideous galvanic life in death ? To cherish
many quasi-human virtues, and wed them all to the
principle that God can be served by believing what is not
true ; to put out the sacred lamp of intellect within you ;
to decide on maiming yourself of that higher god-like gift
which God himself has given you with a silent but awful
charge in regard to it ; to be bullied and bow-wowed out

of your loyalty to the God of light by big phantasms and three-hatted chimeras! Can I call that by the name of nobleness and human courage? This country has been tolerably cleared of Jesuits proper by earnest pious thought and fight, and the labours of the valiant born to us, nor is there any danger of their ever coming to a head here again. But, alas, the expulsion of the Jesuit body avails us little, when the Jesuit soul has so nestled itself in the heart of mankind. What we have to complain of is, that most men have become Jesuits! That few men speak truth to you or to themselves, and with blasphemous audacity pretend not to know that they are lying. This is the full heritage bequeathed to us by Jesuitism; to this sad stage has our battle with it come. Men had served the devil, and men had very imperfectly served God, but to think that God could be served more perfectly by taking the devil into partnership—this was reserved for Jesuitism to effect. Words fail us when we would speak of what the Jesuits have done for men. Probably the most virulent form of sin which the old serpent has yet rejoiced in on our poor earth. For me it is the deadliest high treason against God our Maker which the soul of man could commit. The heart of the world is corrupted to the core by it; a detestable devil's poison circulates in the life-blood of mankind through it, and taints with an abominable deadly malady all that mankind do. Such is Jesuitism, the greatest curse that ever fell on men." (Cheers.)

Compare these striking words of the illustrious Thomas Carlyle with Mr. Dalley's superficial ignorant talk, and what a falling off is there! (Great cheering.) When Mr. Dalley came to talk on the immediate subject of his discourse, namely, the education question, what did he say? His utterances were a combination of weakness and folly unexampled in the history of controversy. In point of incoherence, and absurd inconsistency,

as well as childish imbecility, they were only out-
done by the pastorals of his spiritual overseer and
superintendent, Archbishop Vaughan.   Here is
the essence of Mr. Dalley's philosophy and wisdom.
That the Catholics, he says, constitute one-third
of the people here, and were therefore entitled to
one-third of the educational vote.   Supposing
this to be the case, would the Roman Catholics
of this community, from whose ranks half the
criminals of the country were supplied, agree to
pay half the cost of convicting and maintaining
them?   (Intense applause.)   I do not think I am
out in this matter; I have occasion to know a
good deal about it.   Half the criminal population
of this country, I assert, and I am greatly within
the truth when I state that they are Roman
Catholics.   (Loud   cheers.)   Was the Roman
Catholic community, therefore, prepared to pay
half of the police vote, half of the gaol vote, and
half of the expensive machinery instituted for
the purpose of bringing these scoundrels to
justice? (Loud cheers.) The press of this country
had distinguished itself in exposing the absurdities
of Archbishop Vaughan, and had maintained a
thousand times the sound doctrine that the State
could properly take no cognizance of sect.   The
people were taxed and dealt with as citizens on
equal terms, and not as sectarians; and it was
the height of presumption and ignorant folly for
any portion of the people to step out of the ranks
of the people and assert that they belonged to a
particular sect of religionists, and that, in virtue
of this, they demanded their fair share of the
educational vote, a third, if it happened to be so.
Well, such a position was utterly untenable, and
in the last degree insolent and ridiculous.   (Con-

tinued cheering.) What would it lead to ? It
would result in something like this : Chinamen,
for instance, were pretty numerous in the country,
and they would come forward and demand to be
treated like the Roman Catholics, and have their
share of the education vote whatever it was. The
god worshipped in the Chinese Joss-house was
made of wood. That worshipped in the Roman
Catholic Joss-house was made of flour and water
—(roars of laughter and prolonged cheers)—
which was the more barbarous of the two. The
Chinese could not swallow their god—(laughter)—
but the Roman Catholics not only swallowed
theirs, but they digested it also ; and, by the very
necessity of the case, sent it ultimately floating
down the sewers. (Long continued laughter and
great cheering.) Am I speaking the truth, or am
I not ? (Loud cries of " The truth—the truth,"
and cheers.) If Mr. Dalley's and Archbishop
Vaughan's opinions prevailed, every sect would
claim what they claim for the Roman Catholics,
and we would consequently have the Buddhists, the
Mahomedans, the Mormons, the Spiritualists,
and even the Infidels coming forward to claim
their share of the education vote, which could not
be consistently refused ; and so we would witness
all those conflicting and antagonistic sects sub-
sidised by the State, and disseminating their wild
delusions with the money of the people of New
South Wales. A system of public education was
already established in this country, and I have
always argued that it should be of an entirely
secular character, and this did not in the least
degree imply that religion was thereby necessarily
ignored. The State says that it had the greatest
possible regard for religion, but that in a com-

munity composed of every conceivable variety of
religious sect, it could not undertake to teach
it, but preferred leaving such teaching to the
churches, the Sabbath schools, and the parents
of the children. (Cries of "Quite right," and
cheers.) Even if the community was composed
of only one sect, I would still object to religion
being taught in schools on the ground that they
were not the proper places to teach religion, if
such a thing could be taught. The noise, the
levity, and bustle of a schoolroom were not
calculated to inspire religious feelings, or to promote religious impressions. While giving the
children of the people the incalculable advantages of a good, sound elementary education,
the State relied upon the clergy of the
various churches, the teachers in the Sabbath
schools, and the parents of the children to instil
into their minds the simple beauties of the
Christian religion. (Loud cheers.) Could the
common-sense of this meeting, or of the entire
community, suggest any more rational course?
(Hear, hear.) This system of subsidising Denominational schools would lead to the subsidising of
every conceivable creed, and would, therefore,
lead to the adoption of a system so monstrous
that men of intelligence could not patiently
tolerate it. Besides, State-aid to religion has been
abolished in this country—(loud cries of " Hear,
hear ")—abolished by Act of Parliament. We had,
therefore, decreed that it was wrong to teach
religion in the Church with the money of the
State; how, therefore, could it be right to teach
religion in the schools with the money of the
State? (Cheers.) Were we not acting a most
glaringly inconsistent part in all this, inasmuch

as we were setting up with the one hand what we had knocked down with the other? Archbishop Vaughan had the audacity to assert that the public schools were "seed plots of infidelity, immorality, and lawlessness." I feel so shocked at the cruelty of this atrocious libel and insult to the community—(loud cries of "He lies, he lies," and great excitement)—that I wish that someone would lay a criminal information against him for libel. (Hear, hear.) I would like to see him get six months' hard labour on the roads, and I am sure there is not a man so punished that deserves it more. (Cheers.) Can you conceive the feelings of those mothers and fathers who have their children at our most excellent public schools, on being told by this inflated and shallow Archbishop that they send their children to schools where they are taught "infidelity, immorality, and lawlessness"? A grosser or more infamous insult was never before offered to any community, and justice demands that this Archbishop should be punished for it. (Loud and excited cheers.) He, however, is not done with those libels yet. He would have rough and rougher things yet said of him; and he might rely upon it that this gross insult to the men and women of New South Wales would not be forgotten. The arrogance and insolence of these inflated priests might do very well for the crouching slaves who kneel at their feet, and degrade themselves by so kneeling, but free, enlightened men despise them with their whole souls. I suppose Archbishop Vaughan imagines that he is dealing with those kind of slaves, and hence the palpable absurdity and folly of his several pastoral letters. (Cheers.) A more shallow and intellectually deficient man than

Archbishop Vaughan has never been amongst us, or been so heartily laughed at and despised from one end of the country to the other. (Loud cheers.) Now, to show you how much I am speaking the truth in reference to Archbishop Vaughan's deficiencies as a man of intellect, he says that the teaching of our public schools will make infidels of the children, and this in spite of the priests having one day in seven to cram them with their dogmas; so that the Archbishop is landed in this notable absurdity and falsehood, that merely teaching children reading, writing, and arithmetic, will not only rub out all that can be done in the way of teaching religion fifty-two days in the year, but it will absolutely substitute infidelity for the religion you have attempted to teach every Sunday in the year. (Great laughter.) That is neither more nor less than what Dr. Vaughan says. Give him a number of children every Sunday to teach them all he knows about religion, probably little enough, and let some other man only teach them reading, writing, and arithmetic during the week, and by some occult and magic influence, not only is all Dr. Vaughan's labours knocked on the head, but every mother's son of the children so treated starts up a flaming infidel. (Great and continued laughter.) I suppose rubbish of this melancholy description is also endorsed by the leading Catholic layman, Mr. Dalley. Now I ask you would not the intelligence of a baby, if left to itself, laugh to scorn lay and surpliced lunacy of this kind? I believe the Romish priests of this country, and of all countries, care not two straws about the education of children; they would rather have them uneducated. (Loud cheers.) What they want is the money to deal with as they

like, and it seems marvellous that neither Bishop
Barker nor Bishop Moorehouse, the two Anglican
bishops, seemed to see this. Archbishop Vaughan,
with very vulgar flattery and barefaced adulation,
was spreading the bread of those two Anglican
bishops with layer after layer of a very rancid
quality of butter (great laughter), and the best
of the joke was the two simple bishops did not see
it. It is a matter of small moment to the advocates of secular education what course is taken by
Bishop Barker. (Prolonged cheers.) His advocacy of Denominational schools being supported
with the money of the State will not affect the
views of the Church of England laymen, and if
Dr. Vaughan flatters himself to this effect he is
trusting to a rotten reed. The very backbone of
Protestantism is the free and independent right of
private judgment (loud and continued cheers),
and no Protestant worthy of the name would suffer
for a second the slightest interference by bishop
or archbishop with the free current of his opinion.
(Loud cheers.) But just let us look at this question for a moment from an economical point of
view apart from the nonsensical and absurd views
of Mr. Dalley, and the keeper of his conscience,
Archbishop Vaughan—great heavens! what
a charge for a man to part with! The fearful
expense and extravagance the State was landed in
by its support of Denominational schools, was of
itself more than a just ground to settle the question
against Denominationalism. Just look at this—
in New South Wales there are ninety-four places
where Public schools are established, with varie-
ties of Denominational schools also. Those ninety-
four public schools are more than adequate to
meet all the educational wants of the ninety-four

places, but in every one of these ninety-four places
there are two, and in some places three, Denominational schools set up alongside of the public
schools, to do all the injury to them possible, and
to have three, and in some places four, small in-
efficient schools where one large, effective, and
superior public school would suffice, and would
exist, but for this pernicious principle of encouraging Denominational schools with the money of
the State.* (Loud cheers.) It was fashionable to
call the advocates of secular education the enemies
of religion. This was not true. (Cheers.) The
advocates of secular education aspired to see all
the children of the State well educated, and the
best way to accomplish that was to establish
secular schools where the children of all sects
might be educated together, and grow up in friendship and mutual regard, and as I have already
said the religious wants of the children being
amply attended to in the various churches, Sabbath
schools, and the homes of the children. (Hear,
hear, and applause.) We object, with deep earnestness, to the money of the State being expended
for the support and dissemination of, it might be,
Buddhism, Mahomedanism, Mormonism, Roman
Catholicism, infinitely worse than any of them
(great cheers), and even open infidelity, and this
is what Mr. Dalley, in league with Archbishop
Vaughan, is labouring, in a way, to bring about.
When Archbishop Vaughan's first pastoral appeared, it evoked, from one end of the country to
the other, a universal howl of disgust. (Loud
cheers.) Its flimsy, pitiful logic was torn in
shreds by the press of the country, and public

* Since then Denominational schools have been entirely
abolished in New South Wales.—EDITOR.

meetings were held and public speakers came forward, and with ease cut the ground from under
Dr. Vaughan. The Archbishop, in his next pastoral, with an insolence which absolutely reached
the sublime, stated that the reason of this commotion was that the people " were dazed with the
Roman Catholic truth they had heard from him."
(Great laughter.) From this platform, and in the
presence of this large, intelligent, and influential
meeting, I ask Dr. Vaughan, is it the spectacle of
that mean, ignorant, benighted slave at the foot of
a priest, a poor, wretched, sinful worm like himself,
the one sinful man, God of Heaven, asking the
other to forgive him his sins ? (Prolonged cheers.)
Is this a specimen of the Roman Catholic truth
that has dazed us ? Or is it that other blasphemous farce of a poor, weak, imbecile, old man,
laying claim to the highest attribute of God—
infallibility (continued cheers), and when this
monstrous insult to both God and man is being
enacted, by the assistance of a gang of priestly
knaves, who chuckle inwardly at the frightful
joke, but who have a prodigious pecuniary interest
in seeing it swallowed quietly—the poor old infallible lunatic, on its consummation, is immediately seized with a fit of the gout, and carried
to his bed where he lies sprawling, a picture of
human weakness and impotency? (Loud and
continued cheers, and great laughter.) Is this
the Roman Catholic truth that has dazed this
intelligent community? Or is it the spectacle of
large bodies of men making gods of poor, guilty,
sinful men and even women, addressing prayers
to them, and worshipping them ? I ask again,
will Dr. Vaughan tell us if this is the sort of
Roman Catholic truth that he thinks has dazed

us? Dr. Vaughan had better not lay such a
flattering unction to his soul. The people of
this country hate Popery with a deadly hatred.
They look upon it as a system built upon a foundation of monstrous lies—(loud cheers)—a vile conspiracy against human freedom and human rights
—a low degrading superstition worthy of the
darkest times of savage barbarism—a system insulting to God and degrading to man, and calculated to plunge every people who are cursed by
it into poverty, ignorance, uselessness, and absolute heathenism, speedily resulting in complete
decay. (Loud and reiterated cheers.) Do I speak
truth in what I am saying? (Loud cries of " Yes,
yes.") Let me call witnesses to corroborate my
assertions—I ask you to look at the north and
south of Ireland—the north Protestant, the south
Catholic. In the north all is energy, enterprise,
and active business, commerce and manufactures
flourish, and the people are intelligent and independent. Go to the Roman Catholic south, and
what do you find—neither commerce nor manufactures, nor business of any kind—but you find a
poor, unfortunate, awe-struck people, believing in
all sorts of miracles and supernatural visitations,
living in hovels and " sharing their meal of roots
with the swine." (Loud cries of " True," and
great cheering.) In other countries it is the
same—compare Protestant England, Scotland,
America, and Germany, with Catholic Italy, Spain,
Austria, and Portugal. I don't cite France, because the leading intellects of France repudiate
Popery and priestcraft in all its bearings. (Cheers.)
Mr. Dalley thinks to strengthen the position he
has taken up by citing the concessions made by
such men as Mr. Lowe and Mr. Forster in favour

of his views. I cannot see that this will assist him much. If Mr. Lowe and Mr. Forster have made such concessions, it must have been done in opposition to their sounder judgment, and probably for some purpose—most likely a trick to smooth their way to office, or a bid to catch the Irish vote. Mr. Dalley must be aware that it is not a sound reason to justify our doing wrong because wrong has been done in England. Mr. Lowe and Mr. Forster were to be despised for allowing their anxieties about office to lead them to uphold unsound principles, but I believe the day is not far distant when a thorough reaction will take place in England, and the large and influential body of Nonconformists will strike with deadly effect at this priestly interference with civil government, which threatens to make all government impossible. (Loud cheers.) I cannot help, here, remarking that in my humble opinion, during this controversy about education, there has been a great deal of weak, shallow, ignorant trash talked about the teaching of religion in our public schools. (Hear, hear, and cheers.) It would appear that it has been discovered that the schoolmaster is the only oracle who can be entrusted to teach religion to children. Now if by religion, belief is meant, I am strongly inclined to think it cannot be taught at all. Is it the gift of God—a miracle? It probably may be promoted by the hardships and trials encountered in the journey through life, but to attempt to teach religious belief to the children in schools, would certainly be as hopeless a task as to try to teach them to write plays as good as Shakespeare's. (Loud cheers.) Religious belief is infused into the heart and soul of man by God Himself, in a thousand different ways, and by a thousand different agencies. We all, in this life, feel that we are advancing with rapid strides towards the unknown; and, surrounded as we are by the wonders and miracles of creation, I can imagine no position better calculated to elevate the mind to great thoughts tending to some sort of solution of life's profound mystery. (Loud cheers.) Men are, in most cases, led into religious belief—not by the lessons of schools, or even of churches, but in the great world itself, where adamantine fact preaches sermons to them. When Paul of Tarsus was pursuing Christianity, with the utmost virulence of persecution and with all the fiery ardour of his stern nature, he received his first lesson in religion when that mysterious voice sounded in his ears, prostrating him in the dust, and altering the whole course of his future life. When men struggling through life find themselves at last hemmed in, surrounded, crushed and beaten down by the accumulated weight of many miseries, what inspiration is it that prompts them in their despair to turn their eyes towards heaven for help, not without hope and never without consolation? (Loud continued cheers.) As we sail through the ocean of life without a ripple on its surface, the balmy breezes of prosperity wafting us along, prayers are often a mere assemblage of meaning-less words, and religion an empty name, but when adversity comes, when the tempest rages, when ocean "yawns abyssmal" and destruction threatens, "it is then we begin to understand the sublime language by which the aid of heaven is invoked." (Great cheering.) Even in the darkest abodes of vice and crime lessons are often taught,

impressions conveyed, aye, and even faith implanted
in hearts that would have remained barren and
blighted in the hottest focus of your religious
school teaching. In the school I am speaking of,
the lessons there taught sink deep down into the
souls of men, opening up new regions of thought,
rich in religious lessons not easily forgotten or
effaced. (Enthusiastic cheers.) The presumption
of mitred mountebanks and lay and surpliced
lunacy while speaking on this subject is very
amusing. They imagine they are the sole
repositories of religious belief and can impart it
at pleasure. I remember hearing a mother de-
livering a homily on morality to her son, a boy
about twelve years old; the boy broke in upon
her with—"Mother, it is no use talking if you
have a low vagabond son, no teaching will alter
that. If you have transmitted your own and
husband's honour to him, no contamination or
contact with the world will injure it." This boy
knew more of human nature than either Mr.
Dalley or Archbishop Vaughan, and could
probably have taught them both how simple a
thing was true religion. (Cheers.) Before I conclude, I have one word to say about Dr. Vaughan's
exhortation to fight this battle out at the elections, so let it be, say I, and let every one tainted
with Dalleyism or Vaughanism be marked out for
determined opposition. If those Papists come
into Parliament to vote as their priests dictate,
they deserve to be deprived of the franchise.
(Loud cheers.) No slave has any right to enter a
free parliament, and I trust that every power in
the country will be organized to keep them out.
(Continued cheers.) This is a great and important
question, and every true man is called upon to

fight with his whole soul against the dark superstitions and the grinding tyranny of Rome. Let our societies and combinations in all parts of the country be placed on a war footing and daily increased. Let the friends of secular education unite in the country and in the Parliament, founding their union and action upon an unalterable adherence to the truth and justice of the principle that binds them together, and with this bond of union animating and inspiring them, let us all labour devotedly in the cause. There will then be seen at least one great party in the State, held together by devotion to a principle. Let us have no foolish fears, but with boundless confidence in the justice and righteousness of the principle we advocate, march on, not behind, but in front, of advancing time, with a free and enlightened educational policy inscribed on our banners, untrammelled by every phase of superstition and ecclesiastical chicane, and undismayed by the hollow fallacies of prating bigots, or the more dangerous devices of selfish and designing knaves. (Loud applause.)

PROTECTION.

[On the 27th of March, 1880, Mr. Buchanan addressed a large
audience at the Victoria Theatre on the subject of protecting our native industries. He spoke as follows:—]

MR. CHAIRMAN AND GENTLEMEN,—I have taken the
liberty of calling you together to speak to you on
matters deeply concerning your vital interests.
The earnestness with which I believe in the truth
of what I have got to say will, I have no doubt,
palliate, if it does not altogether excuse, my apparent presumption in calling you together for
such a purpose. One thing I may say, if an
apology is wanted, that I have represented the
people for twenty years in Parliament, and that I
have there been, during all that time, continually
voting and speaking, and I now say that I
challenge any man to point to a sentiment uttered,
or a vote given by me against the interests of the
people. (Loud cheers.) I am a republican, and a
thorough democrat in my political creed, and I
cannot imagine any one supposing that I have
any purpose to serve in advocating the opinions I

am about to lay before you, other than a sincere
desire to advance the best interests as well as to
increase the prosperity and happiness of the
people of this country. (Loud cheering.) The
position and prospects of our mechanics have
always appeared to me in the highest degree un-
satisfactory; large bodies of them continually
idle, and unable, however willing, to find any
regular or continuous occupation; everything
having the semblance of a local industry either
struggling for bare existence or finding itself
suddenly drowned and extinguished by a flood
of foreign importations (cheers;) all workers
in wood, iron, leather, cloth, and many other
materials thrust aside and condemned to enforced
idleness, while the corresponding workmen of other
countries are kept busy and comfortable with our
money. (Continued cheering.) Is there a man
amongst us so blind as not to see that if we
import all we want in manufactured iron, wood,
leather, and cloth goods, the workers in those
materials here must, of necessity, remain idle;
while all the money which we pay for these foreign
importations goes, mainly, as wages to the foreign
workmen, while our own workmen stand at the
street corners in pitiable idleness, watching the
dray-loads of foreign goods rolling past them, and
the manufacture of which goods here should have
given them full and constant employment, good
wages, and all the comfortable happy home accompaniments of a state of things so beneficent and
so just. (Loud cheers, and cries of " True, true.")
I say again, emphatically and truthfully, that if
the people of New South Wales resolve to employ
foreign workmen for all they want in the shape of
machinery, furniture, clothing, boots and shoes,

and many other articles, let them not be the least surprised if they find large bodies of their own mechanics condemned to lives of idleness and poverty. Let them not be the least surprised if they find the country destitute of manufacturing industries, and the people unemployed, hopeless, and despairing. Let them express no wonder if they see our male and female youth growing up with no means of employment open to them, and their prospects for the future dark and lowering. How is it possible for these to be otherwise when a fiscal system is in force by which our whole manufacturing and mechanical community is supplanted by the mechanical and manufacturing community of some other country? (Loud cheers.) And this state of things is justified by Freetraders, forsooth! by the shallow pretext that we can only be producers of the raw material. If there is any truth in this most iniquitous assertion, we want no mechanics here, we want no skilled workmen of any kind. Slaves from the South Sea Islands will do our turn. (Cheers, and cries of "That's what it's coming to.") As far as I can gather, all that the Freetraders have to say in justification of the state of things here described is a few phrases such as "Buy in the cheapest market and sell in the dearest;" "Free Trade benefits the many, Protection the few." But I put it to the common sense of this meeting, even supposing that you can buy the imported article a little cheaper than if it were manufactured here, is this cheapness in any way to be looked upon as a compensation for your armies of idle mechanics and the desolation of your industrial population? (Enthusiastic cheers.) But we deny the alleged cheapness under Free Trade. We say that by a

wise system of encouragement to all our native
industries the competition amongst ourselves
would keep prices fair and equitable. In fact,
in the neighbouring protected colony of Victoria
almost every article can be bought there cheaper
than in Free Trade New South Wales. The four-
pound loaf is twopence cheaper in Melbourne, as
compared with Sydney, although there is duty on
imported wheat and flour in the neighbouring
colony vastly to the advantage of the Victorian
farmers, and essentially to the advantage of the
people of Victoria, as compared with their Free
Trade brethren of New South Wales. It makes
me melancholy to think of the narrow-minded
and narrow-hearted argument used by Freetraders,
that Protection can only benefit a few manufacturers. Protection calls into existence every industry that the country is capable of. It originates
manufacturing enterprises, employing thousands
and thousands of our men, women, and children.
It keeps our mechanics engaged doing all that the
surrounding population wants done. It circulates
all the money that went to pay for foreign imports
amongst ourselves. Who, therefore, can truthfully say that it is a system that benefits the few
at the expense of the many? If Protection enables
a manufacturer to rise amongst us who employs
500 hands and pays them wages which keeps themselves, their families, and their homes in every
comfort, how gross and ignorant a thing it is to
say, as Freetraders say, that Protection only
benefits the few manufacturers. Just look for
a moment at this. Suppose we had no manufactured furniture imported, no boots and shoes imported, no ready-made clothing imported, no cloth
imported, no saddlery imported, no machinery im-

ported, and that the manufacture of all of these
commodities, including ·coach-building and many
other industrial articles, afforded full and constant
employment for every worker in the community,
what a revolution would be created in our whole
industrial system ! What an absorption of all idle
hands ! What an infusion of fresh energy and
strength into every conceivable manufacturing
enterprise ! What an accumulation of wealth
among ourselves, and what a startling metamor-
phosis would be effected in the whole interests,
prospects, advantages, and rights of labour ! (Great
cheering.) I assert that one year's experience of
a system which brought about this state of things
—and I further assert that a judicious encouragement to our native industries would go far to bring
it about—would so change the industrial aspect of
this country, would so enhance its prosperity, progress and wealth, would so invigorate and stimulate
labouring enterprise at its very heart and centre,
that the best and oldest friend of the country
would not know it after one short year's experience of a system so sound, wise, and beneficent.
(Cheers.) Mr. Justice Byles, in his remarkable
and most able work on the " Sophisms of Free
Trade," says—and to make it more clear to you I
will substitute the word " Australian " for
" British "—Mr. Justice Byles speaks thus :—
" The entire price, or gross value, of every home-
made article constitutes net gain, net revenue, net
income to Australian subjects. Not a portion of
the value, but *the whole value*, is resolvable into
net gain, income or revenue, maintaining Australian families, and creating or sustaining Australian
markets. Purchase Australian articles with Australian articles, and you create two such aggregate

values, and two such markets for Australian industry. (Cries of " That's clear.") Whereas, on the contrary, the entire net value of every foreign article ·imported is net gain or income to the foreigner, and creates and sustains foreign markets. Purchase foreign articles with Australian articles, and you then create only one value for your own benefit, instead of creating two, and only one market for Australian industry instead of two. You lose by this policy the power of spending the entire value on one side, which you might have had as well as on the other, and you lose a market for Australian industry to the full extent of that expenditure. It is not a small difference in price that can compensate the nation for the loss. For example, suppose New South Wales can produce an article, say an engine, for £100, and can import it for £99. By importing it, instead of producing it, she gains £1 ; but though she pays for it with her own manufactures, she loses (not indeed by the exchange itself, but by not producing at both ends of the exchange) £100 of wealth which she might have had to spend by creating the value at home ; that is to say, on the balance, she loses £99, which she might have had in addition to the £100 by producing both commodities at home." (Hear, hear, and cheers.) You will remember that when this was quoted at the great Free Trade *v.* Protection controversy,* at the Masonic Hall, Mr. Reid shrieked out in tones that resembled the crowing of a spasmodic cock, " But what becomes of

---

* A controversy between Mr. Buchanan and Mr. Reid—Mr. Reid for Free.Trade, Mr. Buchanan for Protection. The crowded meeting decided in favour of Protection by a large majority.— EDITOR.

the engine?" (great laughter) evidently not
seeing that under Free Trade whatever paid
for the engine went away from us; while,
under Protection, both the engine and what
purchased it remained as wealth among ourselves.
(Cheers.) I do not think that this reasoning of
Mr. Justice Byles can by any possibility be
refuted. Let us take another illustration from
the same high authority, merely using Australian
names, for the sake of a better understanding of
the matter. Suppose we had manufactories in
this country of any importance—which I regret
to say we have not, and never will have under a
system of Free Trade—but suppose the day came
when this state of things was altered, and that
under a Protective system manufactories sprung
up in every district—well, then suppose woollen
stockings to the value of £500,000 a-year are
made at Bathurst, and exchanged annually for
gloves to the value of £500,000 a-year made in
Maitland—the landlords and tradesmen and workmen of Bathurst and Maitland enjoy together an
annual net income of £1,000,000 sterling from
this source. Suppose now that from some real
or supposed advantage in price or quality the
Bathurst people, instead of exchanging their
stockings for gloves from Maitland, exchange
them for gloves from some foreign country, say
from Calais, thus depriving the Maitland people
of their Bathurst market—what is the consequence? It is this, that Maitland loses what
Calais gets; that Australia loses and France
gains half a million a year by the new locality of
the glove manufacture—by its transference from
Australia to France—Australians have half a
million a-year less to spend, Frenchmen have

half a million a-year more to spend. Australian
markets, of which Maitland used to be one, fall
off to the extent of half a million a-year; French
markets, of which Calais is one, are augmented by
half a million a-year. (Loud cheers.) The
Australian glove manufacture, with its half-
million of national net income, is gone from
Australia, where it used to maintain Australians
and Australian markets, to France, where it now
maintains Frenchmen and French markets. Nor
does the mischief end here. On the Maitland
glovemakers were dependent bakers, millers,
grocers, butchers, tailors, shoemakers, &c., with
their servants and families. The migration of the
glove trade from Maitland to Calais ruins all;
they are destroyed like a hive of bees." (Loud
cheering, and cries of "True.") Let me illustrate this subject a little further, by recording a
little bit of trade history, which will enable you
to see clearly what a disaster Free Trade is to a
young struggling country like this. When last
in England I met a gentleman who was carrying
on business as a merchant in a small seaport
town. He told me the following story. He said
he had orders from Melbourne—at this time
Victoria was under Free Trade principles—for
certain machinery to be manufactured at a certain
fixed price. He asked some engineers if they
could execute the order; they declined to do so
at the price. He then had recourse to a clever
blacksmith of the town, whose prospects were at
this time at the lowest ebb, probably not worth
£10. Well, the blacksmith undertook the work
willingly, and executed it with cleverness and
alacrity. The result was that the blacksmith got
a prodigious quantity of this work, his fortunes

rose, large workships were erected, and numerous hands employed. In about ten years the blacksmith had made a large fortune, and he resolved to see the country that had been such a benefactor to him. He consequently took his passage in the ill-fated *London* for Australia, and unfortunately met the fate of almost all concerned in that disastrous voyage. He had appointed the gentleman already spoken of, and who opened up this splendid prospect to him by first employing him, as his executor, and that gentleman informed me that his estate realized £87,000, besides the cost of large and extensive works. He had employed numerous hands in carrying on this trade, who drew high and regular wages. Now I ask this audience to reflect on this for a moment. All this work might, and should, have been done in Melbourne. (Loud and continued cheers.) It went away from Melbourne to employ foreign workmen, and to enrich the foreign manufacturer. If Victoria, at that time, had adopted the wise and salutary principle of protecting its own people, and encouraging its own industries, the £87,000 that was realized at home in ten years would have been realized by a Melbourne manufacturer instead of an English one. The extensive and expensive workshops that were erected to carry on this trade would have been erected in Melbourne instead of the English sea-port town referred to; the hundreds of workmen employed to execute this extensive work would have been Melbourne workmen instead of English workmen. (Great cheering.) So that the prodigious loss to the colony by this little bit of trade history is so palpable that a blind man might see it. (Cheers, and cries of "True.") No doubt it will be said that the English manufacturer could do the work cheaper than the Victorian. Probably he could at a time when Free Trade had struck everything in the shape of manufacturing industry with paralysis, and laid waste the whole industrial prospects of the country. But Victoria has awakened from the delusion of Free Trade; and I know as a fact that, at the present moment, Victoria could turn out the same machinery cheaper than it was at the time imported from England, and cheaper than it could now be imported from that country. (Cheers.) Free-traders cannot answer arguments of this description—they prefer to pass them by in silence. But just let us look a little into the history of this great question, with a keen rapid glance which time necessitates. As far back as the time of Queen Elizabeth, and anterior to that time, no country was so environed by protective laws as England. She was protected at all points, and under this system she achieved whatever wealth and greatness was hers up to the time when she adopted the principle of Free Trade. England's policy seemed to be to create markets abroad for her manufactures, and to protect herself strictly at home from any injuries by importations. Although she herself was wedded to Protection she enforced Free Trade upon all her colonies, including America, then a colony of hers. Ireland was treated in the same way, and looked upon merely as a market for England's manufactures, as was also India and the Cape of Good Hope. At the time spoken of England's treatment of her colonies was very different to what it is now, and the most unpalatable things were forced upon the colonies until open rebellion brought about emancipation and freedom, as in the case of America. The very same spirit shows itself in some quarters in England at the present time, and may be seen in the angry spirit in which the colonial protective laws are condemned, showing that England has no consideration for the interests of the people here, but merely wishes to use the colonies for her own advantage, or, in other words, as markets for the absorption of her manufactures. (Loud cheers.) England turns a deaf ear to the fact that Protection is undeniably benefiting Canada and Victoria; but what is that to her, they have closed their doors against her manufactures, and that is an unpardonable fault, no matter what prosperity it brings to the colonies named. The time was when England would not have permitted this, but in these enlightened times the colonies can govern themselves, and seem to be resolutely bent to study their own interest in whatever legislation they adopt. England may grumble as much as she likes at the loss of colonial markets, but if the colonies are wise they will resolutely secure those markets for themselves—(loud cheering)—and employ their own workpeople in the manufacture of all they want. And who for a moment doubts their ability to do this? (Cheers.) Under Free Trade this will never be done. That system means abundance of work for the foreign workmen, paid with our money, and total idleness and poverty for our own people. Horace Greely calls Protection a system of National co-operation for the encouragement and elevation of labour, and who can deny that this is a sound and true definition? its truth and wisdom illustrated by the practice and experience of every nation on the face of the earth excepting England, and England itself seems for some time past to have been feeling most keenly the injury to herself by her ports being open to every protected country on the face of the earth while theirs are strictly shut against her. In the days immediately preceding the declaration of American Independence the colonists of America were kept in great poverty and distress by all their industries being destroyed, as soon as attempted, by importations from England. No sooner was an industry started than ship-loads of English manufactures pouring in swamped and destroyed it. The people were consequently idle and impoverished; but no sooner was their independence declared, than their first President, the illustrious Washington, in his first message to Congress, most earnestly exhorted them to adopt a stringent system of Protection if they wished to save their country from absolute ruin. But even before this those sagacious men, the authors of the federal constitution of the United States, urgently recommended the adoption of the principle of Protection, as an absolute necessity to the well-being of the State. All the early Presidents of the United States were equally earnest in their recommendation of Protection, as the only policy by which the country could rise to wealth and power. (Continued cheers.) That extraordinary man, Benjamin Franklin, one of the most accurate and most powerful reasoners that ever lived, writes the following letter to his countrymen—it is written from London, 1781. He says:—" Every manufacturer encouraged in our country makes a market for provisions within ourselves, and saves so much money to the country as must otherwise be exported to pay for the manufactures he supplies. Here in England it is well known and understood, that wherever a manufacture is es· tablished which employs a number of hands it raises the value of land in the neighbourhood all around it. It is, therefore, the deep interest of our farmers and owners of land, as well as of the State itself, to encourage and protect our young manufactures in preference to foreign ones if we ever wish to grow in wealth and greatness." Benjamin Franklin you all know was distinguished for the deep subtle character of his reasoning, which led up to his marvellous discoveries in science; he was a thorough practical man as well as a profound philosopher. Well, then, here we have this great reasoner and eminent man of genius, most earnestly exhorting his countrymen, at the very birth of the nation, to adopt without delay a system of Protection to their native industries, if they wish to grow in wealth and greatness. The policy was adopted by the universal voice of the people, every statesman of note from that day to this, adhering tenaciously to the principle, and such men as Clay and Webster spending their best powers in proving its soundness and truthfulness and defending it against the attacks of enemies. Well, then, we sometimes hear Freetraders talk of the wealth and advancement of England since she adopted the principle of Free Trade. But is there in the history of nations any approach to the miraculous and swift advance to greatness and power made by the United States during her short existence? She is about one hundred years old, and, at the present moment, she stands at the very head of the nations of the world, and outstrips them all in her gigantic wealth and in her continually swelling proportions. If anyone doubts this at the present moment, there will be no room for doubt after the lapse of a few years. This great nation owes her present position largely to the wisdom of her statesmen, who would not suffer their people to be kept in idleness while the money that should have paid them wages went to enrich the workmen of another country. The great statesmen of America, from its foundation up to the present hour, did not believe in supporting the manufacturers of England while they left their own to perish. They saw at a glance that they would have no manufactures without Protection. They also saw that if everything they wanted was manufactured abroad, they must of necessity have an idle and impoverished people at home; with one emphatic voice they enacted protective laws, and at the present moment, as well they may, they cling to those laws with more determination than ever. (Great cheering.) Well, here is a country that has had a large experience of the advantages of Protection. It has grown in every conceivable way as no other nation has done. It is composed of a keen, shrewd, sagacious people, alive and sensitive to every injury, and just as clear-sighted in discerning an advantage, and, therefore, those who know this great people must know that if Protection was an injury to them, it would not stand twenty-four hours, or rather would never have been adopted, as the Americans are far too clever a people not to know what is best for them; but written on the mind and heart of the nation, in characters that cannot be erased, are these words, " Protection has been our salvation, and is now our highest hope" (cheers), and the whole nation, while I speak, is more wedded to it than ever. Can it be that a nation like America is wrong in adopting the Protective principle after a hundred years' experience of its advantages, and after every one of her great statesmen and writers, in different eras of her history, vying with each other in extolling the soundness, wisdom, and absolute necessity of its adoption? Surely a fact like this should teach your flippant, shallow Free-trader a little modesty, and lead him to the belief that it is just possible that a nation like America may know what is for her advantage and what is for her disadvantage; and above all, that that shrewd people after long years of practical illustration of the benefits of a protective policy may be allowed to continue it without being called "lunatics," the civilist word that Freetraders have for those who differ from them. America has grown to unprecedented wealth and power under Protection, and the nation seems to be at the present moment more thoroughly satisfied of its immense advantages than ever. But how extraordinary a thing it is that we should have the case of Canada alongside of this great State to illustrate at once the injury and ruin worked by Free Trade, and the prosperity and wealth brought about by Protection. I assert that the history of Canada mathematically demonstrates the truth of both of these propositions. Canada has had a long and dismal experience of the results of Free Trade in the fullest sense of the word, and after a most extensive and all-embracing trial of this principle, she has condemned it and abandoned it. (Continued cheers.) Under Free Trade Canada found that she could not prosper. No sooner did she attempt to establish a native industry than an inundation of imports from the United States and England swept it away. Canada struggled hard to establish manufacturing industries of her own, and again and again attempted to do so, but was always defeated and destroyed by ship loads of importations. She struggled on in this way till hope was at last extinguished and desperation took its place, and the nation demanded in a voice, the tones of which could not be mistaken, either Protection or annexation to the United States. (Loud and continued cheers.) Under Canada's long experience of Free Trade, the people were idle—everything that their mechanics should have made was imported—distress was everywhere the consequence. No manufacturing industries of any kind existed, and the nation was drifting fast towards utter ruin, when the people, awakened to intelligence by the powerful lessons of fact, rose in their majesty and might, and scattered to the winds a Free Trade Parliament and a Free Trade Government. (Loud cheers.) The Government and people of Canada have now, and for some time past, adopted the protective principle with almost electric advantage to the best interests of the people. The moment Protection was adopted by Canada, one man came forward with £100,000 to again set up an industry that had been previously twice or thrice ruined by Free Trade importations. That industry now flourishes in Canada, and employs many hands; those hands would be idle but for this beneficent principle of Protection. Other industries have started up in every Canadian district, and the country prospers and grows in wealth and greatness, while her formerly idle people are now well employed, earning good wages. Just let us pause for a moment to contemplate the significance of this small piece of Canadian history, and see with what irresistible force it comes to the aid of the advocates of Protection. Canada had done all she could with Free Trade; she had tried it for years and years, and, under it, her whole fiscal and industrial system was crushed to utter ruin, and her people left in idleness and penury. She saw alongside of her a stupendous nation which had grown to her unparalleled dimensions of wealth and power by the adoption of a fiscal system which she claims as the main cause of her un-exampled rise. Canada looking, with the eyes of intelligence at all this, roused herself from her lethargy and apparent stupor, and with one supreme effort revolutionized her whole system and adopted Protection as the only means left her to ward off impending ruin and to save the nation from inevitable decay. (Loud cheers.) The nation is, beyond doubt, saved by this policy. Canada, no longer having her markets swamped and ruined by foreign importations, witnesses now her own mechanics and her own manufacturers supplying the wants of her own people. She witnesses a busy, well-employed people thriving and pros-perous, just because she has come to see the advantage of keeping the work to herself instead of sending it, and the money to pay for it, to keep busy and to enrich the labourers of other countries. One would think that a child could see the reason and the force of all this, but Freetraders seem un-able to see anything. I notice one of them, a Mr. Broadhurst, a member of the House of Commons I believe, writes to the Trades and Labour Council of Sydney, which letter was published in the *Herald*, in which he says something to this effect : " That those people who cannot see the advantages of Free Trade—those Protectionists who cannot understand the blessings of Free Trade after reading what can be said in favour of it—must be knaves, or something else." Now I ask you, in all candour, what answer can one make to a man of this description? (Loud laughter, and cries of " None.") That is just my own opinion, and therefore I will leave him to continue his enlightened correspondence with the members of the Trades and Labour Council. I may be allowed here to say all I desire to say about that body. In an agitation of this description I should have thought that the Trades and Labour Council would have been in the van struggling, on our side, for the triumph of our policy. The Trades and Labour Council, at their congress, put forward encouragement to native industries as one of the main objects of their organization; but now, as a body, they decline to interfere because, they say, they are a non-political body. Their principal object is, they say, to guard the rights and interests of labour; this involving the just solution of some of the most difficult political problems of the day, yet this being the prime purpose and object of the Trades and Labour Council, wonderful to relate, they say they are a non-political body. The great political question of State assistance to immigration calls forth the most active zeal of the Trades and Labour Council. I suppose in consequence of its being a non-political body, and I suppose it is because it is a non-political body, discarding politics from its thoughts, that it actually aims at getting itself represented in Parliament, and threatens to put forward its secretary, Mr. Roylance, as a candidate for that high position. (Great laughter and cheers.) Now I ask you, is not this a funny non-political body? The inconsistency and absurdity of this could only be equalled by a teetotal society saying, that while they had nothing to do with the drink traffic, their main purpose was to shut every public-house in Sydney. (Roars of laughter.) I have no objection to the Trades and Labour Council putting forward a candidate for parliamentary honours, and if he is a Protectionist I will support him. But Mr. Roylance is neither one thing nor another, who says that with general politics he will have nothing to do but only give his attention to labour questions. Now what is this but saying that he will not enter Parliament as a representative of the people, but as a mere delegate of the Trades and Labour Council? Mr. Roylance may rest assured that he will get his eyes opened when he first confronts the people. (Loud cheers, and cries of "We'll settle him when he shows up.") So much for the Trades and Labour Council. As a political body it might do incalculable good, and whatever it may say to the contrary, it is a political body, and nothing but a political body, and that to the backbone so long as its objects are what they say they are. (Cries of "True.") Before I made this slight digression I was speaking of the remarkable rise of Canada since she adopted the principles of Protection. Need I remind you that every country in Europe is strictly guarded by protective duties; and that all the great continental statesmen, such as Bismarck, have never dreamt for one moment of even giving Free Trade a trial, so satisfied are they of the immediate ruin

that would follow. What a country India would
be if Protection gave it a chance to rise to manufacturing greatness. But as long as England
rules there India will be reserved as a great
market for her manufactures, utterly regardless of
the poverty and idleness that this brings on her
people. No country in the world offers such
advantages to the establishment of native manufactures, and if they were established by India
protecting herself against foreign importations
that country would speedily become one of the
richest countries on the face of the earth in industrial enterprise and manufacturing wealth. As it
is her enormous population is in the most abject
poverty and ruinous idleness. England compels
them to keep their ports open, and supplies all
their wants. How is it possible, under such circumstances, for any industries to start there or the
people to thrive? But now just let us inquire
how England herself is thriving under Free Trade.
She is the only Free Trade country on the face of
the earth, or, to speak more accurately, in Europe.
According to Freetraders all England's greatness
dates from the day she adopted Free Trade; but
sensible people know that England was a great
nation centuries before this. All England's manufacturing wealth grew under a system of strict
Protection. The nation was made what it is by
the adoption of a protective policy, which existed
up to our own times, and I question if England
would have ever thought of Free Trade but for the
tax on corn. This was an impolitic and an unjust
tax, simply because England could not grow half
as much wheat as would supply her own wants; and
in the face of a famine and a starving people
how could such a tax be for a moment maintained?

It was abolished amidst a ferment of angry feeling, the people's passions being lashed into fierce agitation at the bare thought of such a tax, and in the public turmoil of the time the system of Free Trade which now prevails in England was adopted. No intelligent reader of the history of those times fails to observe that the leading advocates of Free Trade imagined that if the principle were adopted by England, every other country would have followed England's example; and if this had taken place, every other country would have speedily found how completely they had cut their own throats, and how essentially they had served England. But every other country had more sense, and instead of following England's example, they redoubled their protective guard, and set themselves earnestly to the perfecting of themselves in manufacturing art, so that they might, as soon as possible, take all due advantage of England's open door to pour in their own manufactures on her markets. (Loud cheers.) There is not much use in Freetraders producing statistics of England's exports and imports, during her Free Trade history, to prove her great increase of trade, and her great prosperity. What is the use of this, unless they can prove that protected countries, of equal wealth and power, fell away during the same period in a corresponding ratio? We all know that England advanced with giant strides during the last forty years; so did also America, France, and other countries. The Freetraders say Free Trade did this for England. If this is so, will they kindly tell us what did the same thing for America, where Free Trade has no existence? I apprehend that increase of population, the discoveries of

science, the improvements in locomotion, and the
wonders that time works, had much more to do
with England's prosperity than Free Trade. Well,
as a Free Trade country England is left alone in
her glory; and instead of even her own young
colonies imitating her example, they jump at
Protection as essentially necessary to their
existence, and thrive and prosper under it, as
they had previously sunk towards ruin and decay
under their experience of Free Trade. No question about this, that it will take an enormous
amount of injury inflicted on England before she
cries out; her innate strength, her colossal wealth,
her vigorous and energetic people, the rare spirit
of enterprise that impels them, and which seems
characteristic of the nation, will always enable it
to put a good face on the worst of times. But
that England has, of late, cried out in tones of
utmost distress is a fact that cannot be denied.
There is at present serious calamity in the
manufacturing districts of England, and her trade
is weltering in a state of stagnation. A child
might ascertain the cause of this, and it is a
comfort that the English people are not blind to
it. They say they are fighting an unequal battle,
inasmuch as, while their manufactures are ex-
cluded from every country on the face of the earth,
so far as heavy protective duties can exclude them,
yet our ports are open and free to the entry of the
manufactured goods of every one of those protected countries, and on these terms we can no
longer continue the battle. This is true, whatever
Freetraders may say to the contrary. In one year
£64,000,000 sterling of manufactured goods
comes into the free port of England from
protected countries. If England had been pro-

tected that year she would have sold £64,000,000 sterling of her manufactured goods more than she did do. Is it not clear that England's Free Trade brings her the loss of this enormous sale and consumption of her manufactures? And is it in the least degree wonderful or surprising that the English manufacturers cry out when they find their own manufactures thrust aside to the extent of £64,000,000 sterling in one year, and see the manufactures of foreign countries to that amount bought in preference? (Loud cheers.) No wonder the call for reciprocity is loud and long, at the present moment, in England; and it will be louder still as the imports from protected countries flow in upon her, in a stream continually increasing in breadth and depth. The protected manufacturer in America and other countries is guarded against foreign competition, and has the home market entirely to himself, supplying which clears all his expenses and gives him his profits; but seeing England's door gaping wide open, and a free entry, he, with the zeal of a keen man of business, takes instant advantage of the position, so favourable to himself, works his plant to its fullest capacity, supplies the home market, and pours an immense surplus into England's open door. If the English manufacturers can stand this much longer, I will be greatly surprised. It is already causing them to cry out in much agony and even shutting up many of their manufactories, while many are working half time. One of two things must take place, either England must be armed with the same weapon wielded by her competitors, that is Protection, or she must go to the wall as certainly as I speak. England cannot perform miracles, and if other nations have now reached

the same perfection, skill, and ability, in the
manufacture of every commodity that England
has long been distinguished for, how is it possible
for England to continue a fight so unequal, which
must be the case as long as her ports are free and
open to the manufacturers of every nation in the
world, while every nation of the world most carefully shuts the door against a single ounce of
England's manufactured goods coming in upon
them without previously paying a heavy and impossible duty. (Continued cheers.) Can anyone
doubt that England will very soon be compelled
to listen to the voice of distress which rises from
the manufacturing districts, and resort again to
protective duties if she has the slightest notion of
preserving her great manufacturing interest from
total ruin by being supplanted by the enormous
importations of the manufacturers of other
countries? If the late Mr. Cobden had been
alive at the present time, judging from what he
said during his life, who can doubt that he would
have been an earnest advocate of reciprocity?
Listen to those words of Mr. Cobden, uttered not
many years before his death. "What," he says,
" is the cause of England's enormous wealth? The
answer is the cheapness of her manufactures.
What is the cause of her great maritime strength
and power? The answer again is, the cheapness
of her manufactures. What is likely to wrest
this wealth and power from her? I answer only
the superior, or greater cheapness, of the manufactures of other countries." Now this is exactly
what has happened. Other countries, assisted by
energy, zeal, and activity, and the all-powerful
weapon of Protection, and seeing England, through
her Free Trade and open ports, in a position of

enormous disadvantage, have greedily seized the opportunity to inundate the English markets with their own surplus manufactures, made for the purpose, and so undersell her on her own ground to her palpable injury and distress. (Loud cheers.) Freetraders, in deep chagrin, may shut their eyes to this, but the eyes of the English manufacturer, as well as those of the English people, are being opened wider and wider every day, until the ruinous and destructive fact has emerged from dim shadowy obscurity into the clear light of day, carrying with it lessons of wisdom, neither to be contradicted or explained away, and which are at present working out their purposes on the practical, thoughtful, and intelligent portion of the English nation. (Cheers.) The statistics that Freetraders generally trust to, bearing on England's present position, prove little. Since the advent of Free Trade in England, and for a long time afterwards, other nations in their manufacturing skill were not in a position to do her much harm; but as time rolled on they gave their whole attention to perfect themselves in manufacturing skill and industry, and now, and for some years back, America, Belgium, France, and Germany are not far behind her in manufacturing expertness and ability, if they are not actually abreast of her. And, consequently, it is only within the past few years that England has begun to feel keenly the tremendous results to her prospects in the continually increasing flood of manufactured goods that is constantly flowing in upon her from those strictly protected countries. Well, then, here are statistics that carry some meaning with them as bearing upon the present argument. In the year

1877 the exports of England decreased to the extent of £46,000,000 sterling, while her imports increased to the enormous extent of £56,000,000 sterling. This, to my mind, proves that, while the protective duties of other countries reduced her exports, as stated, her own free ports increased her imports by £56,000,000 sterling—or, in other words, Free Trade in England, without reciprocity, cut down her exports by £46,000,000 sterling; while her open ports enabled protected countries to destroy her home markets in her own goods to the extent of £56,000,000 sterling. (Cheers, and cries of "Quite true.") If this game is continued much longer, on the same terms, it requires not the assistance of inspiration to predict that a great change must speedily take place in England's policy, or she will find herself driven to the wall, wrecked and ruined in the notoriously unequal contest—a contest that would ultimately overwhelm England were she ten times what she is in point of stability, wealth, and greatness. (Cheers.) I have now said almost all I desired to say, although the subject is one so large that if I broke other ground the time allotted me here would not admit of me doing anything like justice to the matter spoken of. I will have many other opportunities, I hope, of enlarging upon this, to you and to us all, intensely interesting subject, which, if it were dealt with in accordance with its importance, every man in the country, and notably the working man, would challenge every candidate for parliamentary honours as to his opinions on this vital matter. I may congratulate you on the fact of Mr. Reid having come forward to uphold the cause of Free Trade, and for having published his speech, carefully revised, cor-

rected, and added to. I say I may congratulate
you on Mr. Reid having done this, because now
you know all that can be said for Free Trade
by this Free Trade essayist and honorary member
of the Cobden Club. I desire to say nothing disrespectful of Mr. Reid—far from it, but I appeal
to the intelligence of Sydney whether Mr. Reid's
speech is not pre-eminently false in principle as
well as reasoning. (Loud cheers.) I have no
time to go into detail to prove this, but I saw
a letter by my friend Mr. Hammond, a letter
which he read to me, which left Mr. Reid without
a leg to stand on, and utterly demolished him by
a systematic exposure of his false statistics and
falser reasoning. (Cheers.) Mr. Reid does not
grapple intellectually with the subject, and aim at
solving problems by the force and strength of his
own thoughts; any capacity he shows, in dealing
with this subject, is not intellectual capacity, but
the mere result and offspring of a continuous
plodding among the dry details of Blue Books
which prompts him to attempt to prove his cause
by putting forward figures that could be made,
with ease, to bear the very opposite construction
that he strives to put upon them. As a sample of
the puerility of Mr. Reid's reasoning qualities, he
says this :—" The Protectionists say that labour
is capital : well, climbing a greasy pole is labour,
therefore climbing a greasy pole is capital." Mr.
Reid means this for a very felicitous illustration,
and the best argument he can bring against the
undeniable fact, which to me seems strange that
Mr. Reid should deny, that labour is indeed capital.
The answer to Mr. Reid is a very simple matter,
and is this : climbing a greasy pole is capital if
you are paid for it. Mr. Reid's entire speech

might just be as easily knocked on the head as this
portion of it, and my friend Mr. Hammond has
done this most powerfully and effectively in the
letter mentioned, and which I trust he will publish
in some paper with larger views than the *Sydney
Morning Herald.* To show you how ignorant Mr.
Reid is of the state of things under his very nose,
he says in the preface to his published speech—
"If anyone talks to you of Protection, point him
to your well employed mechanics, their high
wages, and their comfortable homes." (Cries of
"It's not true.") Well may you say that. I tell
Mr. Reid that he is utterly and shamefully ignorant of the subject, I say without the slightest
fear of truthful contradiction that there is not a
country on the face of the earth which could, in
proportion to its numbers, turn out so many idle,
impoverished men as New South Wales. (Loud
and continued cheering.) The labour reports of
the *Herald* and *Evening News* prove this beyond
controversy, and my own personal knowledge more
than corroborates these reports. What faith can
you put in anything that falls from Mr. Reid after
a statement of this description? But I will now
leave Mr. Reid to learn to know better before he
puts forward statements as facts that have not
a vestige of foundation in truth. (Loud cheers.)
Well then, gentlemen, if you believe in the soundness and truth of the opinions I have put forward
in this somewhat lengthy address, act upon them
if you are wise—resist, with your whole force, a
system which leaves you a prey to the cupidity of
foreign countries—act like the working men of
Canada and Victoria, and assert your own power
at the ballot-box—return men to Parliament who
look forward to a higher destiny for this country

than merely growing the raw material to be manufactured by other nations. Rise in your might against a system that necessitates the idleness and impoverishment of well-nigh half the people. Let our mechanics and farmers, and all who wish to see this a thriving manufacturing country, aim their deadliest blows at the system which at present prevails, and which transfers your labour and its emoluments to the hands and pockets of foreign workmen. (Loud cheers.) Never let this great fact be absent from your minds, that open ports mean work for the stranger and foreigner, and poverty and idleness for yourselves, accompanied by stagnation and national decay. (Great cheering.) Look to your children and the dark prospect before them under a system which encourages and prospers the workmen of other nations, while it leaves our own people in poverty and idleness. Never relax your efforts to destroy this system, but continually increase the emphasis of your protest against it. The truth is with you, and in the end victory will crown your efforts. In the meantime let all earnest souls combine in the devoted advocacy of this great cause—the very life of the country is involved in the struggle, and our triumph, which is certain at no distant date, will realize advantages for our people which will challenge the gratitude and obtain the blessings of our own and after ages. (Loud and long-continued cheering, again and again repeated, in the midst of which Mr. Buchanan resumed his seat.)

I

BURNS AND HIS POETRY.

[THE anniversary of the birthday of the poet Burns was celebrated, under the auspices of the Highland Society of
New South Wales, by an entertainment given in the
Protestant Hall. Mr. Buchanan was asked to deliver an
opening address, which he did, as follows :—]

MR. CHAIRMAN, AND LADIES AND GENTLEMEN,—
The theme I have been asked to discourse on,
necessarily for a very short time this evening, is
a great one, being no less than the character and
genius of the renowned Robert Burns, whom
Carlyle designates as a great poet, and one of
the most considerable British men of the last
century. Of all the departments of literature,
poetry is by far the most fascinating. It is universally allowed to be the fruit of the highest and
rarest intellectual capacity. It is in every sense
a divine gift, the inspirations from which have,
in all ages, attracted the warmest admiration of
mankind and embalmed the memory of the writers
in the hearts and affections of myriads of human
beings who were yet unborn when the poets
flourished. Poetry deals with themes that it is

impossible for even the most callous and cold-hearted to be indifferent to. Every varied chord of the human heart is struck by the genius of the poet, and responds with a warm glowing emotion which soothes and lulls the very soul to rest. Every passion in man or woman's nature is roused by the power and spirit of poetry, and alternately melted in tenderness or inflamed with the most ardent aspirations after all that is good, lovely, and truthful. The avocation of the poet is not always limited to the circumstances and events of this world. Sometimes he launches out on the wings of a vivid and powerful imagination, painting scenes and events beyond the gulf which separates us from eternity, and sometimes, with matchless creative skill, depicting the action of angels and the very purposes of God; frequently entering into all the miseries, misfortunes, and mishaps of poor human nature, and gilding even the hardest lot with such sweet, tender touches of sympathy that new courage is infused into the most hopeless and new strength into weakness itself. Again, we have bitter, merciless assaults upon all that is mean and worthless; fierce ex-plosions of scorn and contempt at the hollow hypocritical falsehood of the world; pictures of gentleness and innocence sinking and perishing in the iron grip of despair; noble instances of generous devoted love discarding all selfish con-siderations, and, with a generosity that knows no bounds, offering up life itself in the cause of others. "This world," says Dr. Channing, "with all its prosaic everyday details, is far from being unpoetical. On the contrary, it is full of the very elements of poetry. We have the world itself, in all its everlasting beauty, magnificently furnished for our reception. We have the beauties of nature, in their simple majesty, equally beautiful whether seen in the peaceful calmness of a smiling landscape or convulsed by the fury of a tempest. We have the mighty ocean in its boundless desolation, and, turning to even sublimer objects, we have woman with all her fine and manifold graces, her fulness of feeling and depth of affection; the impassioned tenderness of the marriage tie; the devotion and heaven-born happiness of a mother or father's affection; the wild swelling commotion of the young heart, with all its feverish anxieties and indescribable delights, when the grand master passion of love first visits there, and awakens thoughts of a happiness too vast for earth." All these are poetical, and lift the soul far above the ordinary everyday concerns of life, affording themes for the exercise of the poet's power which, when touched by the magic hand of genius, invariably find a response even in the most obscure and humble of human hearts. The power of the poet is therefore a power of the very highest order, and the rareness of the gift proves its inestimable value. As a master of this high art Robert Burns stands pre-eminent. In the short time that I am allowed for this address, of course I can do nothing more than merely glance at the subject. You all know of the wretched drudging poverty of poor Burns' life from childhood upwards, of his incessant toil without much return, of his short life being, from first to last, a painful struggle with all manner of misfortunes and difficulties under which he ultimately sank, despairing and broken-hearted, in the full vigour of early manhood. Notwithstanding all this, where will you find so sweet a singer?

Where will you find a humorist so overpowering? Or if satire is his weapon, what writer
ever equalled the force and destructive power of
his strokes? He died at the age of thirty-six, in
the prime of early manhood, and his whole life
might be said to have been one long day of un-
interrupted toil. His poems were written after
the labours of the day with body and mind exhausted and worn out with fatigue, and, under
such circumstances, surely it is surprising that he
did so much. It would be in vain to speculate as
to what would have been the product of Burns'
genius under happier auspices. As it is, we have,
as it were, mere short glimpses of his genius, no
sustained effort requiring time and study, to say
nothing of peace of mind, to work it out—as
Carlyle beautifully and eloquently says: "His
sun shone as through a tropical tornado, and the
pale shadow of death eclipsed it at noon." His
works, such as they are, are before the world, and
have been so for nearly a century, and curious
enough no poet, with the single exception of
Shakespeare, has given rise to so much earnest
disquisition, has attracted the attention of so
many men of genius, and afforded a theme for
some of their finest writings. What, then, is
there in Burns' poetry that gives rise to all this?
I say its truthfulness, its naturalness, its masculine force and vigour, its high poetic beauty as
coming from the very soul of a man who saw,
with a clear, penetrating eye, every object he
attempted to describe. There is nothing effeminate about Burns, although no woman was ever
gifted with a keener sensibility. He has a heart
overflowing with love and tenderness to all
animate and inanimate things. He grieves over

the fall of a simple flower, and a wounded hare limping past him in the fields of his daily labour calls forth his impassioned sympathy and his bitter curses at the cruelty of such an act. Carlyle, in his fine eloquent style, says: " A thousand battlefields remain unsung ; but a wounded hare has not perished without its memorial, a balm of mercy still breathes upon us from its dumb agonies because a poet was there." There never lived so gentle, loving, tender a being as the poet, and yet withal so stern and manly a character; he is a favourite wherever he goes, loved by high and low. High born dames of the nobility, duchesses and countesses, are thrown into raptures by the fascinations of his conversation, and pronounce him the most feeling and perfectly well-bred man they ever met—a fine homage to the genius and character of this ploughman—a man whose keen sensitive nature and exquisite delicacy of feeling was well calculated to captivate the sympathy of refined and accomplished women. When Burns comes first to Edinburgh he is only some twenty-seven years of age, and he has scarcely ever looked on any face but that of a peasant. He is a peasant himself, and, up to this time, his everyday companions are the peasantry, male and female, of his country. But, in Edinburgh, he is at once introduced to as noble a band of men of genius, scholars and philosophers, as could be found at that time, or, indeed, I may say, at any time, in any city of the world. Such men as David Hume, the renowned historian and profound and subtle philosopher; Adam Smith, whose great work on political economy altered the policy of nations ; Henry McKenzie, the author of "The man of feeling;" the celebrated Professor Dugald Stewart; Lord Monboddo, the original of Darwin's philosophy; Professor Allison, the accomplished author of the essay on taste; Blair, Blacklock, and many others, including Sir Walter Scott, then a boy of sixteen. Into this splendid society of accomplished men of genius, Robert Burns, just from the plough tail, walked, with no forwardness or flippancy of any kind, but with the consciousness that this was his proper place, and that his genius gave him a right to be here. He deliberately measures himself against the best of them, without a taint of vanity or conceit, but with a self-possessed assurance that he, too, was one of the gifted, and that it was in such society that he had a right to speak. Professor Stewart has left on record that he outshone the best of them in the profound depth and eloquence of his conversation, so much so that the great Hume confessed that he was more than his match in controversy. No higher proof of the remarkable genius of Burns could be given than this. But I have scarcely left myself time to say a word about his poetry. Graphic force and condensed power of expression with a deeply touching pathos are its characteristics. Take one example, the description of a storm in four lines :—

> The wind blew as 't would blaw its last,
> The rattling showers rose on the blast,
> The speedy gleams the darkness swallowed,
> Loud, deep, and long the thunder bellowed.

It was a true poet who wrote that line "The speedy gleams the darkness swallowed." It is simply magnificent in its power of expression and indicates the finest poetic faculty. Take another four lines, among scores of such, on a different theme —

> Had we never loved so kindly,
> Had we never loved so blindly,
> Never met or never parted,
> We had ne'er been broken-hearted.

Surely there is beauty, vigour, condensation, pathos, and true poetry in those four lines.   Lord Byron takes them for his motto to the " Bride of Abydos," and Sir Walter Scott says they convey the complete history of an unfortunate courtship with unexampled felicity and power.   His description of a brawling rivulet, called in Scotland a burn, is admirable, and in point of poetic beauty and descriptive power, superior to a long poem Tennyson writes on the same subject :—

> Whiles ow'er a linn the burnie plays,
> As through the glen it wimpl't
> Whiles round a rocky scar it strays,
> Whiles in a weil it dimpl't;
> Whiles glittered to the nightly rays,
> Wi' bickering dancing dazzle,
> Whiles cockit underneath the braes,
> Below the spreading hazel
>   Unseen that night.

It was also a poet, and a true one, who wrote those lines so beautiful in their expressive force, and so true.   Here is the sort of trenchant power he brings to bear in finishing off a popular actor he saw at Edinburgh —

> Thou art awkward, stiff, affected,
> Murdering nature, torturing art,
> Natural graces all rejected,
> Thou indeed dost act a part.

But it is as a song writer that Burns will live for ever.   Some one has said that Shakespeare is not

more certainly the first of dramatists than Burns
is the first of songsters, and this is true. He
throws off literally hundreds of songs that Shakespeare would have been proud to own, with an
ease and facility in every sense wonderful.   It
would be impossible here to notice the infinite
variety of his songs and their infinite beauty.
" Scots wha hae " stands out universally allowed
to be the finest war ode ever written, a blaze of
fierce fiery energy never to be forgotten, that
should be sung, as Carlyle says, with the throat
of the whirlwind. " A man's a man for a' that "
has been translated and sung in almost every
language, and the name of Burns blessed for
writing it.   Compare the manly sentiment of
those songs with the diseased unwholesome sentiment of a set of songs, the product of the late
American war, such as " Just before the battle,
mother," " Oh, mother, I've come home to die,"
" My mother kissed me in a dream," &c.   I cannot for my life understand what is the meaning
of all this poor prate about one's mother on so
supreme an occasion as the eve of battle.   Burns
does not offer his men much prospect of seeing
their mothers on such an occasion.   No, it is
" Welcome to your gory bed " that he holds out
as an attraction to them, with the consciousness
that they will be fired at it rather than dismayed
by it.   Talking of mothers, a good story is told of
the celebrated British general, Sir David Baird's,
mother.   Sir David was taken prisoner in India,
and the news came to England that, by way of
insulting and degrading British officers in the
hands of the enemy, they were chained to Sepoys
and kept that way night and day.   Some friends
undertook to communicate the sad intelligence to

Lady Baird, Sir David's mother, and having done
so, they were shocked to hear Lady Baird, instead
of being speechless with grief as they expected,
ejaculate in the broadest Scotch "a' weel, God
help the poor wretch that's tethered to our
Davie." "Oh, mother, I've come home to die"
would not be the words used by such a son to
such a mother. If there was dying in the question it would be the field of battle that such a
man as Sir David Baird would select for such a
purpose. In Burns' songs there is no such
spurious sentiment as disfigures those American
songs. In conclusion I have left myself no
opportunity to speak of Burns as a man. I have
nothing to say against his character ; I only wish
that every man who finds fault with his character
were a fiftieth part as good, generous, and kind-
hearted. At this time of day it seems to me a
mere impertinence to speak of Burns' character
as it has been talked of. He was a large-hearted,
unselfish, genuine man, and as such let him
always be thought of, because it was his true
character. The British Government could find
him nothing higher to do than gauging ale
barrels, and on this I cannot help again quoting
Carlyle, for he says with great beauty and true
poetry—"They forgot that a courser of the sun
could not be tamely yoked as a dray-horse—his
hoofs are of fire, and his path lies through the
heavens, carrying light to all lands, not lumber-
ing over mud highways, dragging ale for earthly
appetites from door to door." And so poor Burns
wears himself out in thirty-six years, he dies in
poverty and sadness, fighting with difficulties to
the last, and while he is dying in one room, his
poor wife is giving birth to twins in the next.

His genius the world is still possessed of, and as each year rolls on it adds fresh treasures to his fame. It is now over one hundred years since his birth, and his genius shines, through his works, with as pure and brilliant a lustre as ever, and like Milton's day-star

> Tricks its beams and with new spangled ore
> Flames in the forehead of the morning sky.

This address was much applauded, and at its close the cheering was long continued.

ARCHBISHOP VAUGHAN.

[On Tuesday, the 11th November, 1879, Mr. Buchanan moved the adjournment of the House to call attention to the speech delivered at Balmain, by Archbishop Vaughan. Mr. Buchanan spoke as follows :—]

MR. SPEAKER,—I move the adjournment of the House to bring under the notice of the Government a matter of considerable importance ; I refer to the extraordinary speech delivered by Archbishop Vaughan, at Balmain, last Sunday, and reported in the newspapers of Monday. My duty compels me to notice the tone and style of that speech, and I ask any candid mind to read it and then judge of the propriety of such a deliverance. The manifest tendency of such a speech is to inflame the passions of those who listen to it, and it is not by such utterances that the public peace is preserved. There could be no doubt as to the danger of such harangues. The people were asked if they would not spill their blood in the cause the speaker was advocating—that cause being opposition to the Public School law. The speech had astonished the whole community, and a large proportion of the Roman Catholics were as loud in their condemnation of it as were Protestants. If this speech had been delivered in Germany, in France, or even in Rome, Archbishop Vaughan would have been within the four walls of a jail before twenty-four hours had passed over his head. There are archbishops and bishops, at the present moment, suffering imprisonment in Germany for much less than is involved in this speech of Archbishop Vaughan's. I wish particularly to call the attention of the Government to the matter, and to ask whether this man, or any man, is to be allowed to address language to the people which cannot but have a dangerous tendency. If the speech meant anything it meant that an amended Education Act was expected which they—the people the Archbishop was addressing—were bound to resist, in fact to spill their blood in resisting. Surely this could be looked at in no other light but as an invitation to open and undisguised violence. There have been, in our own times, men imprisoned in England for the use of language in addressing large bodies of the people, less questionable than this. Daniel O'Connell received a sentence of imprisonment for far less questionable language, and it becomes a serious question how far the use of such language as that contained in this Balmain speech could be tolerated by the Government in view of the preservation and security of the public peace. Not only was this imprudence in the use of language characteristic of a large portion of the speech, but the Archbishop aggravated matters by giving outrageously false representations of history, I don't say intentionally, but none the less playing on the ignorance of the people he was

addressing. Those people were blinded as to the
real facts of the case, so that there was a danger
of their being misled into a position where they
might fall victims to the violated law. Herein
lay the thoughtlessness and rashness, and indeed
I might well say the infamy of Archbishop
Vaughan. Under the free flag of England great
liberty of speech was very justly allowed, but he
had yet to learn that under that flag language
tending to endanger the public peace would be
tolerated. There could be no more wholesome
procedure on the part of the Government than to
read this Archbishop a lesson—to bring him to
the bar of justice; and if so brought, he would
venture to say that he would very soon be the
right man in the right place. Really, when we
came to reflect upon this inflammatory language,
we would almost imagine that the speaker was
bereft of his senses. We demanded nothing for
the Protestants that we did not freely give to the
Roman Catholics; and to justify any language
approaching that used by Archbishop Vaughan,
we should have to pass an educational measure
giving large benefits to the Protestant portion of
the people, and systematically excluding the
Roman Catholics from all participation in the
boon. But the reverse of this was the case.
Whatever measure we had passed had been for
the benefit of the whole people, Roman Catholics
as well as Protestants. When we, therefore, found
the whole people standing on the same level of
equality—all participating equally in the benefits
arising from our legislation—how unjustifiable
seemed the conduct of this Archbishop? How
severely must he stand condemned at the bar of
public opinion; how, even among the Roman

Catholics, the unreflecting portion of whom he was so egregiously misleading, must he stand condemned for the language and attitude he had assumed all through this great educational controversy. Now the Archbishop alleged that the Roman Catholics could not conscientiously avail themselves of the educational measure the Government had brought forward. I meet him on the very threshold of his argument by the assertion that this is not true, there being close on 11,000 Roman Catholic children attending our most excellent Public Schools at the present moment. This Archbishop, who prated about tyranny, practised the most abhorrent tyranny over his followers. In the first place he denounced our Public Schools as "seed plots of immorality, infidelity and lawlessness," thereby attempting by false representations to bring discredit upon our Public School system, which is hailed as a blessing by almost the entire population. Who was it, in the case of Mr. Kenna, of Bathurst, that launched damnation at his head because he asserted the right to send his children to what school he pleased? Mr. Kenna had his children at the Sydney Grammar School, as in his opinion the institution where most justice would be done them, and because he refused to take them away from that school at the bidding of the priests of Rome, they refused him on his death-bed the rites of the Church, and threatened him with the refusal of Christian burial. Mr. Kenna was firm and resolute in resisting this unexampled oppression and insult, and although enervated and weakened by disease and approaching death, he never flinched a hair's breadth, but with his last breath hurled defiance at his priestly tyrants. Who can

contemplate without extreme admiration the conduct of Mr. Kenna in thus daring and defying
those priests, and resisting their monstrous demands literally to the death, telling them to leave
his dying chamber, and asserting his manhood
and the right to govern and control his own
children even with his last breath. All honour to
the man who so acted. He died without the
ghostly aid of priestcraft, and preserved his manhood and independence in spite of all the threats
and terrors of Rome. His death may be considered as a triumph over superstition and priestly
tyranny, and his example may well inspire his
Roman Catholic brethren of all classes with
courage and hope. The language used by Archbishop Vaughan at Balmain makes one almost
believe that he is lost to all sense of what is due
to the law which protects him. This was the
opinion of men, uttered at every street corner,
many of them expressing a belief that the speech
was extravagant and dangerous to the public
peace. When we consider how much the speaker
relied upon the ignorance of the people he was
addressing, and how unique and extraordinary
were his interpretations of history, no one could
avoid the conclusion that his passion ran away
with his reason, and left him not altogether
responsible for what he said. Here is an
example of the language he used :—"I will not
conceal from you, or from myself, that there are
signs in the heavens of that which of all things
else in a free country is likely to produce such a
storm as no bishop or priest would be able to avert.
I refer to the spirit of tyranny and persecution
that seems as if they were about to be unchained."
Now, surely, this is unpardonable language to be

used to a mob of excited people, and all because the Government think fit, in the interest of the people's well-being, to establish a system of public education which people may either take advantage of or not, just as they please. One would think the Government was passing an Act to compel Roman Catholics to enter the Public Schools on pain of imprisonment. As matters stand, if the threatened storm came at all, it would come from the Roman Catholics themselves, and, in that case, we wanted neither bishop nor archbishop to avert it. The powers that be were quite sufficient for that purpose, and they would no longer be deserving of that appellation if they were not. The Archbishop talked of the impending storm in a style that led us to believe that his object was intimidation, because the inference clearly was that if the bishops and archbishop were powerless to avert the storm, no other power could do so, and the people would therefore be left at its mercy. If this threatened storm should ever come, which there is not the slightest fear of, Archbishop Vaughan will get his eyes opened at the ease with which it will be dispelled, and its elements scattered to the four winds, without the slightest aid from bishop or archbishop whose spirit I imagine would rather inspire and animate the storm than attempt to allay it. Let honourable gentlemen just listen to this passage from the speech in question: "What did we suffer as slaves and helots for at home? Because we preferred torture and death to acting against our conscience, and to be butchered and disembowelled rather than allow those for whom we were responsible to be tampered with in their faith. We hoped that we had escaped from all forms of tyranny and persecution by coming

K

so far away, where we were told that all were
equal and all were free. The end of the more
brutal form of persecution and of the more culti-
vated is one, it is to destroy our holy religion. I
believe the scientific method is more effective, and
I believe more odious, than the more expeditious
way of tearing out the heart and bowels of a living
and grown man." I ask the honourable members
of this House if they can imagine more outrageous
language than this, addressed as it was to an
excited multitude, and plainly intimating that our
enlightened and beneficent education law was more
odious and cruel in its operation than "tearing
out the heart and bowels of a living and grown
man." This Archbishop seemed very familiar with
the process of disembowelling people and tearing
out their hearts. Probably he remembered that
this was a favourite recreation and pastime of
popes, cardinals, and archbishops in bygone times,
and hence the readiness with which those superfine appliances suggest themselves to the simple
and innocent mind of Archbishop Vaughan. It
was immediately after the utterance of this passage
that he went on to describe an instrument of
torture called the "scavenger's daughter," and
again compared our educational law to the operation of this instrument in crushing out the faith
of the people. How implicitly this priest relied
upon the ignorance of his auditors. Let me
ask him who invented those implements of torture?
Not only the "scavenger's daughter," but the
scavenger himself, and a long ancestry of the
same breed? If he wished to go to the grand
armoury of all sorts of implements of mutilation,
torture, and maltreatment, let him go to the
Vatican. That was where they originated, and

where they were stored ready for use even in this nineteenth century. Archbishop Vaughan seemed to be ignorant of history, or he presumed upon the ignorance of the people to an incalculable extent, when he had the temerity to speak of implements of torture with the history of his Church before his eyes. The sighs and groans of the many victims who have writhed under the tortures of the Inquisition have not yet died away, and cannot be forgotten. What in the name of truth and fact is the history of the papacy? Was it not one long history of cruelty, torture, mutilation, and every conceivable refinement of human suffering? Was not that its true history from the very day of its inauguration, or, more correctly speaking, its apostasy? Nobody would dare deny this; nobody could deny it. Just let the dungeons of the Inquisition be opened, at any period of its history, and look at the poor, mangled, groaning victims trembling in every fibre under the rack and thumb-screw. And who were the authors of all this dastardly work? Let the answer be proclaimed to the four winds. The priests of the Church of this very Archbishop. All history spoke loudly of its infamy, and yet here, in this enlightened city of Sydney, this Archbishop had the barefaced insolence to prate about implements of torture. The Church of Rome was ingenious in the invention of implements to produce and prolong human agony. And to whom were those infernal machines applied? They were applied notably to men of genius, whose grand intellects had made discoveries for the benefit of humanity; and it was because they would not recant their faith in their discoveries, which conflicted with the superstitions of Rome, that those terrible appliances of

torture and death were brought to bear on them.
No Government, no State, no church, no organization of any kind had so signalized itself by cruel
relentless torture and persecution as had the
Church of Rome. This is a fact known to intelligent mankind, and can neither be gainsaid or
denied. And yet this man, Archbishop Vaughan,
talked of the persecution he had suffered, talked of
himself as a helot and a slave coming from England
where, for the last fifty years, a Liberal Government had been in the van in lifting off disabilities
from all sects—from Dissenters and Jews, as well
as from Roman Catholics. All this must be known
to Dr. Vaughan, and his speech at Balmain could
have been intended for no other purpose but to
inflame the minds of his hearers against the education law of this country. Anyone who knew
the history of the world must be filled with absolute wonder on reading this speech of Archbishop
Vaughan's. Did he forget the terror and agonies
of that awful St. Bartholomew's night when wild
massacre ran riot? Did he forget that that was
the result of a Popish plot, which was planned and
deliberated upon for years before it was executed?
Did he forget that, with the sanction and authority
of the Pope, a body of innocent people, men,
women, and children, in the dead of night, when
helpless and asleep in bed, at a given signal, were
ruthlessly slaughtered and mangled by the most
detestable and cowardly acts ever perpetrated
under the silent stars of heaven? Did Archbishop
Vaughan forget these things, or did he think that
we could ever forget them? The record of that
bloody massacre gleamed in lurid flames from the
world's past history, and would not suffer itself to
be extinguished. It would never be erased from

the memory of man, but would stand out high and conspicuous above every event of history, an everlasting monument of the cruelty, cowardice, and infamy of the Church of Rome. But retribution had followed and continues, and ever will continue to follow, as the intelligent reader of history cannot fail to observe, seen in the fact, as a great writer has remarked, that the streets and gutters of the city of that massacre had since periodically run red with the blood of archbishops and priests, thus marking the universal hatred of the act which lived, and ever will live, in the human heart. It would occupy too much time were I to go into the history of the enormities of this Church. Its whole history was one long dark night of cruelty and oppression, blasphemy and bloodshed. Archbishop Vaughan told the people at Balmain that he was ready to spill his blood in the cause. I suppose he meant the cause of resisting our education law. The Archbishop said this when surrounded by a number of friends and when danger was very far away. But when the time of blood-spilling comes, if it ever comes, it will probably require a pair of very sharp eyes to light upon Dr. Vaughan within a mile of it. He is not the man to incur any risks dangerous to the comforts and luxuries of his very easy life. But he had an admirable opportunity of serving his poor flock without spilling his blood. We see him rolling along every day in a rich equipage drawn by two horses—I suppose in imitation of the Apostles. Why does he not sell his carriage and horses, and give the proceeds to the poor? That would be a means of serving the poor Archbishop Vaughan could easily avail himself of. But no, he preferred to keep his chariot. Dr. Vaughan claimed to be a successor of the Apostles. We had received some very grand lessons from the Apostles. Their history was the most glorious extant. But they never kept carriages and horses, and drove about the flowery paths of life, ending in some luxurious and comfortable Apostolic palace. We had also the fact recorded that they never received payment for what they did. The Apostle Paul gave us some information as to what he got in return for his splendid services. Here was a portion of the payment he got : " Of the Jews five times I received forty stripes save one." That was a species of thirty-nine articles that modern archbishops and bishops were not familiar with. "Thrice was I beaten with rods, once was I stoned, thrice I suffered shipwreck, a night and a day I have been in the deep, in journeyings often, in perils of waters, in perils of robbers, in perils of mine own countrymen, in perils by the heathen, in perils in the city, in perils in the wilderness, in perils among false brethren, in weariness, in painfulness, in watchings, often in hunger and thirst —in fastings, often in cold and nakedness." In this beautiful and pathetic language the Apostle Paul tells us of the reward he received ; nevertheless he did not flinch or shrink from his work, but went through it all and on to his ignominious death with a steadfastness and unalterable courage that surrounds his name with a halo of imperishable glory, enabling us to draw a mighty distinction between the grandeur of his life and death and the insolent hypocrisy of his pretended successors. What a difference between the life of the Apostle Paul and the life of this Archbishop. And what a hollow mockery and shallow deception it was on his part to talk of shedding his blood when no one was desirous of interfering with him in the slightest degree. Every intelligent, upright, honest man who read and understood his Bible must come to the conclusion that modern sacerdotalism was a delusion, a mockery, and a most egregious snare. Well, this Archbishop, it seemed, was going to declare war! That was the sum and substance of his speech so far as we could see. I do not understand how it was that none of the Archbishop's friends took him in hand to see to his protection. I know that the Archbishop is surrounded by Irish priests who do not like him, and perhaps the reason why they did nothing to protect him was because they were following the principle that if they allowed him a sufficiency of rope the desired consummation would be secured. But whether that were so or not I ask the intelligent Roman Catholics of this community whether they were prepared any longer to endure the insolence of a dictation which deprives them of the right to send their own children to what school they please? Did they not know that their children in our Public Schools were being made accomplished men and women, that they were receiving a good education, and, knowing that, would they for one moment surrender their manhood into the hands of men who have no right to demand such a sacrifice, and which cannot be granted without degradation and the forfeiture of self-respect and everything bearing the semblance of honour and manly independence. I appeal to the Roman Catholics, in whom I feel a deep interest, not to allow themselves to be trodden down in this way, and I feel sure that if they resist oppression,

above all, the oppression that interferes with the
government of their own children, they will be
happier men and women, with happier homes,
adorned by more enlightened and accomplished
children.   I have felt it my duty to bring this
matter under the notice of the House.   I think
Archbishop Vaughan has used language altogether unjustifiable in this Balmain address.   It
seems to me that nothing but misery can follow
such ill-judged harangues, which may lead those
who listen to them into misery and wretchedness,
because so sure as they come into collision with
the law so sure will punishment follow.   If such
language as I have referred to is persisted in by
Archbishop Vaughan, or any archbishop or bishop,
I hope the Government will adopt means to protect society from such a danger, and to bring the
offenders to justice, whoever and whatever they
may be.   (Loud cheers.)

LICENSING BILL.

[On the 2nd June, 1880, Sir Henry Parkes moved the second reading of the Licensing Bill, on which occasion Mr. Buchanan delivered the following speech :—]

I do not think the Premier can be congratulated upon the Bill he has introduced, or upon the speech with which he has moved the second reading. The speech seems to me to be strangely inconsistent, as well as, in some degree, incoherent. The English statistics to which the honourable member has appealed are not of any moment or value. They only prove that in seasons of prosperity, when the people's pockets were overflowing with money, they drank more than they did when they were empty. The statements the honourable gentleman made about America were as surprising to me as they would be to anyone else who has visited that country. I noticed nothing more notable in San Francisco than the fact that if you go to an office there to transact any business you are immediately asked to adjourn to the bar of a public-house, and there

the business is done. The statement of the
Premier that the Americans do not drink at
meals is without a shadow of foundation. The
action of the State of Maine has been referred to,
but everyone knows that the people of that State
quickly discovered the folly and absurdity to which
they had committed themselves, and had to retrace
their steps. Now there is as much liquor consumed
in the State of Maine as in any other part of the
United States. But, notwithstanding all these
statements, I contend that the consumption of drink
in America is very much the same as in England;
and that in England it is about the same, in
proportion to numbers, as it is in New South
Wales. In spite of all that you can do that
consumption will continue, with little alteration,
till the end of time. But just let us for a moment
consider the inconsistent position occupied by the
Premier in reference to this matter. He says that
the liquor trade is encouraging intemperance all
over the country—these are his exact words. If
that is so, why does he bring in a Bill to legalise
such a trade, to encourage it by stamping it with
legal approval? The Premier's statement is equiva-
lent to saying that a trade which directly occasions
domestic disruption, desolation, and ruin, leading to
the loss of health, employment, character, self-
repect, and the multiplicity of evils which naturally follow in the wake of such a state of things,
should be carried on with all the sanction and
authority that law can give it. The Premier of
this country, who has introduced this Bill, has
introduced a Bill which, on his own showing, will
legalise a trade that encourages intemperance all
over the country; in the name of morality and all
that is righteous, if the Premier believes this,

why does he introduce such a Bill? Surely he would perform his duty more faithfully, would be truer to himself and his opinions if he introduced a Bill to put an end to the trade altogether? The question arises—either this trade is legitimate or illegitimate. If it is illegitimate, let it be put a stop to at once. For my part I think it just as legitimate as any other trade, and on that ground I cannot see the justice of demanding a license fee to carry it on. The Bill before the House does not attempt in a single instance to do what might be done by a Government who understood the question and its duty in reference to it. The object of the Government should be to license houses kept by men of high character, the houses containing ample accommodation, rather than to harass the trade with innumerable annoyances and petty degrading insults at the hands of police officers. It is a most outrageous thing that you license a person of admitted respectability and character to carry on this business, charging him a heavy fee annually for so doing, while, at the same time, you let loose the police upon him to break down his door at any hour of the night ; the police, by this Bill, being authorised to do so if there is any undue delay in opening the door when called on, the undue delay being a matter for the judgment of the police. How can you hope for men of character to take their families into a house exposed to an outrage and degradation of this description? I am sure such things will not be countenanced by any member of this House who understands and respects liberty. The Bill does not attempt to put down mere drinking kennels or shanties, in fact it encourages them by authorising the magistrates, if they think right, to dispense with every necessary accommodation, so that, under the Bill, a public-house may be licensed with nothing but a bar to drink at, and thus the worst defect of the present system is retained, the Bill leaving untouched the lowest type of drinking dens. This trade might be made a great comfort and advantage to the public if only first-class hotels were licensed, and all mere drinking houses swept away. If men of character and respectability applied for licenses for any houses having the necessary accommodation, the licenses should be granted without fee of any kind. I cannot see on what principle of justice this trade should be singled out for special taxation, a taxation from which all other trades are exempt. The Premier will probably justify the tax by saying that we are dealing with a trade which is demoralising and ruinous to the best interests of the people. I hear some honourable gentlemen cheer this remark; but if this is true, why do you license it? What can we think of men, who, holding such opinions, give their votes to license a trade that brings desolation and ruin upon large masses of the people, and undermines and saps the foundations of human virtue and integrity? This is an important measure, but its provisions are such as could never have been devised by any person who had the slightest appreciation of what was due to the free and intelligent society that surrounds him. Just let me shortly point out a few of the very gross things that this Bill contains. Under the 8th clause a witness who refuses to be sworn is to be liable to sixty days' imprisonment, and so also is a witness who absents himself when called upon to give evidence. The man may be detained by

illness, and not be able to attend, and yet he is to
be liable to a fine of £50, or sixty days' imprisonment, if he fails to appear. If a witness be
disrespectful to the chairman of the licensing
board, probably some inflated blockhead who may
have no proper idea of the responsibility of his
position, or what really constitutes disrespect, a
penalty of sixty days' imprisonment is the consequence. The proposal which the Premier, in introducing the Bill, seemed to justify—namely, that
a policeman shall have the power to break into a
public-house if the landlord does not open the
door promptly—is a detestable power, and I
cannot imagine how any Minister of the Crown
could deliberately sit down and draw a clause so
arbitrary and oppressive. The publican may be
fast asleep in bed, in the dead of night, and if he
does not promptly answer the summons of the
policeman, which he cannot hear, he is to be
subject to this outrage. The Bill goes on to
provide that the holder of a license shall not be
allowed to supply liquor to a prostitute; but how
is he to know a prostitute if one comes into his
house? and is it because she is a prostitute that
she is not to be allowed a glass of liquor? If
this is the reason, it would be equally valid in
preventing her being supplied with meat from
the butcher or bread from the baker. It is
this pitiful, wretched meddling with the rights
of people that I most complain of in this Bill.
The ignorance displayed by the friends of it is
superlative, and those cruel and galling attempts
to interfere with the rational liberty of individuals
meet you at every turn. I would prefer that the
matter of granting licenses should be placed in
the hands of the District Court Judges; but, if a

Board is preferred, as the Bill takes all sorts of care that no one having any interest in public-houses should sit upon it, it would be only justice to exclude teetotalers. This Bill, it will be observed, deals with a variety of matters besides the liquor traffic, greatly to its detriment. It would have been well had the Bill dealt with liquor licenses only, but no one can blind his eyes to the fact that this measure aims at putting an end to the Sunday evening lectures which have for some time past been delivered at the different theatres in Sydney. Those lectures, I am informed, because I never attended any of them, affect to deny the Christian religion. Yielding to no man in respect, veneration, and love for the simple beauty of that religion, I think we can all very well afford to allow all opinions free scope. To attempt to coerce or put down any adverse opinion by any other weapon than fair argument, is at variance with the spirit of the age, and should be discountenanced by all lovers of free speech. The days of pains and penalties for the free expression of one's thoughts have long since passed away, although the spirit of those dark times seems to be revived in the clauses of this Bill which strike at these theatre lectures. According to the Bill, lecture halls must be licensed, and if not licensed the lecturer must have permission from the Colonial Secretary before he can deliver his opinions to the public. This seems a retrograde and barbarous movement, a pandering on the part of those responsible for this Bill to the narrowest and bitterest spirit of persecution. The same spirit that would close a man's mouth against the free utterance of his thoughts would enclose his body within the four walls of a prison, or burn it at the stake, in pursuance of their dark and be-nighted intolerance. The truth has nothing to fear; the more it comes in contact with false opinions the more certain is their destruction. Free inquiry should be everywhere encouraged, and will go on in spite of the combined despotisms of the world, as well as the small tyranny of this very contemptible little Bill. The Premier, in his speech, seemed to argue against these Sunday lecturers being allowed to continue their lectures because, he argued, as the people won't suffer the plays of Shakespeare to be performed on Sunday nights, he did not see the justice of allowing lectures to be delivered on that night denying the truth of the Christian religion. I question very much whether the people would object to the plays of Shakespeare being performed on Sunday nights; but even suppose they did, that would be no valid reason for closing the theatres against accomplished and intellectual men, speculating upon the truth or falsehood of all that is offered for the acceptance of human belief. It would be well for all parties concerned to meet the conclu-sions of free inquiry and put them down, if they can, by argumentative force and not by brute force, and I, for one, believe that, in such an en-counter, the grand truths of the Christian religion have nothing to fear. The plays of Shakespeare are among the best educational agencies of which we have any knowledge, and any man who pur-poses to perform the great works of the English dramatists ought to be allowed to do so without a license. This oppressive principle of the Bill has been extended to concerts and ball-rooms, and is a most harsh and uncalled-for interference with the innocent enjoyments of the people. The

House ought to exact an apology from the Premier for putting such provisions into the Bill, provisions worthy of the ages of persecution, when argument was answered by imprisonment and death, and the right of free speech strangled by a wild and savage fanaticism. Although this Bill deals with these important matters spoken of, still, in the main, it is intended to settle the principles upon which this drink traffic shall be suffered to continue. One would think this a simple enough matter, and so it would be if the Government would only license respectable houses, of ample accommodation, kept by respectable men, and, above all, see to the establishment of a system by which the adulteration of the liquor sold shall be constituted a crime, and punished with imprisonment. It would be also an advantage, which I observe the Bill recognises, to see to the size of the measures used by the publican in serving out his liquor. There have, of late years, been some extraordinary inroads upon the standard measures, inroads which have always tended to diminish the size of the vessel used. I observed, no later than this very day, this sort of measure used in a public-house, and so struck was I with its insignificance, that I brought it away with me for exhibition in this House, and here it is. Now I ask honourable members did they ever see a more miserable, attenuated, consumptive-looking abortive article; one feels horrified at such an abomination when the days of pints and quarts are remembered, and I am glad to observe the Bill enforces a return to those substantial measures. In what I have said I have pointed out only a few of the defects of the Bill, and I know the honourable member for the Lower Hunter will supply what I have omitted.

The principle of the Bill is radically wrong, and the details are such that they will continue the very defects that the Bill was introduced for the purpose of abolishing. Let me say a word or two to the teetotalers before I conclude. This class of society seem to suppose that it is the number of public-houses that creates the demand for drink— it is exactly the opposite. Surely all reasonable men will admit that it is the demand for drink that creates the public-houses. Suppose there are 100 public-houses in the principal street in Sydney; if you close fifty of them what result do you bring about? The teetotalers tell you that by such a procedure you reduce the consumption of drink one-half, but common sense tells you that you do nothing of the kind; but more likely you leave the consumption of drink exactly as it was, with this difference—that you drive the consumption of the fifty houses you abolish into the coffers of the fifty you allow to remain. In the language of a celebrated writer, those advocates of the reduction of the number of public-houses, believing that by so doing they reduce the consumption of drink, " mistake the cataract that breaks the stream for the fountain from which it springs, and are content to refer the fruit to the blossom without taking into consideration the germination of the seed and the underground working of the root." Of course, if you reduced the number of public-houses to a large extent its effect upon the consumption would be felt, but I believe a reduction of even thirty per cent. would occasion no perceptible difference in the consumption. You may reason as you like, but to the end of time you will never be rid of sin, you will never be rid of misery, and rely upon it that men will murder themselves

L

by excess in drink as by other excesses, as long as
the world lasts. Remove every public-house from
this city to-morrow, and innumerable private stills
will be established where poisonous drinks will be
fabricated, detracting infinitely more from the
well-being of humanity than the trade as it now
stands would do were it doubled or trebled. As
long as you have to deal with this world you will
have to deal with poor, frail, struggling humanity.
You will have to deal with men who have not the
firmness to resist the temptations of drink. You
may persuade the drunkard, and rescue him from
his danger and distress by making him a total
abstainer—the only hope for him—but you will
never succeed by imposing severe restrictions,
even if these restrictions are upheld by all the
solemnity that attaches to an Act of Parliament.
If the public-houses are not called into existence
by the demand for drink, any number of them
can do no harm. Men don't drink in consequence
of the presence of a public-house; they drink
from inclination, strong in some men, liable to
become a disease in others, and a disease characterized by an insatiable and devouring craving
which hurries its victims to sure and certain
perdition. This excess carries its own remedy
with it. If the unspeakable tortures of the ordeal
do not, with frightful agonies, drive the unhappy
victims back to total abstinence, and consequent
safety, the horrors of a painful and terrible death,
either in the madhouse or the gutter, will drop the
curtain upon a picture not more tragic than it is
appalling. As far as I have observed, and I have
given much thought to this subject, there are
three classes of drinkers. There is a very large
class, in all countries, who do not care for drink

in the least degree, who have rather an aversion
to it than otherwise, although they take a glass
when it is going. They have no liking for it, and
seldom take more than one or two glasses at a
time. There is another very large class, everywhere to be met with, who like good wine, who
have an infinite relish for it, enjoy it with rare
gusto, and take it as regularly as they take their
food, and, to all appearances, with as much advantage. They never dream of excess, and mean to
end as they begun. Millions in every large
country reach extreme old age under such a
regimen. These two classes form the bulk of
every country, and would be in no degree injured
if every second house was a public-house in the
towns where they are resident. There is also a
third class, comparatively a very small class, who,
from some cause or other, speedily fall victims
to this their deadly enemy. They cannot control
themselves—drink seems to deteriorate and destroy
every good quality in them. They have no happiness
but in excess. Moderation is hateful and painful
to them. Their nature and disposition, originally
good, become corrupted; all their finer feelings
obliterated, their moral perceptions blunted, all
delicacy and sensibility destroyed, and nothing left
them but an overpowering and ungovernable desire
for the accursed thing that has brought such ruin
and destruction upon them body and soul. I do
not care how originally pure and honourable a
man's nature may have been, a persistence in this
course of excess will metamorphose him to a
felon; will force him to the performance of acts
from which at one time he would have shrunk as
from a loathsome leprosy; will sink him to the
lowest depths of grovelling meanness, and often

leave him no door through which to pass away save that opened to him by suicide, the madhouse, or the gallows. Well, then, this is the class for which the advocates of total abstinence work, and for which such measures as the one we are now considering are forced upon us as a necessity. The public-houses, as I have already said, are harmless and powerless to do the other two classes the slightest injury, and I would, in solemn earnestness, ask what possible chance have you of serving this third class unless you could shut up every public-house in the land? If one remained the drunkard would be served, even if he had to climb mountains and swim rivers to reach the spot. For this class there is only one remedy, but it is a most effective one, namely, strict and inviolable total abstinence. This can save them—nothing else can. Legislation can effect nothing here. Those who trust to it to save the class I am speaking of, are trusting to a falsely grounded hope. The drunkard who is reformed is driven into the harbour of reformation by insufferable pain and terror; if he is not so driven, he is driven to hell with a thousand demons at his heels, expiring amidst the most appalling surroundings and accompaniments. The man who weathers a storm of this description thinks twice before he again exposes himself to the same disaster. If the lesson is thrown away upon him, and he continues his drunkenness, it will be repeated with the horrors and ills of it deepened and intensified, resulting in a bitter and tragic end. The fate of the drunkard is so terrible that all good men pity and deplore it. When once a young man finds this habit of drinking gaining upon him, if he is wise he will turn his back upon it for ever, or he may rest assured it will overwhelm him. I am sure honourable members of this House will excuse me if I try to picture the beginning and end of the drunkard, in the hope of inspiring terror and alarm in the minds of those who may be approaching the threshold of this fatal path. A young man of decent and honest parents begins life with high hopes and expectations. He is most attentive and devoted to business, and stands high in the opinion of his employer, as well as all who know him. He is always dressed with punctilious neatness, and is seldom to be found absent from his home after business hours. He is high-spirited and manly in all his acts, and everywhere a favourite. From some cause or other, not easily discoverable, an entire change comes over his whole conduct. He has taken to drinking habits, a thing unknown to him before; he is seen to frequent public-houses at nights where no possible chance ever found him a short time previously; by-and-bye he is never to be seen anywhere else of an evening. Those habits and late hours soon begin to tell on him. He is often not punctual at his business in the morning; sometimes late hours and drink prevent him appearing at all. He has now to drink through the day, and is frequently absent from duty for that purpose; those absences bring the eye of his employer upon him; he is spoken to severely on the subject, which drives him to despair and greater excess; it ends at last in his dismissal, with a lost character, broken health, and ruined hopes. He is now a pitiable object, wandering about from public-house to public-house without purpose or object, his appearance bleared and blighted, his sunken blood-shot eyes and bloated

face the very image of haggard misery. His
dress, formerly so neat and clean, is now dirty,
tawdry, and slovenly, and only serves to intensify
and bring out in strong relief the fatal ravages of
excess. He seems to be entranced—chained down
to absolute inaction, and powerless to make the
slightest effort towards his emancipation from a
thraldom so degrading, or to strike one solitary
blow in furtherance of his restoration to honourable and manly action. Alas! what a picture,
visible, no doubt, everywhere, as well as here in
Sydney. The end of this unfortunate being's sad
history is not far to seek. His whole business in
life is now drink; he emerges from his wretched
home in the early morning and crawls to the
public-house for drink—food is his aversion; he
sits there the whole blessed day, the very picture
of a drivelling idiot which excess has reduced him
to. He seems powerless to move, and is only
roused from his lethargy that the house may be
shut up. He makes an effort to stand and steady
himself, and, having armed himself with a bottle
of spirits, he reels onwards to his dismal home ;
having arrived there, without an attempt to
undress, he falls heavily on his wretched bed,
clothes, boots, hat, and all, and is soon in a state
of apoplectic stupor, instead of the " innocent sleep
that knits up the ravelled sleeve of care." In
this perturbed state all manner of loathsome
shapes and things, and wild, hideous phantas-
magoria pass through his fevered and troubled
brain. In the excess of unbearable suffering he
starts to his feet, affrighted, with an alarming
and agonizing cry, trembling from head to foot,
and perspiring at every pore. He gropes about

for the bottle of raw spirits he brought home with him, seizes it with avidity, gulps down the half of it, and falls back senseless on his bed of exquisite torture. This cannot last long: convulsions soon seize him, and, while writhing in one of the fiercest paroxysms, he is at last laid at rest, and lies there a ghastly corpse, with an expression on his dead face that might appal the devil. The most melancholy feature in all this is, that if such an unfortunate has a mother near, I think I can see her, as the body moves slowly away to its last home, holding up her hands in silent thanksgiving to Heaven that the grave has at last closed over all that remains of a son who was only an eye-sore and a disgrace to her and a nuisance and a misery to himself and everyone else, while she is painfully conscious that the poor misguided, helpless victim has left this world "abhorred, self-hated, hopeless for the next, his life a burden and his death a fear." Those who think that such measures as the one now under consideration, or any legislation whatever, can reach the class here spoken of, and represented by the picture I have attempted to paint in colours not a whit too vivid, will speedily find out their mistake. If the tortures of excess do not cure the victim, there is nothing so certain than that they will kill, and it is equally certain that, as long as the world lasts, men will discard the lessons of experience and perish miserably under this influence, so ruinous and destructive to humanity. I cannot see my way to support the Bill before the House. Its irritating and impolitic intermeddling with the business and everyday rights of the people, its unnecessary interference in matters that might well be left alone, the arbitrary and oppressive spirit which characterizes it all through, must be hateful to every enlightened member of this House, and as a necessary consequence meet with their unequivocal condemnation.

[The Government withdrew the Bill at the conclusion of the debate.]

SUPPLEMENTARY FINANCIAL STATE-MENT.

[On the 16th June, 1880, the Treasurer made a Supplementary Financial Statement, in which he proposed an export tax upon wool, a tax upon stock, and a tax upon coal. Mr. Buchanan addressed the House as follows, on these proposals :—]

SIR HENRY PARKES is the Premier of a Free Trade Government, he calls himself a Freetrader, he, in fact, has received the Cobden medal, which, by-the-bye, after what has happened, I would advise him to return without delay ; and now just let me bring under the notice of the House what this so-called Free Trade Government has done within the last few months. What I say of the Government is this, that being, notoriously, professed Free-traders the truths of Protection have gained such an ascendancy, and commanded so much support in the country that, in deference to this principle, the Government is compelled to purchase what machinery it wants from local manufacturers, in order to give employment to our own mechanics, although they say they can purchase the articles

cheaper from the importer. Protectionists could
do no more than this. The Government have just
placed an import duty on beer, and abandoned
their excise duties on the home-made article; this
is the very essence and soul of the protective principle. The Government have also abandoned the
convention with South Australia, afraid of the
competition of that colony. They last week proposed a royalty of so much a ton upon coal, but
being told that such a tax would act prejudicially
upon our rising industries, they changed it into an
export duty. Now, I ask this House what does all
this mean? You are mostly all Freetraders, and
yet you are insensibly forced to the adoption of
protective principles, from no pressure unless it be
the pressure of truth and plain common sense,
which leaves you no other alternative than to
follow their dictates. There is something in the
highest degree interesting in the spectacle of this
Free Trade Parliament and Free Trade Government forced to the adoption of the protective
principle under the pressure of the simple truth
that circumstances force upon them, and without
the presence of any strong protectionist party in
this House. No greater homage was ever paid to
the truth of the principles of Protection than to
see this powerful Free Trade Government adopting and putting them in force of their own free
will, as the only means left them by which the
prosperity of the country might be maintained,
and its credit upheld. The policy of the Protectionists in this country is a very sound and simple
one. It is *ad valorem* duties, retrenchment, and a
fair rental for the public estate. If this policy
were adopted we could abolish the Stamp Act,
and we would require no other taxation than that

we receive through the Customs. But just look
at the position of this Free Trade Government,
and the inconsistencies and incoherencies it is involved in. Does the injustice of the present proposals of the Government not strike everyone as
absolutely monstrous? A class is to be singled
out for heavy and specific taxation. An export
duty on wool is to be levied, and a tax of so
much a head on sheep and cattle is to be inflicted
in violation of every known principle of taxation,
and to the extreme and unjustifiable injury of a
class of the community. The justification of all
this is, according to Sir Henry Parkes, that the
class in question does not pay an adequate rent
for their runs. They, at all events, pay all the
rent they are asked to pay, and if this is not sufficient, surely it is not their fault, nor does it
redound much to the credit of the Government
that, while admitting that the rent paid by the
squatters is inadequate, they have never made the
slightest effort to raise it, but now, in a fit of
ignorant reckless desperation, strike at a special
class of the community and inflict it with a heavy
and direct burden, from which all other classes
are exempt, and this is done, forsooth, because it
has pleased the Premier to say that the Government has resolved not to go to the Custom House
for any further taxation. I assert that this
singling out of any class of the community for
special taxation brands with complete incompetency the authors of those financial proposals;
and the amusing part of it is that the Government is forced to resort to those unjust, clumsy,
and ruinous propositions through the preposterous
fear that its Free Trade character would be com-
promised if it went to the Custom House for any

further revenue, a Government which has already
purchased from the home manufacturers all the
machinery it wants, although it has to pay dearer
than it could get the same article from the importer, and which shrinks from its original proposal of a royalty on coal through the fear of
injuriously affecting our young rising iron industries, and which, while imposing an increased duty
on imported beer, abandoned its proposal to tax
the home-made article through the imposition of
excise duties. I think, after this, the less said
about the Free Trade character of the Government the better. The Protectionist party is certainly not strong in this House at present, but I
believe it is strong, and growing in strength, in
the country. The Protectionist action of the
Government in the way I have pointed out has
certainly not been brought about by any formidable display of voting power on the part of the
few advocates of Protection in this House, but is
due entirely to the self-evident truths which the
Government, coming in contact with the veraci-
ties, has not failed to perceive. But a Government
which is neither Protectionist nor Free Trade, but
which may be driven by necessity to adopt or
violate either principle, is always a danger to the
community where it exists, and hence we find the
present Government, in its intellectual helplessness and despair, driven to the injustice of
pouncing down upon a section, or class, of the
community, and fastening burdens upon them on
the ground, as they say, that they are rich and
can bear them. Is not this the argument of a
burglar? Surely this House will never consent to
these proposals, backed as they are by arguments
of this description. Taxation should light equally

on all classes, if possible, and no system of taxation seems to me so fair as *ad valorem* duties, which, while bringing possibly a large revenue, will undoubtedly stimulate the rise of various manufacturing industries in the country. As our land revenue has been frequently pointed to as an evidence of our great prosperity and wealth under Free Trade, I hold it to be my duty to take this opportunity of thoroughly exposing this transparent fallacy. Before I leave this part of the subject, I believe I will make it clear that our land revenue—that is, the money derived from the sale of our public lands—is more a proof of the unsoundness of our land law than anything else. It is well known that we have had Government after Government wilfully shutting their eyes to the financial position of the country, and recklessly going on with extravagant expenditure when they knew that the condition of things was rotten to the core. The sale of our lands for the last six years, I am informed, brought in three millions sterling per annum, and this we always called revenue, which it, in reality, was not. The statement that it was revenue was constantly sent home to England, while we were boastingly comparing our position with that of our neighbours in Victoria, and gasconading about the success of our Free Trade policy, as shown by a revenue of five millions sterling. I would here ask do those boasters ever ask themselves what would have been the position of Victoria had she been blessed with a territory as large as ours, and could have raised three millions sterling by the sale of land? As it is Victoria is far ahead of us in every conceivable way. She has more employment for her labourers

and mechanics, and infinitely more activity in
trade, while manufacturing industry flourishes
there under the fostering and nourishing influence
of Protection. But the question I would like
strangers to understand is, what do these extensive land sales of ours represent? The people in
England most erroneously imagine that they
represent the successful settlement of the people
on the public lands. It will be my duty here to
show that instead of that being the case, these
sales of land represent no settlement, but that the
land is purchased and used as a weapon of offence
as well as defence, and may be said, with great
truth, to represent the undying animosities of
two classes of the people, which a ruinous and
destructive land law had brought into violent and
disastrous collision. No one will deny that the
pastoral interest of this country is a source, if
not the main source, of our national wealth—that
it absorbs a vast amount of labour, gives rise to
the commerce of our port, and may be looked
upon as essentially the backbone of the country's
prosperity. Well then, I say, in passing a Land
Law, or any law, this great fact should have been
looked to, and every care taken to conserve an
interest the importance of which to the country's
well-being is so transcendent. But this was not
done. By the Land Law of 1861, passed under a
gust of passion, the pastoral interest was uselessly
and without reason well-nigh destroyed. Instead
of keeping the agricultural and this great interest
separate, which might easily have been done,
with mutual advantage, the two interests were
brought into direct collision, and have been
waging an incessant war from that day to this,
pretty much to the serious injury, and, in many

individual cases, to the ruin of both interests. The free selector, under the law, invades the squatter's run, it may be at several points; if the squatter cannot prevent this his ruin is inevitable. He consequently proceeds, by every means that the law will allow, to harass and annoy the free selector, impounding his stock, and ruining him by actions of trespass. Sometimes the squatter is forced to buy the free selector out, and this process is often repeated upon him by the same man. I need not say that I am as warm a friend of the free selector as any man in this House or in the country, and I say unhesitatingly that, under this wretched Land Law of ours, the free selector is an infinitely greater sufferer than the squatter. Scarcely a selection is taken up that is not found, two or three years afterwards, to be invalid in consequence of being on some other person's property or on a reserve. No later than to-day I put into the hands of the Minister for Lands a letter from a selector who, after being in possession of his selection for three years, and after fencing and improving it, and rearing his family upon it, was told that it was on a reserve, and that he must leave. Only the other day a Bill was passed through this House to validate one hundred and sixty selections of this description, and probably there are five hundred others which have not yet been discovered. In the face of such facts who can hesitate to condemn a law which brings about such results? The squatters all over the country, finding themselves invaded in every direction by strangers squatting down on the best parts of their runs, have lost no time in drawing the sword in self-defence—they have used the Act for their own preservation. They

have become free selectors themselves, and have
purchased large portions of their runs, in different
places, using them as fortresses to annoy, and if
possible destroy the free selector; by judicious
and well-selected purchases of land they have
hemmed the free selector in—made it impossible
for him to move without a trespass, and involved
him in costly legal proceedings the moment a
chance offered. This is the state of things as
they exist at present, and as they have existed
since the passage of our infamous Land Law.
The land which has been bought during the last
six years, and which has brought us three millions
sterling annually, has been bought by the squatters,
not that they wanted it, but simply to be used by
them as a means of destroying the free selector,
so that instead of this enormous land revenue
representing a wholesome settlement of the people
upon the lands of the country, it represents no
settlement whatever, but is proof positive of the
ruin of the squatter, brought about by his being
forced to purchase land he does not want, and
to borrow money to purchase it, paying heavy
interest, nine per cent., to the banks for the loan.
This, then, is the real truth about our splendid
revenue, said to be the results of Free Trade.
Our Land Law, undoubtedly the worst in the
world, has placed two interests in violent antagonism, leading to an agrarian war all over the
country. The free selector's fate is to sustain a
few years of this war, and then sink into utter
ruin, leaving the squatter master of the situation,
but only for a short time, as he has soon to
encounter another invader who is served in the
same way. The enormous purchases of land
which the squatters have been forced to make

have brought them, as a body, to the verge of
bankruptcy, and this land revenue which we have
boasted so much of, and put forward as a proof of
our prosperity, in reality expresses and means
nothing but the ruin of a great interest, and the
pernicious character of that law which will be
truthfully described by the future historian of
this country as a Land Law that blighted and
withered the two great interests of the State, and
has acted as a more formidable barrier against its
progress than any combination of causes could
possibly effect. But it seems that now the
squatters are unable to purchase any more land,
and so, our land sales having failed, the Government is now forced to think of some new taxation
to meet an anticipated deficit, and hence the proposals now under consideration—proposals in
themselves grossly unjust, embodying all the
worst features of class legislation, and striking
a heavy blow at the very vitals of our great producing industries, which should be encouraged
and fostered rather than weighed down by the
pressure of unbearable burdens. I say that this
odious taxation should be resisted by the intelligence of this House—that the atrocious sentiment
of the Treasurer and the Colonial Secretary that
the justification of this taxation is the wealth of
those on whom it is inflicted is a sentiment so
infamous in its rank injustice and reckless,
ignorant wrong-doing, that no intelligence will
hesitate a moment in visiting it with its utmost
condemnation. We are now, I suppose, on the
eve of a general election, and let the Government
go with those extraordinary financial propositions to the country—propositions involving a
programme of extravagance, class taxation and

M

export duties—and let them be met and answered with proposals of retrenchment, *ad valorem* duties, a secure tenure to the squatters, and a fair rent for the public estate, and if wisdom guides the constituencies, who can doubt as to the decision? The Government is all weakness and hesitation in regard to this important matter of finance. The members of it have no fixed or clearly defined principle, but are driven from one absurdity to another as defeat after defeat overtakes them. The time was when any Government found its financial policy scattered to the winds under a tempest of dissent, that resignation would instantly follow such a catastrope, but no such event takes place now. The Government seems to be quite content to see its various financial proposals condemned by the House, and is quite prepared to swallow the accompanying humiliation upon the one condition of being allowed to retain office. Well, it is a mercy that this Parliament is at its last gasp, and the constituencies must inevitably soon be called upon to create another. If my words could avail anything, I would say to the people, Remember our unprecedented revenue from the sale of land is at an end, the capacity to buy is exhausted, but the stimulant to purchase still remains. The squatter will now have to fight the free selector without the mighty aid of land purchase, and while that mutually destructive war still continues the people have only to look around to see armies of idle mechanics kept idle by a never-ending stream of foreign importations flowing in upon them and striking with paralysis the hand of industry in every part of the country. If this will not awaken the people from their lethargy, let them think of their children and of their fate in the future, with a terrible danger hanging over them in the total absence of any means of honest employment, and the dark, bleak, blighting prospect of—it may be—the bush for the boys, and the streets for the girls. How on earth can it be otherwise when every article that they should make is imported, and every pound that should pay them wages is sent to pay for such imports? I exhort the people in every district of this country to ponder well over this weighty matter before they part with their votes at the impending general election, and vote for the men who will encourage and foster our native industries. It is a matter in which the very fate of your children, and your children's children, is wrapped up and involved. The principles I advocate would go far to secure them constant and honourable employment, and would be a constant source of happiness and comfort to the many fathers and mothers who cannot fail to see how dark a prospect lies before those who are so dear to them—so long as we are burdened and afflicted with a fiscal policy which blights and withers every industry as soon as it attempts to rise, and carries away our wealth to secure the happiness of foreigners. Truths so plain and self-evident cannot fail, ere long, to arrest the attention of the people of this country; and I trust that every patriotic feeling, and every manly intelligence, will come to the rescue, and return men to the next Parliament whose lofty aims will reverse the old worn-out policy of giving all to the foreigner, while every home industry languishes and dies, and every second man we meet knows not from where the next day's work is to come. I have thought it my duty thus to address the House, as I have no faith in the Government. To the people I therefore look, and if they still remain blind to their interest and duty in reference to this great question, I will at least have the consolation of having laboured in a great cause, and in the thought of a high-minded, patriotic intention. (Loud cheers.)

PROSTITUTION.

[THIS address was originally delivered as a lecture on the above
subject. It afterwards appeared, in a condensed form, as
an article in the *Sydney Morning Herald*.]

THE subject I propose to speak upon to-night is
one that must interest every well-wisher of his
species. Looking at the matter as it is to be
seen all over the world, one can observe, even on
the surface, such an indication of acute misery,
wretchedness, and indescribable wrong that a
deeper investigation of the subject only leads to a
most ample confirmation of one's preconceived
ideas. To witness so many young girls, the
flower of their sex, openly sacrificed to a system
so pernicious is well calculated to enlist the
sympathies of humanity, and to rouse the purest
feelings of charity and philanthropy in aiming at
its amelioration, if not at its entire abolition.
The victims of this atrocious system are generally
the finest and most beautiful of their sex. Their
very beauty and attractiveness is the primary
cause of their fall. Simplicity and innocence,

allied to a fascinating, handsome figure and
beautiful face, is too conspicuous and attractive
an object to escape the designs of reckless,
daring, unprincipled wickedness, and hence the
ruin that is often wrought, and the life-long
misery that is often entailed by the successful
snares which every dastard thinks he is entitled
to lay for the unwary, and the impunity with
which he knows his villainy can be accomplished,
so far as the law is concerned.   Could seduction
be made a criminal act, and I know of no felony
more atrocious, and punished by severe imprisonment, a considerable check would be imposed on
the cowards who only look upon a beautiful and
unprotected young girl as fair game, and as a
prime object on which to exercise their unbridled
and ungovernable animal propensities.   One feels
something like a sickening sensation creeping
over him as he witnesses, in our large towns,
those poor girls plying their wretched vocation,
knowing, as we all must know, the speedy and
dreadful end of such a career.   I do not suppose
that there are many who now listen to me who
will be disposed to deny that the evil I am speaking of is one of the most frightful and destructive
scourges society has to deal with, nor will they,
I think, refuse to admit the difficulty of proposing
any plan for its repression, and even if no plan,
at present, occurs to me for that purpose, still,
something will be gained by merely calling attention to the subject, so that philanthropic men and
women may be induced to take it into their
serious consideration, and, if successful, even in
this, I doubt not some good will result from thus
pressing the matter upon public attention.   The
evil, to speak in plain terms, consists in that

strong tide of prostitution which seems to flow, and never ebb, in our large colonial towns. Few people, of any observation, will be prepared to deny that this evil, or, at all events, the public exhibition of it, exists in Sydney, for instance, in a much larger degree than in any town of the old country of similar dimensions; and surely it is worth while to try and ascertain the exact cause, or causes, of this. The rulers in many Continental cities have felt themselves so utterly unable to cope with this evil that they have, by licensing it, taken it under their own control, and have succeeded in bringing it under stringent regulations and a severe surveillance if they cannot altogether destroy it. I am altogether opposed to this plan on the simple ground that neither the State nor any other power should give the slightest countenance to vice or immorality of any kind; and if the participators in the evil I am speaking of find that dreadful disease and life-long punishment follow their iniquity, I unhesitatingly say let it be so; it is the wholesome edict of a wise Providence which ordains that all violations of the moral law shall be followed by punishment as certainly as "the thunderbolt pursues the flash." Speaking of the matter in reference to our own great city, I mean Sydney, I will never believe, and I ask you all to go along with me in this unbelief, that any young woman in this country is forced to resort to prostitution as a means of living. And there are thousands of the very humblest class who would die rather than submit to the infamy of such a life, who would slave the flesh off their bones, in the humblest capacity, sooner than sink themselves beneath the contempt of the most worthless, and bring dishonour and shame on the name they bear.   In the large majority of cases, women are forced into this destructive path by a false step in the first instance.   Many feel disinclined to a life of patient, humble industry, and listen to the voice of temptation falsely, and fatally, believing it to be the signal for their emancipation, while not a few fall victims to the perfidy of men. Those men, under the pretence of making honourable proposals to them, take advantage of the confidence thus engendered to consummate the ruin of their poor unhappy dupes, who are then abandoned, covered with shame, shunned and despised by every heartless wretch who apparently delights in the thought of their degradation. Such unfortunates are now in a dreadful plight. Left without character or friends, with the fierce execrations of those who once knew them ringing in their ears, and publishing their shame far and near, is it in the least degree surprising that, in the unequal strife, the poor, unhappy girls are borne down, and ·seek, in the wild, reckless, whirling dissipation of the town, oblivion of those sorrows that are known to themselves alone ? This class of unfortunates are to be pitied indeed, and many of them might easily be rescued by kind words and timely interference.   Notwithstanding that dire necessity compels them to live a life of infamy, they frequently retain much purity and innocence of thought and feeling, and in their quiet moments no one but themselves knows of their agony and how they loathe and detest the life which the harsh and un-Christian laws of society force them to continue in, by rendering it impossible for them to do anything else.   Just let me picture to you the case of a

young girl situated as I have indicated. She
confides her inmost soul, her character, her all,
to the honour of the man she loves; she would
sooner doubt her own existence than doubt his
truth and fidelity. She is full of implicit, trusting confidence, and can imagine or apprehend no
evil from the man she would die for. In an evil
hour, and under a whirlwind of passion, she falls,
and is at the same time betrayed, deserted, and
abandoned, most heartlessly, by the only being
in the world who could restore her to happiness
and peace of mind, and who has it in his power
to rescue her from inevitable ruin. But instead
of being so dealt with, she is left to struggle
alone with the overpowering misery of her position, not the least part of which is the burning
thought of her pretended lover's execrable villainy.
Many a cowardly wretch, miscalled a man, who
acts thus, thinks he has done something great,
and, according to his own base notions, something manly. It is a crime which the laws of
this world take no notice of, therefore there is no
want of cowards to perpetrate it; but it is, nevertheless, a crime than which I know of none more
calculated to inflame the anger of Heaven, often
receiving the most signal and exemplary punishment in this world, but, whether or not, certain to
meet it, with all its consuming severity, in the
next. But just let me here stay for a minute,
to ask you how does society deal with the
unfortunate girl and her unmeasured wrongs? It
shuts in her face, and bars, every door against her;
closes up every avenue, by entering which she
might hope to regain and retain an innocent and
virtuous position. It stamps her with the brand
of its deepest detestation, and, by treating her

stupendous calamity with a heartless levity and
indifference, leaves her to perish in pain and
wretchedness, and only too glad to escape through
the door that death so mercifully opens for her.
Such things force us to reflect how little of the
spirit of true Christianity exists in the world.
God help the poor girl so situated, so far as the
mercy of this world is concerned. A beautiful
story is told of the great Edmund Burke. Coming
home one night with his illustrious friend, Samuel
Johnson, they passed a poor unfortunate young
woman fainting in the street. They stopped and
tried to help her, although they both could see
that she was one of those unhappy women who
live by prostitution; this in no way arrested their
desire to administer relief, and seeing no readier
means of attaining that charitable object, Burke
nobly resolved to take her home with him, and
forthwith conveyed her to his own house, and
there, by kind and Christian treatment, nurtured
and restored her, and saved her by directing her
steps on the right path for the future. No
grander act in the grand career of Edmund Burke
than this. It was an act worthy of the beneficent
founder of our common Christianity, and was
the very embodiment and realized essence of
Christianity itself. But as I have asked, and
shown, how society deals with the unfortunate
girl, just let me put the same question to you, and
ask how does this same rigidly righteous and
virtuous society—I, of course, speak of the world
in general—deal with the man, the author of this
fearful wrong inflicted upon the unhappy girl?
It receives him with smiles and caresses. His
crime forms no bar to his admission among the
highest circles; mothers and fathers knowing

well the whole story never dream that their daughters and themselves are insulted by the presence of so unworthy a wretch. They hear the story of his infamy, and talk of it as a piece of harmless gallantry, while the unhappy broken-hearted victim of this cowardly villainy, to give it its right name, is pining in wretchedness, and sinking unnoticed in sorrow and despair. So much for the justice and righteousness of this world. After this, might we not be almost led to believe that its censure is as little to be regarded as its applause? In fact, I have sometimes thought that when the applause of the public was very enthusiastic in favour of any individual, there was pretty sure to be found some falsehood or want of genuineness in the conduct thus applauded, and *vice-versâ*. Of course, there are exceptional cases of thorough-paced nobility of conduct that the public never make any mistake about. A very large proportion of the unfortunates who infest the streets of our large cities at night, and who may be seen flaunting about elaborately dressed and apparently joyous and happy, are very young girls, most of them native born. In numerous instances, those girls are induced to follow this course of life from seeing nothing but the fair side of the picture, if it has such a side. They see girls whom they had formerly known in service dashing about at theatres and other places of amusement, expensively dressed, with all the airs and appearance of fashionable ladies—the ravages which vice and disease have made upon them in a great measure obscured by gaudy attire and every conceivable artificial appliance. Under such circumstances, the apparent independence and freedom of their career attracts the thoughtless and giddy, and thus recruits the fatal ranks of prostitution. We see those poor girls of an evening, painted and decorated and richly attired, their spirits heightened by stimulants, and their eyes flashing and sparkling with the consequent excitement. Inexperienced youths, and young lads from the country, are overwhelmed by the spectacle; they stand transfixed in admiration, and, as far as any thought of resistance is concerned, they seem to be enchanted, fascinated, and undone. The girls are not slow to see this, and, in their sweetest manner, complete the business by luring their victims to the dearly-bought and unhallowed delights of some wretched back slum, which is all these poor girls, with all their finery, can call home. If some of those misguided youths could only drop in upon any of those girls in the morning, before they have had time for painting and decoration, what a sight would meet their previously deceived and deluded senses. Suppose any of the enchanted youths were to call upon the most bewitching and lovely of the ladies who so entranced them when seen at night sweeping along with the distinguished and graceful ease of a duchess. Well then, having sought out her squalid, poverty-stricken home, and entered it, behold the poor, unhappy girl on her wretched couch, her head splitting with never-ceasing pain, her nerves shattered and unstrung, and her finery tossed about the bare room in every direction. As she attempts to sit up, to see who disturbs her, what a frightful, debauched, battered look meets your gaze. Her eyes are bleared, blood-shot, and painfully languid, the paint of last night runs in streaky seams over her haggard face, which is pale, ghastly, and almost livid. Dreadful and deadly sickness overwhelms her the moment she raises her throbbing head; she gulps down brandy to alter this, and sinks back on her wretched bed suffering the tortures of the damned. She spends the whole miserable day thus, and towards evening, with the assistance of stimulants, she makes a languid, painful effort to array herself in her most fascinating style. At length, with difficulty, she completes her toilet, and, with a farewell application to the brandy bottle, not dreaming of such a thing as food, she makes for the scene which is hurrying her to perdition. But what a wretched, dishonouring, and degrading life it is at best. I waive altogether the infamy and sinfulness of such a career, and ask every young woman to look at this. It is a life which, under the most favourable circumstances, will speedily consume and destroy health, the most priceless blessing we know of. In almost every case an incredibly short time suffices to deface and deform the appearance, however beautiful. When this beauty and attractiveness leaves them, then the iron, red hot, enters their very souls. Neglected and thrown aside by the most worthless, spurned and despised by all, their poor, unhappy hearts sink within them; they become objects of loathing even to themselves. Disease of the most virulent character, long neglected, fastens its merciless talons upon them, and, with minds racked and tortured by never-ceasing remorse, they crawl into some wretched den of infamy, far removed from all who once knew them, and there, in an agony of bodily pain and mental anguish, with no kind friend to whisper a word of comfort to them, or in gentle, loving tones to point to brighter days and a happier fate beyond the grave, they expire, generally amidst the oaths and execrations and wild revelry of wretches whose humanity is scarcely recognisable from the ravages of vice, disease, drunkenness, and the filthiest debauchery.

> " So the struck deer, in some sequestered part,
> Lies down to die, the arrow in its heart,
> Reclines unseen in coverts hid from day,
> Bleeds drop by drop, and pants its life away."

Such is the fate of nine out of ten of the girls I have been speaking to you about, and he would be indeed a benefactor to his race who could devise some means to rescue these poor girls from this danger, and deter others from certain and disastrous shipwreck by embarking on a sea so fatal and so deadly as that of prostitution.

CHRISTIANITY.

[The following address was delivered by Mr. Buchanan in the Temperance Hall, Sydney, to a very crowded audience. It was so cordially and warmly received that a number of gentlemen waited on Mr. Buchanan and asked him to re-deliver it, which he agreed to do, and it was again delivered in the same Hall to a crowded and enthusiastic audience :—]

LADIES AND GENTLEMEN,—Some eighteen hundred years ago there appeared upon the earth a man of singular virtue with the startling statement in His mouth that He was the Son of God. He makes this statement with great meekness and modesty ; He never swerves from it a hair's breadth, but clings to it with uniform and reso-lute tenacity to the last. He predicts His own cruel death, and announces Himself as the Saviour of the world. He never hesitates to claim a direct commission from Heaven. He is born into the world by miraculous agency ; He recognises no ties of human relationship, but speaks of a uni-versal brotherhood founded upon the love and worship of God. He attacks with unrivalled

vigour the prevailing religious systems, and
founds a Church so simple and so pure in its
constitution and principles that a child might
understand and love it.

During His short life, reaching to thirty-three
years, He promulgates the purest and most
exalted system of morals the world has seen.
In all His dealings with human nature He rises
infinitely above it. All that mankind strive and
struggle after is looked upon with absolute indifference by Him. He is born poor, and poverty
accompanies Him through life. He associates
with the poorest of the poor, and selects His most
trusted friends from that class. He never cringes
to the rich or the most powerful in authority, but
to their faces assails them with truths of the
most unpalatable character. He raises all in
authority against Him ; drives to madness the
priesthood of the time; stings them to the soul
with a relentless plainness of speech and a caustic
severity which, in all literature, stands unequalled
for its crushing and consuming power. All human
objects, struggles, purposes, and efforts are ignored
by Him so far as He is Himself concerned. He
has come to found a system by which humanity
may be comforted, guided, made happy here, and
inspired by the certainty of everlasting happiness
with Himself in Heaven hereafter. This grand
purpose He pursues with a constancy and fidelity,
and a devotion so sublime in its singleness of purpose, that all men marvel at the spectacle. His
life is spent amidst continual persecution and
danger ; it is entirely occupied in relieving
human distress. His pure heart overflows with
exhaustless and universal love, and the simple
though grand religion which He promulgates is

all summed up in the words—" Do unto others as
you would that they should do unto you." He
flatters no man with the hope of any human prosperity or worldly advantage in espousing His
cause ; on the contrary, He tells them that His
own fate would be theirs—that he who would
save his life in the next world must lose it in this.
If they are rich men He tells them to go and sell
what they have and give to the poor, and take up
their cross and follow Him. He exhorts them to
an implicit, unwavering faith in God, who clothes
the lily in all its simple beauty, and feeds the
birds of the air, who neither toil nor spin, and
asserts that the same care and attention would be
devoted to them if they threw themselves upon
His mercy and beneficence with a single-minded,
all-absorbing, earnest faith. The people were
carried away by the simple beauty of this teaching, and saw in the deep earnestness and noble
bearing of the Teacher something that made
them feel more than they could either understand
or express. And so He continued the preaching
of His grand and elevated system of charity,
forbearance, and love, not without danger to
Himself, as He is frequently brought in collision
with the powers that be, and this at the instance
of the arrogant, intolerant priesthood of the day.
On those occasions His calm, dignified bearing,
His superhuman wisdom and Divine aspect, strike
His judges with awe and terror. He breaks the
charge in pieces by one or two laconic sentences,
pregnant with meaning, and walks away, leaving
judges and audience silent and thoughtful, and
only able to mutter, with an indefinable apprehen-
sion or fear—" What manner of man is this?"
When attacked by His priestly and self-righteous

N

assailants in the course of His wanderings, He
sometimes breaks upon them with the power of a
thunderbolt, strikes into the very inmost soul of
them, laying bare the blackness of their hearts;
ruthlessly tears the mask from their faces, and
with a sharp, incisive, murderous invective, strikes
them dumb and prostrate. On those occasions His
assailants soon find they are in the presence of a
power that never before dwelt in human nature;
His keen searching eye penetrates every refuge of
falsehood; His intuitive knowledge of every
movement of the human heart, and every expression of the human face, enables Him to hold up
before His opponents their true pictures, and the
graphic power by which they are painted covers
them with self-convicted confusion and admitted
defeat. His conduct in dealing with the outcasts
and lost ones of humanity, with whom He constantly associates, contrasts in the most striking
manner with the same conduct of the professedly
religious of that day, and of all days up to the
present hour, and He esteems them much fitter
objects for the reception of His truth than the
rigidly righteous, who outwardly display a flaming
zeal for the worship of God, but inwardly are full
of all manner of unrighteousness and deceit. In
His life of suffering and dejection He is often
without the means of relieving the pangs of
hunger, and His home is frequently on the cold
ground, in His own touching words, " having no
place to lay His head." As His beautiful and con-
solatory system gained ground enemies thickened
around Him. The priests of that day, jealous
of the large-hearted liberality of His doctrine,
and fearing the subversion of their own hollow
superstitions, dragged him before the tribunals

on charges of blasphemy and sedition, but His spotless life and immaculate character, combined with the calm, dignified intrepidity by which He met them, paralysed his judges, and sufficed for the moment to avert injustice and wrong. The hatred of the priests, however, succeeded in inflaming the passions of the mob against him, and their narrow, malignant hearts were often gratified by the spectacle of His ill-usage and insult. He bore all this with never-failing patience and equanimity, and in His deepest humiliation offered an example of resignation and fortitude which was more divine than human. His life was now in constant peril; nevertheless, with splendid courage and unwavering zeal, He preached and taught His grand doctrines of love, mercy, and forgiveness. He called His few followers around Him, and told them of the cruel death which He knew would shortly overtake Him. He exhorted them to fidelity and constancy in the cause when He was gone, and exhibited before them infallible proofs of His divine connection, cheering and animating them to the highest pitch of fidelity and devotion, and arming them with a superhuman courage to meet the trials and miseries which He well knew they would all soon have to grapple with. He is at length arrested, without a shadow of foundation in justice, and dragged before a judge, who has gained an immortality of infamy by his conduct on the occasion. The judge, Pilate by name—let us name him in order to execrate him—finds no fault with the pure-minded Divine Being before him ; and yet the dastard orders Him to be flogged, and ultimately hands him over to the tender mercies of an ignorant, intolerant Jewish rabble to be murdered in cold blood, with every accompaniment of cruelty and brutality. He meets His fate with a calm, unostentatious courage and a dignity and exalted piety which drew forth the admiration and sympathy of His persecutors. His death, painful and horrible at best, was aggravated and embittered by filthy and brutal insult and every circumstance that could deepen its ignominy and degradation; and yet, amidst all this injustice and cruel wrong, and while writhing under the tortures of a fearful death, He turns His mild, benignant face to Heaven and breathes an earnest prayer to God to forgive His persecutors on the ground that they knew not what they did. Thus perished the man Christ Jesus, and " if ever God was man or man God, He, indeed, was both." Could His murderers have known that from that time and to the end of time their illustrious victim would be worshipped by all grades and classes of people as the God and Saviour of the world how they would have shrunk from the perpetration of their crime ! We are now eighteen hundred years distant from the consummation of that foul deed, and in all countries millions of human beings are moved to tears and deepest worship at the bare mention of the name of Jesus. His beautiful life and touching story can never die, and so long as the world lasts humanity will lean upon Him and cling to Him, under all circumstances of prosperity or adversity, as its hope and consolation, and as the shining light that will dispel the terror and the darkness of futurity. In pausing for a moment to contemplate the character of Jesus we are struck by its amazing singularity. Since the creation of the world nothing resembling it has appeared ; not only is this so, but ranging through the realms of fiction we find no conception that bears the remotest likeness to the poor, dejected, broken-hearted wanderer of Judea. Men like Shakespeare, Dante, and Milton, with all the strength and splendour of their far-reaching powers, while portraying every conceivable phase of human character, have, by the exercise of their vivid imaginations, soared into regions beyond death and the grave, painting, with amazing power, scenes and events beyond ordinary conception; yet with all their splendid faculties, especially in their portraiture of human nature, they have imagined nothing approaching the faintest likeness to the character of Jesus of Nazareth. Let us search all history, ancient or modern, investigate the literature of all countries, in all ages, and curious enough the same fact will be elicited. If I am asked for proofs of the divine character of Jesus, where shall I find them if not in His life and actions? Show me such another life since the beginning of time. Where shall we find His all-embracing love, His sympathetic zeal in relieving human distress, His patient endurance of suffering, His perfect purity of thought and spirit, the beauty and grandeur of His moral teaching, illustrated by His spotless life and character, His steadfastness and intrepidity in the face of danger, His sublime courage in the presence of death? All this is remarkable enough as exemplified in the life of Jesus; but when we come to reflect upon the object of His life, and the consistent and persistent devotion to that object through all manner of trials and sufferings, which He knew to be the only reward He would meet with in this world, then we begin to be struck with His superhuman character. In looking at this character, we find, from first to last, a rigid and unbending integrity, maintained and practised at the expense of every worldly comfort and every worldly advantage. We notice a calm, deliberate intention to pursue a course antagonistic to the prevailing systems of His time and in defiance of all consequent danger. We observe a sweetness and gentleness of character, and a uniform humility associated with a stern and enduring courage, which never for a moment shrinks or quails before any danger however formidable. We see this poor, forlorn, friendless Being inspired with the sublime thought of rescuing mankind from all manner of debasing superstitions, and planting in their hearts a true knowledge of the nature and character of the Creator of all things, pointing out to them a means which not only secures their peace and happiness here, but assures them of a happy destiny beyond the grave. In the performance of this grand duty never before did humanity witness such singleness of purpose, such unselfish devotion, as was seen in the daily life of this dauntless apostle of freedom and philanthropy, and great moral teacher; privations, cruel hardships, toil unceasing are the daily accompaniments of His short, sad history. He is frowned upon by all in authority and continually menaced by danger, yet with what determined purpose He advances on His course. Is there nothing divine in all this? Is there nothing remarkable in His systematic contempt for the things of this world so dear to humanity? We don't find Him cultivating the society of the rich and powerful, and living a life of luxury under their protection, which He might easily have done, but, on the contrary, grinding poverty is His lot, and it is His pride to take, literally, in His arms the victims of loathsome disease with a view to their relief. What a noble trait in His character is this warm sympathy with those suffering from the pangs of disease! What boundless solicitude for their restoration to health and happiness is displayed in His every act, and what an inflexible purpose He shows in treating the poorest of the poor with as much, and even more, consideration than the powerful and wealthy. The best argument for the divinity of. Jesus is to compare His life with the best specimens of humanity that have ever appeared in the world. Nothing approaching to the complete and perfect picture of all that is pure, simple, elevated, and holy, as exemplified in the life of Jesus, has ever appeared in the world before or since. That life stands alone in the world's history, and can be accounted for in no way but by the fact that there dwelt in it and inspired it the great Spirit that called all things into existence, and which presides over the destinies of the world and all that it contains. It is curious to notice how afraid most men are of the adverse opinion of their fellow-men, and how often they are cowed by this fear into silence on matters as to which honest speech is urgently demanded. The very constitution of human society forces men into an attitude of deceit, double-dealing, and hypocrisy; they are compelled to make a show of acquiescence as to things which they inwardly condemn, but silence is imposed upon them through fear of imperilling their worldly position and prospects. There is, consequently, a prevailing tone of falsehood in almost all that is done or said in the world; and the man who dares set his face against this, does so at the risk of injury, and it may be ruin, to what he calls his position and interests. Whole nations profess to worship Jesus Christ, and to be guided by His principles and doctrines, but let any man attempt to put these principles into practice and he would be scouted and buffeted out of existence—the very penalty Jesus Christ Himself paid for the transcendent blessings He conferred upon humanity. The principles enforced with such matchless zeal and enthusiasm by Jesus, while the world professes the utmost devotion to them, are at war, and deadly war, with the whole system and constitution of human society ; and the reason of this is obvious enough, and may be found in the grovelling selfishness of humanity, which never can or will understand the unexampled purity, the self-sacrificing virtue, and the high moral grandeur of the character of Jesus. Although this is the case, a large portion of the world have agreed, with a singular unanimity of opinion, to regard the doctrines and principles of Jesus Christ as the highest and most valued moral teaching known to humanity, however far their practice may be removed from such an opinion, a cheap way and a way dear to mankind of gaining a reputation for sanctity. There are, however, occasionally some men who make an attempt to realize in practice the religious principles they pretend to hold. These men are generally very rich men, who have reached that period of life when the shadow of death rises ominously before them, and they begin to see how impotent and useless are these hoarded treasures ; and now, in a fit of panic, aim at smoothing their course to the next world by dedicating immense sums to public charity amidst the plaudits and worship of the multitude. The whole proceeding is dictated by the most contemptible fear, and is often a cruel wrong to surviving relatives. There are some, even in the prime of life, who give of their vast wealth £1,000 to the hospital amidst all manner of eulogistic newspaper paragraphs and clouds of human incense; yet the act puts them to not the slightest inconvenience, and is not to be estimated, in point of moral value, with the act of the poor mechanic who gives his threepenny piece. The mechanic's gift is, of course, considered beneath notice, but the £1,000 donor is raised to a pedestal of saintship, and so extravagantly belauded, publicly and privately, that in due time another £1,000 is given, eliciting another barbarous roar of human applause about nothing, and filling the air with the "hallelujahs of flunkeys" and the newspapers with fulsome plaudits of an act not worthy of being associated with so sacred a word as charity. Such a man might very easily give £1,000 occasionally to the hospital, or other public institution, and have not one particle of genuine charity in his whole composition. We are told authoritatively that a man may give all his goods to feed the poor and even his body to be burnt, and still be without charity. There can be no true charity without a sacrifice, and the mere giving of a £1,000, while thousands are still held in possession, is not the charity of Jesus Christ, nor does it bear the remotest resemblance to it. It may pass current with the world as charity, and be applauded to the echo as such, but when put to the test of Christ's demands it will be found to be mere vanity, or more likely a cunning policy adopted for the purpose of purchasing a reputation, so that a readier admittance may be obtained to public confidence with a view to ulterior objects. In tracing the lives of the very best of men how frequently does the cloven foot of their human nature appear to mar and distort their very best actions! How little difference, in reality, is there between the best and the worst, and when tried by the test which Jesus Christ applied, how completely both are reduced to the same level. The prevailing aspect of the world is falsehood, and falsehood is the very essence of human nature. Truth is a principle to be acquired, and no man does acquire it but after a frightful struggle against the falsehood of his nature; that falsehood is never eradicated from the nature of men, but lurks there ever ready with its suggestions, its temptations, and insidious efforts to obtain mastery, and more or less tincturing the thoughts, actions, and conduct of all men. Let any observant man look around him, and he will soon find ample corroboration of the truth of what is here said. There is scarcely a trade or occupation to which man turns his attention but is based upon falsehood and deceit. From morning till night men labour to overreach each other, all arrayed in the disguise of honesty, but all propelled by selfishness, avarice, and overruling, imperious necessity. From this sickening scene of fraud, hyprocrisy, and double-dealing, how refreshing it is to turn to the simple purity and genuineness of the life and character of Jesus. What a sovereign contempt do we see here for all that interests and animates mankind to effort! What nobility of purpose is revealed in His every act and deed! No taint of sin or selfishness, or human weakness of any kind, mars for one moment the dignity and moral beauty of His devoted life. He has no two faces, one for the rich and powerful, another for the poor and helpless. He does not recognise the distinction between them, so visible to humanity; and is equally in earnest whether administering a rebuke to the highest functionary in the land, or tending and nurturing, with the most loving solicitude, some poor, diseased, helpless outcast. It is certainly a remarkable fact that no human being has appeared on the earth before or since the appearance of Jesus that bears the remotest resemblance to Him. He stands out so conspicuously from humanity, is so infinitely superior to, and so different from even the very best specimens of human nature, that the conclusion is irresistibly forced upon us that He had a divine nature as well as a human one. But whether God or man or both, the dignity and majesty of His sublime figure will for ever move before our imaginations; the purity and unselfish devotion of His simple life will ever attract a spontaneous worship; and the cruel injustice of His tragic end will, to the end of time, thrill the souls of men as they mourn over the fate of so much goodness and so much glory. Say what we will, argue and philosophize as we may, reason with all power, human or superhuman, we shall never erase, in the slightest degree, the indelible mark which the life and death of Jesus has left on every age of the world since His birth. We shall never be able to deduct one iota from the divine power of that life and death to soothe the trials and brighten the hopes of the poor, to comfort the oppressed, inspire the hopeless, cheer the dejected, and enable them all to issue from their last struggle with their last enemy irradiated by the consciousness and crowned with the glory of conquest. During the lifetime of Jesus He founded a Church, and after His death His followers and disciples spread that Church over a large portion of the earth. The doctrines of the Church were very simple, and consisted merely of faith in Christ, that He was the Son of God and died for all. His apostles preached nothing else but this, one of them saying—"I resolve to know nothing but Christ's death and crucifixion." The ministers of those Churches, whom they called elders, were appointed to that office from the possession of no worldly learning or accomplishments, but from an earnest faith in Christ's life and death. On appointment to this office they did not deem it necessary to give up their secular labours by which they supported themselves, nor was there any instance of one elder being appointed to any Church, but always a plurality. The idea of being educated in the worldly schools to this priesthood, and following it as a profession or means of living, never crossed the mind of Jesus or one of His followers, and would have been looked upon by them as a monstrous prostitution and open blasphemy. The crafty priesthood of modern times quote one or two isolated texts, such as " the labourer is worthy of his hire," to justify their wholesale extortion and plunder of the people. The example and direction of the Apostle Paul on this vital subject are entirely thrown away upon them. While it was notorious that every preacher in the Church of those days, as a matter of vital principle, laboured with his own hands at his secular occupation to support himself, the Apostle Paul directs them in their travels to take, in the shape of meat or drink, whatever was voluntarily given, and adds —" For the labourer is worthy of his hire." But from his birth till his death he worked for his own living at his secular occupation, and never dreamt of or imagined such a state of things as prevails now. Let us hear the great Apostle himself on the subject, because, in speaking on it, he is not only perfectly plain and explicit, but emphatic and conclusive beyond doubt or question. This is what he says—" Nevertheless we have not used this power"—the power to take money for preaching—" but suffer all things lest we should hinder the gospel of Christ." Again he says, ." But I have used none of these things, neither have I written these things that it should be so done unto me; for it would be better for me to die than that any man should make my glorifying void." In the same place he says—" What is my reward, then? Verily, that when I preach the gospel I may make the gospel of Christ without charge." In the same strain he writes to the Thessalonians—" For ye remember, brethren, our labour and travail, for labouring night and day, because we would not be chargeable to any of you, we preached unto you the gospel of God." In the second epistle to the same Church he writes—" Neither did we eat any man's bread for nought, but wrought with labour and travail, night and day, that we might not be chargeable to any of you, not because we have not the power, but to make ourselves an example unto you to follow us." Besides the trials and sore persecutions which befel Paul in the exercise of his ministry, and which he terms "the things that were without," he found a serious occupation for his mind and attention in that which he says "cometh upon me daily, the care of all the Churches." Yet we see that, notwithstanding that serious charge of the oversight, not of one Church, but of all the Churches, he did not deem it in any way incompatible with that duty that he should labour and work with his hands that he might be burdensome to none. Accordingly, when he came to Corinth, and met with Aquila and his wife Priscilla, he abode with them, and wrought, because he was of the same craft, for by their occupation they were tent-makers, and there, although he resided with them and was maintained by them, he wrought with his hands at their business of tent-making, that he might not be chargeable to them. He refers particularly to his conduct in this important point, in a manner so clear and conclusive that if gospel truth had been the object of the various Churches of the world, they would have had no difficulty in arriving at it. In his remarkable address to the elders of Ephesus, whom he sent for to Miletus, and after declaring that he was pure from the blood of all men, as he had not shunned to declare to them the whole counsel of God, and exhorting them to take heed to themselves and all the flock, he says—"I have coveted no man's silver or gold or apparel. Yea, ye yourselves know that these hands have ministered to my necessities and to them that were with me. I have shewed you all things, how, that so labouring, ye ought to support the weak, and to remember the words of the Lord Jesus how He said—'It is more blessed to give than to receive.'" Surely nothing could be plainer than all this, or, to a candid mind, more satisfying or convincing, but it is all thrown away upon our modern Churches. This is one of the main sources of the degeneracy and corruption of Christianity, and so our modern clergy turn their backs upon the Apostle Paul, and close their ears against his noble and self-sacrificing doctrines, while they, with greedy avidity, clutch at the lucre, and, in many instances, to an extent which stamps them as the veriest impostors and charlatans the world has seen. We see, then, how simple was the constitution and doctrine of the Church founded by Jesus—a body of earnest men brought together by the power of God's truth over their consciences. Their grand doctrine was belief in His life and death; they were all earnest believers, and this was the only qualification for appointment to the ministry. I wonder how many of our modern clergy of our Established Churches possess this qualification. No educational qualifications availed anything for the ministry of Christ's Church. A man might have been the most accomplished scholar of the age and it would have in no way recommended him for admission to the Church, far less to the ministry. Whatever his accomplishments, if he lacked the faith by which mountains are moved he was but a "sounding brass." The Apostle Paul, in the language I have already quoted, shows clearly with what indignation he repudiated the idea of a minister of Christ receiving payment for the performance of his duty. He performed that duty without charge, and, in his own touching language, here is a portion of the payment he received for it: "Of the Jews five times I received forty stripes save one. Thrice was I beaten with rods; once was I stoned; thrice I suffered shipwreck, a night and a day I have been in the deep. In journeyings often, in perils of waters, in perils of robbers, in perils by mine

own countrymen, in perils by the heathen, in
perils in the city, in perils in the wilderness, in
perils in the sea, in perils among false brethren ;
in weariness and painfulness, in watchings, often
in hunger and thirst, in fastings, often in cold
and nakedness." When we reflect upon this and
listen to the modern pretenders prating about performing the work of their Master, many of them
drawing thousands of pounds yearly in consideration of the pretence, how the soul of every true
believer and genuine reader of the New Testament
is filled with scorn and contempt! And what a
contrast when we look at the various religious
organizations of our own day and compare them
with the Church of Christ and His immediate
followers. That Church, with no paid ministry,
with every member an earnest, devoted believer,
ready at any moment to lay down his life in the
cause, and exposing it in spite of the knowledge
that the bare profession was certain to result in
loss of comfort, property, liberty, and life. When
we reflect that this Church and every one of its
adherents were, from the first, marked out for the
most relentless and bitter persecution, at the
instance of all the powers of the earth ; that the
Apostles, almost to a man, met a cruel and violent
death ; that all who took any part in it must have
first made up their minds to certain ruin and sore
destruction, to be hunted from place to place,
imprisoned, flogged, spat upon, insulted in every
vile manner, and ultimately tortured to death.
Under such circumstances what a guarantee had
we for the sincerity of those devoted men ! What
a pure and genuine worship must have ascended
to heaven on the assembling of this band of heroes !
What a divine inspiration that must have been

that armed them with the sublime courage to
brave the bitterest hatred of the mightiest
monarchs of the earth, to laugh to scorn
dungeons and racks, and to hold aloft the banner
of Christ with rare constancy and firmness,
amidst poverty and hunger, torture and insult,
desolation and death! Estimate, if you can, the
power of that principle of worship, inspired by the
life and death of Jesus, which had laid hold of
these men, prompting them to consider all things,
life itself, as lost for His sake. In all history
there is nothing so grand or so thrilling, and,
curious enough, notwithstanding the persistent,
continuous, and frightful persecution to which
the Church of Christ was exposed—notwithstanding the formidable character of the powers arrayed
against it, and the wholesale murder of its
adherents, wherever they could be found—in
spite of all this we see it burning only with a
clearer and a steadier lustre, as the efforts to
obscure and extinguish it were redoubled. This,
then, was a Church worthy of its pure and divine
Founder. It was a Church which left every man
to act upon his own conviction—nay, demanded
that he should do so. "Let every man be fully
convinced in his own mind" was the very soul of
the system. There were no priests here arrogating
to themselves a monopoly of the knowledge of
Christ, and pretending that it could not be
imparted to anyone without their aid. Each
man was responsible for his own belief, and was
taught and exhorted to search, study, and investigate for himself. Their one dogma was Christ's
death and resurrection, and they never tired ex-
patiating on the glorious theme. Their doctrines
were simple and beautiful, consisting of brotherly

love and mutual aid, bearing each others' burdens. No treasures were laid up on earth, but the poor were the recipients of each one's surplus. No thought was expended on the future, and, having food and raiment, they were all required to be content. The Church struggled on nobly, making many converts, in the face of the most appalling persecutions and under the most grinding tyranny. Persecution and the sword were in full cry after it when an event took place that altered everything, and laid the foundations of that vast fabric of corruption which took the place of the pure Christianity of the persecuted Church and prostrated the whole human mind, where it prevailed, under a priestly thraldom which is visible, in a mitigated form, at the present hour. The event referred to was the conversion to Christianity of the Roman Emperor Constantine. This event corrupted the pure struggling Church to the very core, and raised anti-Christ to his throne. After Constantine's conversion all persecutions of the Church ceased, and just in proportion as it had been hunted and oppressed by the kings of the earth, in the same proportion was it now, by them, nurtured and fondled, and in every way supported, protected, and patronised with results which I shall attempt to portray presently. I have tried to sketch the true and only Church of Christ in as faithful and condensed a manner as possible by merely reflecting the facts of the New Testament. It is now left for me to paint the corrupted Church which superseded the purity and simplicity of Christ's system after Constantine's conversion, or. so-called conversion, and which has been more or less the curse of humanity from that day to this. Under this monstrous incubus mankind has groaned for ages, kings and priests have used it for their own aggrandisement, and through it man's intelligence has been struck with paralysis, his body enslaved, his spirit broken, and his whole character degraded almost to the level of the beasts that perish, while priests have rolled in luxury and licentiousness, and amused themselves by inventing new devices for the further degradation of humanity and to rivet the almost universal thraldom. In these days there are signs abroad that the reign of the priest is at end. May God, in His mercy, open the eyes of poor blind humanity to see the depth of their corruption and treachery, and the happiness and peace that are to be found in an earnest, life-giving faith in the simple beauty of the pure Christianity of the New Testament. We have seen what a noble struggle the Church of Christ made against the powers of the world, and what a splendid and dauntless courage animated its followers. The handful of poor men who threw all that men hold dear to the winds for the sake of the grand truths they upheld, their unswerving fidelity to those truths, their inflexible firmness and constancy under cruel punishment, the devotion with which they offered up their lives in the cause, the fearless intrepidity with which they ignored all earthly considerations, stamps them as the noblest characters and the grandest heroes of history. Their Church was integrity itself, as well it might have been, every member being there at the cost of his life. No money rewarded their ministry, but the loss of everything was cheerfully endured for the sake of their belief. It was a Church for virtue to glory in. The preachers poured forth their souls in burning earnestness, and struck conviction to the hearts of all listeners. The intense zeal and boundless devotion of every man of them bore down every obstacle, and kept the flame of Christ's righteousness alive when every earthly power was bent upon its eclipse. This Church was existing in all its purity and strictness of discipline when the Roman Emperor Constantine ceased to persecute it, became a member of it, and upheld it. The effect of this was, as I have said, to corrupt it to the very core. The Emperor's example was everywhere followed, without the slightest reference to principle or conviction. After the Emperor joined the Church there was no road to place or power but through membership of it. Every knave took his cue from the Emperor and joined the Church, deeming it the most politic course he could adopt. Crowds of scheming libertines, unprincipled impostors, and designing politicians entered it without a thought of anything but their own worldly advantage in so doing. In one word, the floodgates were at once opened for a full, broad stream of corruption to roll in, and the pure Church of Christ and His apostles became an implement of government, a machine, through which, the priesthood became the hirelings of kings, and both united for the simultaneous plunder and oppression of the people. This has continued to this very hour, and has stimulated the deepest hatred of priests and their craft in the hearts of all enlightened, true men. The Church of Christ was thus almost entirely obliterated; its doctrines, constitution, and practice trampled under foot, and a most appalling spiritual tyranny set up in its place. The new priests soon let it be known that it was no part of their programme to live in poverty or to depend upon the voluntary contributions of the people for support. They became the paid officers of the State, and began by exacting the tenth of every man's earnings to keep them in luxury and affluence. The original upholders of the purity of Christ's Church had all disappeared, under imprisonments and death sentences, and their successors, with the aid of kings and civil rulers, enforced their atrocious plunder of the people by legal process and, if necessary, by military force. The provision of a tenth of each man's earnings was soon found inadequate to satisfy the rapacity of those priestly vultures, and in due time, with the aid of the temporal power, they laid claim to and obtained large tracts of the finest lands, which afforded them princely revenues for all time coming. In the meantime their numbers were increased immensely with every variety of rank and grade, from the mere novice up to him they called the head of their Church, whom they also created a temporal king. Their whole proceedings were without a shadow of foundation in the Word of God, and this was so well known to them that the reading of the Scriptures was prohibited, and the Bible became a sealed book to the people. Every monstrous fable and blasphemous dogma were then taught as the Word of God, the priests telling the poor, unfortunate people that no one was competent to understand the Scriptures without a priest being present to interpret. The whole substance of Christ's beautiful and simple doctrine was lost and swallowed up in this terrible corruption and apostasy. The thing at length became so spurious and rotten that the priests did not care to conceal their profligacy and licentiousness.

For some reason, unknown to God's Word, the priests were prohibited from marriage, and it requires no vivid imagination to picture the frightful grossness and profligacy that this detestable rule induced. Open and undisguised immorality among the priesthood was the rule, and it was followed by a train of consequences too horrible to mention. Religious houses were established for the reception of men and women, who thus retired from the world. The women saw no human beings but the priest, and in all countries this infernal system produced results from which the soul of man shrinks with horror. Every device that human invention could think of was put in practice by the priests for the purpose of raising money. Not content with the splendid provision already made for them, they pretended to forgive sins and sold this forgiveness to their poor dupes for money. They also granted indulgences for money, that is, on payment anyone got liberty to do as he or she liked for a specified period. Even the dead were turned into coin, and large exactions made from the deluded survivors in order that the priests might secure the repose of the souls of the departed. The revenues from these sources were enormous, and enabled the priests to live lives of rare luxury and licentiousness. An embargo was laid upon education, and the discoveries of science were silenced on pain of death. A system of confession of sins to the priests was introduced, by which the secrets and private affairs of all families were disclosed and used for various atrocious purposes. Under this frightful system the entire body of mankind, where it prevailed, were sunk and lost. The human mind was hopelessly enslaved; all right of free thought gone. The priesthood hung over the people stupifying them with a deadly malaria from which there was apparently no recovery; all independence annihilated, no one ever dreamt of thinking for himself, far less attempting to throw off the stigma and torture of this infernal, blighting, soul-destroying tyranny. This state of things continued for centuries, and well-nigh succeeded in entirely extinguishing human intelligence. The priests reigned supreme, and saw with delight the mass of the people prostrated at their feet in hopeless thraldom. Such was the state of the world when what is called the Reformation burst upon it with a terrible explosion. A priest of unrivalled ability and rare courage, Martin Luther by name, had long looked upon all he saw with feelings of profound disgust. The abuses of the so-called Church, and the libertinism and glaring immorality of the clergy, had filled his soul with loathing, and, being an earnest, true man, he assailed the monstrous fabric of superstition and corruption with all his splendid ability and unconquerable courage, and never ceased until he had split it in two and shook it to its foundations. Luther was in every way fitted for this gigantic task, and played his part with the spirit and devotion of the early martyrs. Priestcraft received a deadly blow at his hands, and at this day we owe to him the right of free thought and emancipation from the shackles of a galling, priestly oppression unendurable by enlightened men. The new opinions spread in all directions, and were espoused by the intelligence of every land, and reformed Churches set up in all countries. However little we may value the character of those reformed Churches, as compared

with the simplicity and purity of the Church of
Christ, we cannot fail to glory in the event that
struck down the colossal spiritual tyranny that
had so long degraded and oppressed mankind.
The reformed Churches did not dream of going
back to the Scriptures, which were now opened
for the perusal of the people, for their model in
founding a Church. Had they done so we would
have had something very different from what now
prevails. They took for their model the system
they had left, and retained many of the leading
abuses of the original apostasy. Let us take the
Church of England, as by law established, as an
example. It seems to be the merest mockery to
talk of it as a reformed Church. Its connection
with the State, to begin with, gives the lie to the
dying declaration of Jesus Christ, " that His
kingdom was not of this world." Where is the
authority in Scripture for such offices as their
archbishops and bishops with their enormous
revenues ? The Archbishop of Canterbury has
£15,000 a year, and the bishops, to be within
the mark, say £3,000 each. Are not these a
remarkable set of followers of the meek and
lowly Jesus, who had not, on this earth, where
to lay His head ? Consider that those magnificent revenues are wrung from the people, in many
instances, in spite of their repudiation of the
Church and dissent from it; and yet we find
those bishops and archbishops have the effron-
tery to take the name of Jesus in their mouths !
As a means of extortion and plunder, the Church
of England at this moment stands unrivalled ; the
Church of Rome scarcely surpasses it in rapacity.
The reformed Church lays hold of the tithes, and
has property in all towns, besides splendid revenues

from the best lands in the country. This " Cormorant Church " preys upon mankind from their birth till their death. The livings of this Church are mostly in the hands of the aristocracy, and are often sold in London, by auction, to the highest bidder. As the result of this system the most worthless and profligate men are frequently appointed to very rich livings. This, then, is what is called the reformed Church of England. Is it not monstrous that the people, who have access to the New Testament, should tolerate a system of this description? Do men pretend to exercise their judgments upon religious matters at all? or do they accept, without inquiry, whatever is placed before them for their belief? The Bible might never have been written for aught there is in the constitution and practice of the Church of England to be found there. And what are all intelligent men forced to pronounce it to be but a mere political machine set in motion by men who are bribed by the State to use it as a means of upholding kingcraft and aristocracy, and for the purpose of keeping the people in ignorance and awe? There are no men so ready to call out Atheist as the bishops and clergy of this church when anyone raises his voice against it. The true Atheist and practical opponent of Christ's religion is the man who dares to open his mouth in defence of the Church of England and its multiplied abuses. We have seen the large revenues drawn by her bishops, in open defiance of almost every word that fell from the lips of Christ. I wonder if any of those bishops ever thought of the passage, " Go and sell what thou hast and give to the poor, and take up your cross and follow Me." To be sure they did, only to laugh at it. Take up their cross!

The cross they take up is generally large instal-
ments of their yearly pay to be devoted most
religiously to their own luxurious comfort. One
of their number, I observed some time ago, died
leaving behind him the enormous sum of £200,000.
What a sum to be imprisoned at the instance of a
bishop! Of course, this bishop had a beautiful
conception of the text, "Lay not up treasures
upon earth" or "Having food and raiment, let
us therewith be content." Had that bishop's
faith been as strong in Christ as it was in
his money, what a happy man he would have
been! I wonder how he felt when he passed, in
rags and wretchedness, the beggars in the street!
If he ever prayed, I wonder if his prayers were
only limited to the preservation of his treasure!
And now that he is dead and before his God, may
we not rely upon the fact that his soul is in the
company of other rich men, where cold water, for
cooling purposes, is in considerable demand?
Just let us suppose for a moment that this bishop
had been a Christian man! What a world of
tears he might have dried up with a tithe of that
sum—what an infinity of distress he might have
alleviated had Christianity lived in his heart!
And what a consolation, when the inevitable
stroke of death came upon him, to reflect that the
bulk of his fortune had been expended in carrying
joy and comfort to many a desolate hearth, and
pouring balm into many a wounded spirit! Under
such circumstances how smooth the pillow of his
death-bed! With what calm placidity could he
have faced the last enemy, his dying couch surrounded by visions of faces beaming with smiles
of the most ineffable gratitude, and whispering in
his ear the hopeful words —"Fear not, inasmuch

as you did it unto us, you did it unto our blessed Saviour," the dying man's greatest anxiety, if he had any, being a pardonable impatience to be ushered into the presence of the God he had so faithfully served, and whose teachings he had so practically followed. But let us look at the picture as we may suppose it to have actually existed. Behold his Grace lying on the bed of death, his whole soul torn to pieces, in an agony of despair, at the thought of leaving his vast treasure, which I have no doubt had occupied him every moment of his life in accumulating. See him, frantic with anguish, with nothing but his money to console him, and the searing fact entering like red-hot iron into his soul, and telling him, in the most unmistakable manner, that it was futile and powerless for such a purpose, and that a few hours, perhaps, must tear it for ever from his cramped, narrow, polluted, miserable heart. See what a vivid expression of fear and alarm overspreads his dying face at the bare idea of looking to such a source for consolation! Mark the agony that is depicted in his every muscle as he thinks he hears the words already ringing in his ears, " Depart from Me, ye cursed." And see him, at last, sink paralysed into death with the apparent consciousness that his brief heaven was now over, and that his eternal hell was about to begin! And so will it be with every pretender to Christianity who luxuriates on the spoils of the people, and preaches the gospel as a mere profession, and makes it a means of amassing wealth. Although, in the Church of England and Scotland, there is a departure from many of the grosser errors of the Popish superstition, still anyone who looks at those Churches will see at a glance what manifold abuses leaven them from top to bottom. We see the Scriptures entirely discarded as a means of guidance by their founders. We see doctrines and practices pervading both Churches entirely unknown to the Word of God; we see the clergy of all grades, hired and paid by the State, and acting, collectively, more as an engine of government than as Churches, far less than as Churches of Christ. Against this scandalous system the Scriptures are continually witnessing and protesting, but their voice is drowned by the clamour of an army of priests who share the gigantic wealth of those human inventions created for the purpose of giving stability to the political system of England and other countries, and for aiding kingcraft and aristocracy in the compassing of their nefarious ends. So we have always seen the priests of those Established Churches, particularly those of England, acting on the side of wealth and power, and arrayed against the people on all political questions of vital concern to them. On all questions of reform, originated for the purpose of extending the people's influence, the clergy of the Church of England were always their bitterest opponents. Even when the question was the transcendent one of cheapening the bread of starving millions the clergy of whom I am speaking fought to the last against the beneficent reform. What cared they for the struggles, the trials, the privations of the poor, in comparison with the smile of the Lord to whom they owed their livings? What was it to them if fathers and mothers cried for bread to save their dying children, and cried in vain, so long as they, by their action, laid the foundation for another and a higher step in the ecclesiastical ladder? Those Churches exist by the power of the State; take away that power, and they fall to the ground, stone dead—no power but State money giving them the semblance of life. Their influence on the people is insignificant, and their very rottenness and enormity has created a wider-spread infidelity than all other causes put together. The Established Church of Scotland, while not defaced by the manifold abuses of the Church of England, still it cannot escape from the charge of being a branch of the kingdom of anti-Christ, inasmuch as the Scriptures has been a closed book to the founders of it so far as it contains anything in common with the Church of Christ. Its very State connection proves that it was never intended that it should be constituted in accordance with the principles of the Church of Christ, whose kingdom, He so repeatedly said, was not of this world. The advocates of this State alliance with the Church have constantly, and most falsely, asserted that religion would go down but for this alliance. Granted, that the spurious thing that passes with them for religion would vanish on the withdrawal of this money support. But can they shut their eyes to the glorious struggle maintained by the early Christians, not only without any such support, but in the face of an organized system of the most virulent persecution, rained down upon them with all its fierce and virulent force, sweeping away their liberties and their lives? The few poor men who upheld Christ's pure system under circumstances so terrible were true believers in Christ and His word, and this is the only secret of their devotion. The modern pretenders are true believers in pounds, shillings, and pence; hence their lukewarmness and utter absence of all response to their ministrations on the part of the great mass of the people. Large masses of people, indignant at the palpable prostitution of Christ's gospel, as seen in the practice and humdrum action of the various denominations, have turned away from them, and may be seen in hordes on any fine Sunday enjoying the beauties of God's creation, at all times calculated to inspire a higher worship than that which is generally induced by listening to some poor creature narrowing down the large-hearted maxims of Jesus Christ to the pitiful dimensions of his own insignificant, paltry soul—the consolation to this picture being that the congregation are for the most part oblivious of all that is going on, they having come under the mesmeric influence from the moment of the preacher opening his lips. It seems to me wonderful how this conspiracy against Christ's truth is not seen through even by the most ignorant; and, above all, it seems to me wonderful how the clergy can maintain their ground in the face of all that can be said against them. Even in quiet, sedate Scotland the Established Church clergy obtain their livings by the most questionable means. In the towns they tax the people of all sects for their support, and if anyone refuses to pay, which is frequently the case, he is sent to gaol, or his goods are sold off at a ruinous loss. In Edinburgh the spectacle has been seen of a respectable citizen dragged off to gaol, handcuffed like a felon, because he refused to contribute to the support of a Church he did not belong to, and the doctrines of which he hated and despised. I myself have seen serious riots

over this in Edinburgh. I have seen a man's
furniture dragged into the street and sold under
the protection of military force to pay the clergy
of the town. On those occasions the fiercest
hostility to the system was evoked, and the
clergy were talked of in a way that would have
done them good to listen to, while the military
were attacked by an angry multitude, and the
furniture smashed to atoms before their faces.
This rather than that the ecclesiastical cormor-
ants should touch a farthing by the sale. Fancy
ministers of Christ, so called, living by such
means! Imagine those impostors ascending their
pulpits on Sunday with the knowledge of all this,
and that honest citizens were lingering in gaol
because they refused, most righteously, to contribute to the support of a Church they had
nothing to do with. If the New Testament had
any meaning for these insolent pretenders, how it
must sting them; how true is the Scripture,
" They impose heavy burdens upon men grievous
to be borne, but they themselves will not touch
them with the point of one of their fingers."
And again, " They devour widows' houses, and
for a pretence make long prayers." My hearers
will observe that up to this point I have only
spoken of the Church of Christ, the Popish superstition, and the political machines, miscalled
Churches, of England and Scotland. There has,
of course, been large disruptions of the three last
named institutions by dissent, most, if not all, of
the dissenters leaving them on account of their
strong belief of the truth of the charges I have
levelled against them in this address. This dissent has spread all over Europe and America, and
has become most formidable in its dimensions and

power. The dissenting Churches have again and again been dissented from, and there seems to be a continuous effort to fight back to the pure simplicity and truth of the original system. In all the large bodies of Dissenters, they retained much of the error contained in the Churches they had left; but some of the later dissents made effort to organize themselves on the primitive model, with more or less success. The fundamental error of those large bodies of Dissenters was their failure to see how unscriptural it was to make the preaching of the Gospel a profession by which a living was to be obtained; and what terrible results of indifference and rottenness the practical operation of this principle produced. The knowledge of God is not a thing that can be taught in schools, as many shallow people suppose. The existence of faith is a miracle, and exists nowhere but where God implanted it. Every true believer on the face of the earth at the present moment, and in all past time, must have undergone identically the same process by which the Apostle Paul was converted. Paul was one of the most relentless of Christ's persecutors, and in a moment, while thus engaged, his whole thoughts and belief were revolutionised and changed. He saw, as if by a flash of electricity, the simple gospel of Christ in all its everlasting beauty, and Christ Himself as the God and Saviour of the world; and on this splendid truth breaking in upon his darkened mind he says, with intense emphasis, "Henceforth I conferred not with flesh and blood, but became a preacher of the faith which once I destroyed." It was no human influence that brought about this conversion, and every human being who is brought to a knowledge of God's truth is so brought by the same power and the operation of the same process which wrought so mighty a change on the moral life of Saint Paul. Is this principle, I would ask, recognised by any of the many Churches we see around us? Do we not see in all cases young men asked by their parents to become ministers of the various Churches as the most likely means to obtain a living? And what are the qualifications deemed necessary by men for this profession or trade? A university training, consisting of the acquisition of a knowledge of the wisdom of men, which is foolishness with God, and when this is attained they are generally appointed to the charge of a Church. They are not brought to this by the power of God's truth over their consciences. They may be, and frequently are, entirely without belief on the subject, and have taken up the profession as a mere trade by which a living is to be obtained for themselves and families. What wonder, then, under such a system, that the pulpits of almost all the sects are characterised by sleepy, sluggish indifference, and a total absence of all vitality or animation. The clergy are not in earnest because most of them are unconverted, their belief being a sham, not a reality. They preach, not as the early Christians did, from undying and devoted love, but for the lucre that rewards them. Is the whole thing as we now see it, in our established and large dissenting Churches, not, therefore, an egregious mockery and hollow pretence as compared with the stern and noble reality that I have already, most feebly, attempted to picture? Looking round upon what is called the religious world, what do we see? We perceive innumerable sects

P

upholding antagonistic systems, every one of them
putting forth their own creeds and confessions as
their guide and rule, to the prejudice of the Holy
Scriptures. " In vain do they worship Me, teaching for doctrines the commandments of men "—
the clergy, in many instances, receiving princely
revenues, and, in every instance, considerable
salaries for preaching the Gospel of Christ, which
Paul said he did without charge. Let us take our
own capital, Sydney, and look for the results of
all this paid preaching. Sydney may be looked
upon as the head-quarters of the clerical army,
where the Generals and all the rank and file are
present; and here, if anywhere, some result
should be visible. Well, then, in this very Sydney,
we find our gaols crammed to the door, crime
rampant, female prostitution overloading our
thoroughfares to a degree that has frequently
called forth the animadversions of the press,
drunkenness in rare glory, and every species of
juvenile delinquency, male and female, flourishing
with exuberant fruitfulness. Let the clergy of
all denominations look at this, and acknowledge
their impotency. It is no answer to this state of
things to keep up this continuous psalm-singing,
and, as Carlyle says, " this assiduous Sunday
organ-grinding." This is a very poor reply to the
demand for something like earnestness and faith.
We want a clergy totally the reverse of what we
have, and we shall never get this until there is a
return to the truth as Christ and His apostles
preached it. Sooner or later the thing must be
exploded; the people already see its utter hollow-
ness, and the clergy know they have neither influence or power. They will, no doubt, point me
to the fact of their churches being crowded on

Sundays. For my part, I am never there to see; but, taking it for granted, let me ask them to deduct those who are there in deference to the cant of a spurious respectability. Let them deduct those who are there to further their worldly interest—those who are there to see and be seen—those who are there from sheer vanity—those who are there to see their sweethearts, if not to meet them—and how many do the clergy think would remain as being there to worship God in spirit and in truth? But do the clergy not admit the truth of what I am saying when, by their spasmodic efforts to bring about from time to time what they call a revival of religion, they confess that the religion they profess to teach is fainting, if not dying? If this is not the case, what use for a revival? The clergy have a sad task before them in attempting to revive that which never existed. They know all this as well as I do, but something must be done for their money; and this is the curse of that money, that it is not legitimately earned, and has brought the clergy of almost all denominations into contempt in the eyes of all earnest readers of, and true believers in, the New Testament. We see the clergy also busy forming what they call societies for the promotion of morality. Is this not a plain confession that their various Churches are failures for this purpose? If their Churches were any good for the purpose of promoting morality, surely there would be no occasion to resort to other means; but it is because the clergy find their Churches are total failures for the purpose that recourse is had to those new societies. The day, I hope, will soon come, for the sake of all concerned, that this making a profession of preaching the Gospel of Christ, as a means of obtaining a living, may be discarded by all honest men. It is thoroughly unscriptural and wrong, and has done more to retard the advance of Christ's truth than any other cause known to me. It has demeaned and lowered the clergy, and many of them seem conscious of it, and confess as much by their looks. Let the clergy, therefore, seek to earn their bread in some more reputable way; and then let them enter the pulpit animated by the zeal of those noble ones of old, and preach the glorious Gospel of Christ as He and His apostles preached it, " without money and without price." We may wait long enough for this and other reforms in the various Churches, but so long as they remain as they are, they will be simply tolerated, and that is all. The cold-hearted indifference as to religious truth which prevails so widely among the people has its root in the self-seeking designs of the clergy and their marked selfishness, together with the palpable insincerity of their entire action and attitude. It is difficult . to imagine how it could be otherwise when religion is degraded into a mere handicraft, and followed as a profession or trade by which a living is obtained. I have no objection to all this going on; but if it is to continue, let them shut the Bible once and for ever. Don't let them any longer pretend that the Bible countenances the " feigned words " by which they make merchandise of it, and falsify it for their own interested purposes. Although the world, which notoriously prefers falsehood to truth, may smile and approve, there is a time which may yet come when the clergy will be taken in their craftiness. To that time and place let them be relegated strictly to abide their fate. I would here also remark upon the unscriptural character of the titles the clergy arrogate to themselves—the Reverend, the Very Reverend Father in God, his Grace the Lord Bishop, and so forth. Would any of the clergy kindly tell us what portion of the New Testament justifies their assumption of such preposterous titles? Are they not rather unequivocally condemned by the whole spirit of God's word, "He who will be greatest among you shall be least?" Was the Apostle Paul ever addressed as his Grace the Lord Bishop? And yet we find herds of men, who can read and apparently have their senses about them, falling on their knees before a poor sinful worm like themselves, while "may it please your Grace" falls from their recreant lips. I charge those men, if they can be called such, with turning away from the Gospel of Christ, and accepting the gospel of men. I charge them with allowing poor weak, culpable sinners like themselves to come between God and their consciences, and with allowing upstart insolent, as well as ignorant, priests to thrust all manner of lying fables into their idiot heads as the truths of God. These are serious charges! Yet how true are they. If the poor dupes I am speaking of would only read their Bibles for themselves, and if they do not do so they will have to answer to God for the omission, how they would spurn the impostors who live by deceiving them. As for the clergy, it is in vain to address argument to them; they are too well paid, their position is too comfortable, their vestments are too soft and fleecy, their luxurious, idle life is too enjoyable to be relinquished without a death struggle. I have often imagined the spectacle

when final judgment will be awarded, when all
those Popes, Cardinals, Archbishops, Bishops,
Reverends and Right Reverends are called upon
to give an account of the deeds done in the body.
What a picture to imagine them standing in the
presence of Christ and His Apostles, and to be
told, with bitter scorn, "I know you not; you
rolled in wealth and luxury while on the earth,
and blasphemously drew it all in My name; you
prostituted My gospel and falsified it for your own
base advantage; you ground princely revenues
out of the poor and applied them all to your own
selfish ends. You basely betrayed Me in your
every act, and now you are here to answer for it."
Imagine the cowardly terror of the sneaking,
selfish crew, as those words fall like forked
lightning upon them; but there is no escape
here, they are struck dumb, and vanish out of
sight under the terrible words of the sentence,
"Depart from Me ye cursed!" Could the
wretched victims of those designing knaves who
are "fooled to the top of their bent" by the
schemes and devices and lying wonders of priestcraft—could they, I say, only open their eyes and
look the matter fairly in the face, how monstrous
would their delusions appear; how they would
hate and despise the charlatans by whom they
are deceived and plundered, and what a relief if
they could only shake off the priestly incubus
under which they have so long groaned and
weltered. Many causes have contributed to the
frightful corruption of Christianity which we see
on all sides of us. A fruitful cause of this I
have already pointed out—that of the kings and
rulers of the earth making use of it as an
implement of government. All State-subsidized

Churches may therefore be looked upon as in no way entitled to be considered as Christian Churches at all, but rather as political organizations, or a higher order of police, hired and paid to promote the preservation of the peace, and to keep down all political restlessness or agitation on the part of the people. The Scriptures are entirely abandoned by them as a means of guidance, although they affect to use the Bible as their sole guide to save appearances, yet their prayer-books and catechisms, and confessions, and creeds, are invented and used for the purpose of superseding it. In what part of the Scripture shall we find authority for such an officer of the Church as the Pope of Rome? And in what part of the Bible shall we find his infallibility promulgated? An infallible priest at the head of a pretended religious organization, built upon a foundation of monstrous lies and grovelling delusions that the intelligence of a baby, if left to itself, would laugh to scorn, is a notable invention of human villainy in every way calculated to subserve the ends of its inventors; those ends being plunder, extortion, the enslavement and degradation of the people, and their own luxurious comfort and elevation above all that is called God. How long is man's intelligence to remain so clouded and besotted that it allows itself to be played upon after this fashion? Well may those priests be alarmed at the prospect of the schoolmaster getting abroad. Well may they dread the power of education, and struggle so hard to stifle the efforts of good men to rescue the people from their brutalizing influence. Wherever those priests have been with their vile teaching, the same luxuriant crop of ignorance, helplessness, and crime may be reaped;

the same black, benighted superstition springs into
existence; the same paralysis of human intelligence and human progress prevails, and we
observe a poor, helpless, awe-struck people believing in miracles and apparitions, and leaving
and expecting all their obvious duties to be
performed by such supernatural agencies. Is
it, therefore, an unpatriotic work to labour to
bring this reign of priestcraft to an end? The
intelligence of mankind in this very century is
slowly but surely sapping the foundations of all
the strongholds of the priest. A yell of agony
comes from the enemy's camp as every fresh
weapon is forged for this purpose. Priestcraft
may well tremble in these times, for never
before was the artillery of truth more formidable or served with greater precision than
that which is at present directed against, and
playing upon, its citadel. No doubt members
of the different sects will agree with me in all this
because they themselves have not gone, perhaps,
so far in the abandonment of the Scriptures as
their guide and rule. But surely they have gone
far enough in this direction. I have already repeatedly spoken of the degrading and unscriptural
proceeding of prostituting the preaching of Christ's
Gospel into a mere trade by which a living is obtained; and I charge all the leading Christian sects
with appropriating only so much of the Scriptures
as will suit them, while they attempt to mutilate
and distort the remainder into conformity with
their own worldly and self-seeking views. Take,
for instance, that passage of Scripture beginning
with "Lay not up treasures upon earth." The
whole chapter is a most earnest exhortation to
save no money over and above our immediate

necessities, and in carrying out this rigid procedure those who practise it are cheered and
comforted with the assurance from Christ's own
lips that they would be tended and cared for by
the constant and watchful love of their Heavenly
Father who would never allow them to want. Do
the Churches believe this? Unquestionably they
do not; they get away from it by attempting to
say it is not to be taken literally. The whole
chapter will bear nothing but a literal interpre-
tation, and is a necessary and inevitable result of
all Christ's teaching and example. All Christ's
genuine followers are required to be content if they
get food and raiment, and it is just as monstrous to
suppose Christ Himself hoarding up money in a
bank as to imagine anyone who professes to be a
follower of His doing so; and the man who professes to be a folllower of Christ, and at the same
time lays up treasures upon earth, is to all intents
and purposes an unbeliever and a hypocrite engaged in the impossible task of trying to serve
both God and Mammon. "It is easier for a
camel to go through the eye of a needle than
for a rich man to enter into the kingdom of
Heaven." This language is plain enough, but do
the Churches believe it? No, they do not, nor
any other portion of Scripture which calls upon
them to take up their cross.

The joys of Heaven are offered to the rich man
on the one condition that he sells what he has and
gives to the poor. There is no escape from it—
"Go and sell what thou hast and give to the poor,
and take up your cross and follow Me." The man
to whom this was addressed went away sorrowful
because he had great possessions. From that day
to this, doubtless, millions upon millions have gone

away sorrowful from the same cause.   The alternative, according to the clergy, is the torments
of hell.   Now if this was accepted, in the faintest
way, by human belief, how quickly would every
rich man professing Christianity rid himself of
his superfluous dross.   And the reason he does
not do so is because he is an unbeliever at heart
who would like very well to get to Heaven and
escape from hell, but hesitates about the price
because he has no assured belief in the reality of
the bargain.   Considering the short and fleeting
nature of human life, its precarious tenure at all
times, and the tremendous eternity beyond, what a
momentous question for human decision, whether
that eternity is to be one of bliss or one of torture !
And if the torture could be avoided and the bliss
attained by laying up no treasures upon earth, but
expending the surplus on deeds of charity and
goodness, what a maniac would that man be who
retained a shilling beyond that which would provide him with food and raiment, with which he is
bound to be content if he believes the Bible or is
a follower of Jesus Christ.   Are we not then
forcibly driven to this conclusion, that when we
see a rich man professing to believe in Christianity
and still retaining his money we see an unbeliever
and an impostor who has no faith in Christ's words,
but an abundant faith in the filthy lucre which
is the real object of his worship and affection?
All this the clergy try to explain away by saying
that it is not to be taken literally ; but as they
have in this way explained away almost the whole
Bible, the next best thing they can do is to try to
explain away Christ, who must be a sharp thorn in
their sides and a constant reproach to them so long
as their whole system is so entirely opposed to

His. It is amusing to see the rich men trying to compromise matters by subscribing largely to build new churches and towards all charitable objects; but Christ has signified in the clearest language that such trickery and cunning will not do. There can be no charity without a close imitation of Christ, so far as it is possible for sinful humanity to imitate Him; and the idea of a professing Christian with thousands of pounds laid up in banks is a more monstrous anomaly than that of a teetotal agitator starting a public-house. The position of the clergy is becoming every day more and more untenable, and it is not difficult to predict what their fate will be during the next fifty years. They must either return to the simplicity of Christ's doctrine and practice, or they will be dismissed by the indignant voice of public opinion. They may take to the frantic ringing of their church bells as the only resource left them to silence the earnest remonstrances of the people, but, so sure as I speak, their occupation, as it now stands, is gone. The public, when once alive to the plain teaching of Scripture, will suffer no paid emissaries of selfish worldlings to usurp the position of Christ's ministers, and to cloud and obscure His beautiful and simple doctrine by their own fables and inventions, as embodied in their creeds and confessions, their decrees and catechisms. The Scriptures are open to all men, and so plain that " he who runs may read." But this state of things would not suit the game the clergy had to play, so they tried to make out that the whole thing was a deep and almost insoluble mystery; they called it divinity, theology, &c., and appointed Professors in Colleges to teach it, and pretended that no man

was competent to preach the Gospel of Christ
unless he had undergone a preparatory training
in those schools, that Gospel, be it remembered,
being simply : " Do unto others as you would that
they should do unto you." The clergy have
laboured most assiduously, both by precept and
example—and when I speak of the clergy, I mean
the Protestant clergy as well as the Popish clergy—
professing and practising nothing but legerdemain, to teach the people the possibility of serving
both God and mammon. There is not one of
them who dares either practise himself, or teach
the people to practise, the doctrines of Jesus
Christ. Let me see the clergyman who will
excommunicate any of his members who " lay
up treasures upon earth," or " who takes any
thought of to-morrow," or " who is not content
with mere food and raiment." If these doctrines
are not carried out literally it is because they are
not believed in, and so, therefore, the clergy don't
teach them, as it would interfere with the service
of mammon so dear to mankind, the clergy in-
cluded. But if the clergy don't teach them,
Jesus Christ and all His Apostles taught them,
and, what is more, put them in practice to the
very letter, and demanded the same self-denial
from all who pretended to follow them. " Go
and sell what thou hast and give to the poor,"
&c., was a test that the man with great possessions shrank from. He, it would appear, thought
to serve both God and mammon, but Jesus Christ
undeceived him quickly, and he went away
sorrowful. This test is as applicable now as
then ; but the clergy don't think so, as it would,
if put in force by them, probably destroy their
trade entirely ; and so they go on cutting down

the Scriptures to suit their own convenience, and making it abundantly clear that whatever service they give to God shall in no way interfere with their more devoted, their more earnest and congenial service to mammon. I have often thought of that passage in Matthew's Gospel where the devil attempts to overthrow the virtue of Jesus Christ: "Again the devil taketh Him up into an exceeding high mountain, and showeth Him all the kingdoms of the world and the glory of them; and saith unto Him, All these things will I give Thee if Thou wilt fall down and worship me. Then saith Jesus unto him, Get thee behind me, Satan: for it is written, Thou shalt worship the Lord thy God, and Him only shalt thou serve." Although the devil was completely defeated here, he was by no means dismayed. He made the same offer to the clergy, and it was by them greedily accepted, with the annexed condition of falling down and worshipping him, and hence all we see. Well, then, what is the aspect of the world we see around us? The simple and life-giving religion of Jesus Christ is abandoned by men, under the pernicious teaching of their priests, as requiring too many painful sacrifices to be practised, and we observe gangs of priests and parsons living on the substituted imposture. These priests, as they walk through life, must often notice an angry expression of interrogation on many a face: "What are you doing for the money you draw?" "Did the Master you pretend to follow draw any money for the work that He did?" "Would you do a hand's turn in His cause minus the money?" "Why not betake yourselves to some useful labour by which your stomachs may be appeased and your bodies

clothed, and not barter away the truths of God
for the dearly-loved filthy lucre ? Do you imagine
your transparent play-acting is not seen through,
and laughed to scorn by every intelligent man
living ? " The answer the clergy give to these
interrogations is to get up what they call a
revival of religion by resolutely working their
spiritual bellows and blowing heartily until
fanaticism, mixed with lunacy, flames forth in
ghastly, lurid colours, dying out as rapidly as it
was kindled, and leaving our lunatic asylums
well stocked with the unhappy victims. Messrs.
Moody and Sankey have a good deal to answer
for touching this matter. The coarse, vulgar
ribaldry employed on those occasions is sickening
enough. The disgusting familiarity of the various
preachers' style in speaking of sacred things would
be simply laughable were it not so shocking
and revolting. The name of Christ is bandied
about with a levity myriads of miles removed
from genuine piety, and the whole scene is, from
first to last, the most lowering, degrading, and
humiliating spectacle the eyes of intelligence ever
rested upon. And so the clergy are satisfied with
a revival of this description, taking advantage of
an extensive derangement of the human stomach
to aggravate and inflame human fears; and this
is their apology for the money they draw. This
is the " be all and end all " of their functions,
and the justification of their idle, worthless lives.
If the clergy aspire to the respect of mankind,
instead of courting their contempt, their course is
a plain one, although not an easy one. Follow
after the example of Christ and His Apostles, and
if this requires more courage than any of them
possess let them throw down once and for ever

their cowardly pretence, act the part no longer of
sheer impostors, " assume a virtue if they have it
not," and seek in honest labour to serve God in
spirit and in truth. Labour is worship, as has
been said of old, and the labourer if he is worthy
will get his wages ; but to be paid for praying, or
even for preaching, and to exact this in the name
of Christ, is so flagrant and gross a thing that the
being who does it must, as a condition precedent,
have divested himself of all belief in Christ or His
teachings, and recklessly entered the arena oblivious of everything but the one grovelling and
sordid consideration which seems to be the Alpha
and Omega of all ecclesiastical organizations under
heaven. And so it will be till men are roused from
their stupor and open their eyes to see clearly and
measure accurately the worth of the charlatans
who come to them under the preposterous pretence
of attempting to save their souls while their own
well-clothed and well-fed bodies and comfortable
livings are the only things in jeopardy. Was
there ever, in this world of sham and delusion,
anything imagined so comical and preposterous as
the spectacle of a poor wretched worm, a miserable, fussy, pragmatical thing of clay approaching
a fellow-sinner with the portentous statement that
he has come to save his soul, or even to assist at
an undertaking so extraordinary ? And yet do
we not know that shoals of people believe that
poor blockheads, like themselves, have this power,
and do actually implore their assistance in emer-
gencies. What can we say to this but call loudly
for education to make men and women of what the
clergy, with their hollow teachings and nefarious
trickery, have all but transformed into " dead sea
apes "? How different from all we see was the

Church of the New Testament, where men were appointed to the ministry from no educational acquirements or successful scholastic examinations, but from an intense and earnest zeal in Christ's cause, where no money was offered or received for preaching the gospel, but each man laboured at his secular occupation and found the means of support by so doing! Have we seen anything approaching to this under the worldly system of a paid hireling clergy, who in many cases, as the result of the system, follow it as a means of living without reference to belief at all? Have we seen the very faintest resemblance on the part of the modern, pretended, upholders of Christ's cause to the glorious band of devoted men who upheld His Church amidst all manner of danger and distress, and sealed their devotion to it with their blood? Here, in this Church, invisible as it is at the present time on the face of the earth, I cast my anchor, believing firmly and most sincerely that there is neither comfort, safety, nor satisfaction in any of the numerous and various shams that prevail. Looking around, then, on the various temples that have been raised in the name of Christ, we shall scarcely find one on which He would not have turned His back and despised as an unreal mockery and a hollow pretence. If, therefore, I, and those who think with me, can find no Church that we can conscientiously enter, surely we are no losers thereby. Have we not got the great world for a church, with sermons in every breeze that blows and in every flower that springs? Have we not got the most immortal discourse ever pronounced on this earth, the Sermon on the Mount? And with its splendid morality and everlasting consolations animating and sustaining us, let us walk through life humbly, though firmly, under the shadow of Christ's righteousness, wish the fear and love of God ever present to us, but with no fear of man whatever.

[This address was highly appreciated, and much applauded by two very large audiences.]

TITLES.

[ON Tuesday, 18th January, 1881, Mr. Buchanan moved, in the Parliament of New South Wales—(1) That in the opinion of this House the conferring of titles upon any of the people of this country is inconsistent with the spirit of our democratic institutions, and ought to be discontinued. (2) That the above resolution be communicated by address to his Excellency the Governor for presentation to her Majesty the Queen. In bringing forward this motion Mr. Buchanan spoke as follows :—]

MR. SPEAKER,—I have thought it my duty to have this motion considered in the interests of the people of this country. Nothing can be imagined more ridiculous and contemptible than to proceed any further with the practice to which I take exception, and for that and other reasons I think we ought respectfully to suggest to the imperial authorities that it be discontinued. There can be no doubt that the conferring of titles upon the people here is inconsistent with the spirit of our democracy; that it is an insult to our democratic institutions; and that it tends to sap the foundations of all true manliness and independence by setting up false objects of ambition for the attraction of the people as well as spurious objects of respect. I think—and I believe all rational men will join me in thinking—that the conferring of titles at the rate this is being done at present, and reflecting upon the class· and character of the people who are obtaining them, is calculated to bring about no other result than the deterioration of society in this country, certainly far enough gone in that respect already, and not to be improved by creating a vain, vulgar, ignorant set of titled nonentities, who, in most cases, achieve the worthless distinction by a systematic servility and grovelling meanness, prompting them to prostrate themselves before authority, absolutely soliciting the contempt that so often greets them, thinking themselves only too well recompensed by being allowed for a short time to breathe the same atmosphere as the poor titled worm they venerate and worship. This system which I am condemning has grown to such an extent of late that it demands a check from this Parliament. Can anyone doubt that it tends in a great degree to the injury of that wholesome spirit of manly independence which should prevail in a young rising democracy like this? The existence of titles has exercised a very sad and pernicious influence on the people of England, inasmuch as it has lowered the character of the people by leading them to form the most erroneous views as to where they should repose their respect and esteem. I can scarcely imagine anything more despicable or mean than a vulgar Englishman's worship of a lord simply because he is a lord. An Englishman of the type to which I refer, like Sir Pertinax, could not stand erect in the presence of a titled person, no matter how worthless or contemptible that titled person might be. When I say Englishman I, of course, include Irishmen and Scotchmen, who are, if anything, a shade worse than their brother donkey of England, and who may be seen any day offering up incense to every insignificant, contemptible thing of clay who, in many cases, has earned a title by playing the part of a mean pander, destitute of every feeling of honour, and every manly, upright, independent principle. Those things, I believe, had a most enervating and deteriorating effect upon the people. Titles had exercised that influence in England, and I do not wish to see the same injurious influence at work in this country. On every ground of policy and principle titles should not be allowed here. But I take the highest of all ground, and assert that the conferring of titles is at variance with the spirit of our common Christianity, which recognised no such thing. Not only is this so, but the great Founder of Christianity repudiated the idea of accepting a title, and positively rebuked the person who addressed Him as " good master;" not even considering it right that He should take that title, although no human being that ever lived deserved it more. Clearly, then, Christianity placed a ban upon all such absurdities, and even when the Apostles were contending as to which was the most distinguished or first in point of rank and status, the Saviour of mankind settled the question most effectually by saying that the first should be last and the last first, and that the least amongst them should be the greatest, thereby levelling all their towering ideas of vanity and ambition, and setting His face against the practice to which I now call the attention of this House. The whole system of Christianity is founded on the purest principles of democracy. The practice of conferring titles had been resorted to in England, as in all countries where the monarchical principle pre-

vails, for the purpose of upholding the interest of
kings, and blinding and bribing the people at a
cheap and easy rate; but not only had it corrupted
society in England by setting up false objects of
public esteem—not only had it done all I have
said in the way of injuring and deteriorating the
strong masculine sense of the people, but it did
all this for the purpose of maintaining and
upholding kingcraft as well as priestcraft, with all
their accompanying wrongs and crimes that have
so desolated the different ages of the world's history. Were not the professors of religion enlisted
under the same banner, and bribed with money as
well as title and rank to take office under this
system? Titles were not only conferred upon
laymen, but also upon clergymen, some of whom
were addressed as " your Grace," "your Eminence," "Right Reverend Father in God," and so
forth, thus adding blasphemy to the pitiful farce
they were playing. Those titles were not and
could not be conferred in the interests of religion,
because the clergy, having allowed themselves to
be hired into the service of kings, to assist in upholding monarchy in all its unprincipled extravagance and open robbery, it was thought to please
the worthless men who thus acted by conferring
on them titles and enormous revenues, and by
thus appealing to their swelling vanity and base
cupidity they became the willing tools and instru-
ments of every conceivable tyranny and oppression
as well as every vile and dastardly plunder of the
weak and helpless. And so the people of England
groan under the oppression of a titled and privi-
leged class, temporal and spiritual—an idle, do-
nothing aristocracy, engaged almost entirely in
the preservation of game to shoot at their leisure,
while the poor people are perishing around them

in a life and death struggle for bare existence. But let me ask what are their paltry titles at best? There are great historical names in England of an eminence and lustre so enduring that the highest title known fades away into insignificance and total eclipse in presence of their simple grandeur. What title could do anything but obscure the illustrious names of Cromwell and Hampden? Imagine Cromwell calling himself "the Earl of Baconfat," by way of advancement and distinction. There were men in England who had steadfastly set themselves against the idea of titles, and had point-blank refused to accept them. Faraday and the grand old Thomas Carlyle, and many other eminent men of genius, spurned from them the bare idea of a title, and carried their own glorious names with them to the grave. No title dims and obscures the name of William Ewart Gladstone. Mr. Disraeli, it is true, had recently taken refuge under a paltry title, and I have no doubt that if they had covered him a foot thick with titles his true character would be visible through them all, and he would appear as he was, "mosaic to the very watch chain." The names of Fox, Pitt, Burke, Cobden, and Bright would go down to the most distant posterity untarnished by any contemptible title. Their names are free from this degradation, and in their simple majesty command a respect and regard deeper than that accorded to the holder of the highest title in the land. It would thus be seen that, even in England, the very hot-bed of this system of title-mongering, there were high-minded, independent men who would not suffer their names to be degraded by such folly. Those men had only to say the word in order to obtain the highest title at the command of the Sovereign, but not one of them did so. They preferred the simple untitled name given them at their birth, and which they had covered with a glory in the presence of which the highest titles paled into invisibility and utter extinction. This being the case in England, one might have thought that there would have been no attempt to create a titled aristocracy in this country. But there has been such an attempt seriously made even to create a House of Peers here. I speak advisedly when I say that a deliberate attempt was made to create peers of this realm of Australia. If this idea is ever realized in practice, I trust that the titles of our peers will have some character and meaning about them. So much am I interested in this that I have gone the length of preparing a few titles which are not more characteristic than they are beautifully euphonious, and, I doubt not, will give entire satisfaction. I would like to ask those people who are so fond of titles how they like " His Grace the Duke of Burglary;" "The Most Noble the Marquis of Manslaughter;" "The Right Honourable Lord Robbery;" "Viscount Perjury;" "Sir Petty Larceny, K.C.M.G.," &c. Whatever honourable members may say of these titles, they will, at all events, admit their appropriateness as entirely characteristic and descriptive of the aristocracy of Botany Bay. There is a title given to some people here which consists of putting the letters C.M.G. after their names. I believe this title is much coveted among the "wealthy lower orders," as they have been very aptly styled, and is, occasionally, conferred upon publicans, aldermen, Government clerks, including the butler and head servants at Government House. Those are mainly the classes who aspire to and generally receive this title of C.M.G. It is, however, sometimes given to fussy people

who are always hovering about the skirts of great
men, performing the duties of valet most religiously. One man, we all know, was made a
C.M.G. for taking charge of a few toys and dirt of
that description at one of those great public shows
that are so common in this era ; while another
received the title for making himself conspicuous
at all sorts of public ceremonies, and for organizing
banquets and testimonials to himself and other
nonentities. These are apparently the description
of services in recognition of which this title is
conferred. It has now become so low that I
question if it would be accepted by any person
above a publican or a Government House servant.
But surely it is in every degree contemptible and
degrading to the country that its people should be
imposed upon to this extent, and it is high time
that Parliament interfered with a strong remon-
strance. For my part I intend to protest against
these titles in every conceivable way. In point of
principle they are both wrong and absurd, while
they bring ridicule and contempt upon those on
whom they are conferred. Thomas Carlyle says, in
one of his great books, "The first spiritual want
of a barbarous man is decoration, as indeed we
still see among the barbarous classes in civilized
life." Do we not see the truth of this exemplified
in the sort of people who decorate themselves with
this little bit of ribbon from England? And do
we not see the distinction, if it can be called such,
sunk to the lowest depth of dishonour and worth-
lessness, a byword and mockery in the mouths of
the people generally? I trust this motion may be
carried, and the Government of England told
emphatically that we wanted none of their contemptible titles here—that here we were an
honest democracy, respecting men for their worth

and integrity, and knowing no higher or more honourable or enviable title than that of an honest man. But it was amusing to observe some of the more prominent of the men who accepted those titles here. One would have thought that our silly, empty-headed, pretended Tories, for there are such beings here, would have been the only candidates for those pitiful distinctions. No one would have ever imagined that our chief Radicals would have been the most eager of the people to caricature themselves after this fashion. But, to our extreme surprise, we find two of our most distinguished Radicals, Henry Parkes and John Robertson, metamorphosed into Sir Henry and Sir John, at their own earnest solicitation, thus showing what a vulgar vanity dominates those two men, and how essentially they belong to the valet species. Mr. Francis, late Premier of Victoria, refuses this so-called honour, and so comforts us with the assurance that everything that is genuine and manly has not altogether departed from us. Mr. Francis gives his reasons for refusing the paltry distinction of knighthood almost in the terms of this motion now before the House, namely, that those titles are inconsistent with our democratic institutions. What a contrast is here exhibited between the conduct of Mr. Francis and our Radical Robertsons and Parkes's, to say nothing of our Irish rebels. The Parkes and Robertson case was bad enough, but that of the Irish rebels brought consuming and destroying ridicule upon the whole pitiful business. Some of those Irishmen were tried as rebels in Ireland, and now look at them kneeling at the feet of the power they alleged had oppressed their country, and accepting from the hand of the oppressor this wretched distinction.

In the whole history of titles conferred, can any honourable member of this House imagine anything so absolutely humiliating as those Irishmen, or any one of them, accepting the title of knighthood from the English Government? Was it for this that John Martin and the stern John Mitchell suffered transportation for life and had sentence of death passed on them? Was it for this that those Irishmen themselves stood in the criminal dock in Dublin ready to pour out their lives in their country's cause? Just look at those patriot Irishmen arraigned in the felon's dock, ready to die in the cause of their oppressed country, and then turn your eyes upon them kneeling at the feet of the very power that they had just stigmatised as the oppressor of their country, and accepting from the hands of what they and their associates denounced as the base, bloody, and brutal oppressor, a title that should fasten to their names the odium of an everlasting infamy. Well might the young Ireland patriot ejaculate, pointing to the humiliating and degrading spectacle : " The flaming patriots who so lately scorched us in the meridian shine temperately to the west, and are scarcely felt as they descend." I can conceive nothing more absolutely despicable than the action and conduct of those men amongst us who covet and run after those wretched titles that England scatters so freely around. The best of the joke is that hitherto they have mostly been obtained by rampant Radicals and democrats of a very vulgar type—a set of men whom I often think must be made of the same sort of clay that urinals are made of, and who, in their encounter with true men, cannot complain if they are met on that understanding, and, in theory, at least, put to the same use.

With regard to our two Radicals, Sir Henry
Parkes and Sir John Robertson, surely those two
men would have been held in higher esteem and
regard had they led the way in refusing this small
distinction. They, however, allowed their very
small vanity and native littleness to overpower
what good sense they had, and now they are
doomed to carry on their shoulders for the term of
their natural lives "the barren burden of knighthood." Why, the thing is so contemptible that
the late Charles Kean, the actor, shrank from the
humiliation of knighthood, and bravely refused
to degrade his name by such absurdity. The
authorities thus failing to humiliate the stage,
descended among the fiddlers, and so the leader
of the orchestra became a member of the order of
knighthood. It is curious to note that after Henry
Parkes and John Robertson had accepted this title
the moment they appeared before their constituents
they were both rejected, proving that the sound,
manly sense of the people despised them for degrading in their own persons the good sense and manhood of the country. I trust that the members of
this House will be true to themselves, and not
suffer the country to be further degraded by the
dispensing of those small titles. The motion
before the House is in the interest of the country's
honour, and, if carried, will tend to the elevation
of the people by inspiring them with a nobler
ambition than seeking after distinctions so vain
and unreal. Let the people of this country understand clearly that there is no title or distinction
comparable to that of an honest, upright character, which neither kings nor queens can confer,
but which add the purest lustre to royalty itself.
Let the people of this country stand upon their
own worth and merit, emulating each other in

their high aims and objects, recognising no titles but those of probity and honour, and prizing those above any title that power can confer, while at the same time turning their backs upon the wretched distinctions of the mother country, which have neither sense nor meaning, but are invented for the purpose of upholding the craft of kings and priests, and to aid in the subjection and enthralment of the people.

[This speech was received with much applause and laughter, but the motion was defeated by a large majority.]

OPENING MUSEUM AND PUBLIC LIBRARY
ON SUNDAYS. ·

[ON Tuesday, the 29th March, 1881, Mr. Melville moved the
following motion :—" 1. That in the opinion of this House
it is undesirable that the Museum and Public Library
should be opened on Sundays. 2. That the foregoing
resolution be communicated by address to his Excellency
the Governor "—on which occasion Mr. Buchanan spoke
as follows :—]

MR. SPEAKER,—I think honourable members must
be struck with the very poor deliverance we have
just listened to, by the total absence of all argument and a disinclination on the part of the mover
of the resolution to encounter this subject and
deal with it from a New Testament point of view.
How is it that all of those very righteous people
who stand out for a strict and literal obedience
to the fourth commandment shun all reference to
the New Testament view of the matter? Is it
because the New Testament dictum is dead
against them, and totally destructive of their
gloomy and fanatical theories? Some people
do not like to touch upon what they call the
religious aspect of the question, but there is no
question at all if you leave out the religious con-

siderations attached to it. It is religion that makes it a question, and what I will aim at showing in what I have to say is that religion, the religion of Christ, is with us in doing well on the Sabbath day. The promoters of this resolution found all their argument upon the strict words of the fourth commandment. But the fourth commandment in its strictness cannot be observed by any of us. Observe that day as required by the terms of the fourth commandment and the world would be brought to a standstill—not a dinner would be cooked, not a bed would be made, not a house would be swept, not a vehicle would be visible in the street. All ships would stay their onward course and lie listless for twenty-four hours, and the world would be plunged in gloom and stagnation, productive of indescribable misery and wretchedness. But I ask, Is this fourth commandment binding on us as Christians? I say it is not. The fourth commandment speaks of the seventh day, which is Saturday, and insists' that that is the day to be observed in the fanatical manner described. Well, even the supporters of this resolution do not observe Saturday as a religious day at all, and by this practical act prove that the fourth commandment is abandoned by them as a guiding influence. The fourth commandment says, " Neither thou, nor thy son, nor thy daughter, nor thy manservant, nor thy maid-servant, nor thy ox, nor thy ass, nor the stranger that is within thy gates " shall do a single thing on the Sabbath day. Is not this continually broken and violated by all classes of the people, religious and irreligious? What clergyman hesitates a moment in setting his servants to work on the Sabbath day, cleaning his boots, cooking his dinner, and performing all the work incident to housekeeping? And do we not see crowds of carriages, in every large city, driving up to the church doors on the Sabbath day, blocking up the thoroughfares with their chariots, their servants, their oxen, and their asses? What becomes of the binding nature of the fourth commandment in the estimation of those very religious people, who would, in all probability, vote to close our public libraries and museums against those who believe they do well in frequenting such places on Sundays, the only day that offers them an opportunity for such visits? The commandment refers to the seventh day, yet on this day they acquiesce in the opening of theatres and of places of business, and the ordinary business of life is carried on upon this day exactly the same as on the other days of the week. Does this not prove that, among Christians, the seventh day is abandoned as a holy day, or day of worship, or rest? And if this is so, as all must admit, what is the use of asking us to be bound by the strictness and severity of the fourth commandment when they themselves, in their practice at least, entirely repudiate it? This cant and humbug about Sabbath observance, as it is called, is an old story, as old as Christianity itself, and curious enough, the very men who in our day make all this noise about ceremonial observances of days and seasons are the representatives of the men who stickled for the rigid observance of the Sabbath in the time of our Saviour, and even attacked and denounced Jesus Christ Himself as a Sabbath-breaker as well as His devoted Apostles. But Christ turned upon His self-righteous assailants and consumed them by pouring on them a flood of the most caustic and bitter

sarcasm ever uttered by human lips. Our Saviour
first reasoned with them with admirable clearness
and vigour, telling them that if they had known
the meaning of the text "I will have mercy and
not sacrifice, they would not have condemned the
guiltless." I question if either the clergy or the
humble mover of the resolution now before us
understand the meaning of the text quoted. The
plain meaning is this, that while the Old Testament system was one of sacrifice the New Testament system was one of mercy, and it was this
more kindly and beneficent system that Jesus
Christ introduced, to the destruction and entire
abolition of the cruel, hard-hearted, rigid system
of Jewish rites and observances. Jesus Christ
said it was right to do well on the Sabbath day,
and this in answer to the charge of Sabbath-
breaking brought against Himself by the Sabba-
tarians of that era; and is there anyone that
doubts that if our Saviour appeared in these days
that His large-hearted liberalism would not be
hated and despised and He Himself insulted, ill-
used, imprisoned, and even murdered by the very
party represented by the mover of this resolution?
Our Saviour described that party in ever memorable language, painting their pictures in colours
so vivid, and with an eye and hand so steady and
unerring that, tested by eighteen centuries of
time, the universal judgment is that the work is
pre-eminently a masterpiece. I cannot refrain
here from giving the very words of this masterly
picture of the religious Pharisee and hypocrite,
the assailants of Jesus Christ, because their very
counterpart is to be found in the noisy, narrow-
scheming hypocrite of our own day and time,
above all among large sections of the clergy and
their religiously arrogant followers. Are not

those who would prevent a working man, or any
man, from attending a public library or museum
on a Sunday one and the same with the arrogant
hypocritical impostors who accused our Saviour
of Sabbath-breaking because He healed the sick
on a Sunday? Are they not the same whom
Jesus Christ pilloried for ever as insolent pretenders? Can they shelter themselves from the
application of that language which, in its withering, consuming severity, laid bare their brethren
of old? Do they for a moment pretend that they
do not see themselves painted to the life in the
assertions that they "bind heavy burdens grievous
to be borne and lay them upon men's shoulders,
but they themselves will not touch them with one
of their fingers? But all their works they do to
be seen of men, they make broad their phylac-
teries and enlarge the borders of their garments,
and love the uppermost rooms at feasts, and the
chief seats in the synagogues, and greetings in
the market place, and to be called of men Rabbi,
Rabbi. But woe unto you hypocrites, for ye shut
up the kingdom of heaven against men! For ye
devour widows' houses, and for a pretence make
long prayers; therefore ye shall receive the
greater damnation. Ye compass sea and land to
make one proselyte, and when he is made ye make
him tenfold more the child of hell than ye are
yourselves. Woe unto ye hypocrites, for ye make
clean the outside of the cup, but within it is full
of extortion and excess! Ye blind hypocrites, woe
unto you, for ye are like unto whited sepulchres,
which indeed appear beautiful outwardly, but are
within full of dead men's bones and all uncleanness;
even so ye also appear righteous unto men, but
within ye are full of hypocrisy and iniquity; ye ser-

pents, ye generation of vipers! How shall ye escape the damnation of hell!" If Jesus Christ hurled this terrible invective at the heads of those hollow hypocrites who found fault with Him because He cured the sick on Sundays, and with His Apostles because they plucked the ears of corn while walking in the fields on the same day, how much more would He launch it at their modern representatives who blame us for opening libraries and museums on Sundays for the improvement and elevation of the masses. "It is lawful to do well on the Sabbath day;" those are the words of Jesus Christ, and, as far as this argument is concerned, they settle it entirely in our favour. The man who spends a portion of his Sunday in studying the rich literature of England in our free public library, or walks quietly through our museum studying the works of God's creation there exhibited, cannot be said to do otherwise than well in this. If this is so, we have the sanction of our Saviour, in the language quoted above, that it is lawful to do it, and under such circumstances we can well afford to despise the buzzing, noisy, narrow hypocrites who are so fond of displaying an outward zeal for religion, but inwardly are just exactly what Jesus Christ said they were. When I said those people displayed an outward zeal for religion, I was sadly mistaken; religion they know little or nothing about, and if they did they would not appear in our Parliament with motions of the description now under consideration. Outward and public observances is their idea of religion, and in proportion to the noise they make in brawling over those questions, and to the amount of public attention they attract to themselves, do they feel satisfied of the purity of the religious feeling by which they are inspired;

they bless God continually that they are not as other men, and look down with a lofty disdain upon all who venture to come between the wind and their spurious sanctity. I have felt it my bounden duty to consider this question from a religious point of view, because I was convinced the sanction of the New Testament was strongly with us in repudiating the insolence of those Pharisees both ancient and modern. I think I have made it pretty plain that both religion and common-sense, as well as common humanity, are strongly with us in opening up all innocent sources of recreation and amusement on the Sabbath day—that the cold-blooded, narrow, sectarian bigotry, always rampant on occasions like this, shall have no voice in this free Parliament—that its sour, hateful, fanatical visage is as repulsive to us as its teachings are cruel and heartless, and as far removed from the pure religion of the New Testament as from the prospect of contributing in the slightest degree to the public happiness or well-being. I shall say no more upon the religious aspect of the question, believing as I do, and also believing that I have demonstrated that all its sanctions are with us in providing innocent modes of instruction and recreation for the people on the Sabbath day. Our opponents affect to think that opening libraries and museums on Sundays is getting in what they call the thin end of the wedge, and that this is merely a preliminary to the complete secularization of the Sunday, and the forcing of the labouring population to work on that day just as on any ordinary day, and so result in the working man being deprived of his day of rest. This argument has been seriously used by the friends of Jewish ceremonial and rigid observances, and doubtless accepted and believed in by people who don't think for themselves. Its absurdity and fallacy can be seen at a glance by people of the least reflection. Why, it is difficult enough to get men to work a fair day on week days, far less attempting the hopeless task of getting them to work on Sundays. Let any employer of labour only attempt to work his men more than eight hours a day on the ordinary week days and he is instantly met with strikes and rebellion and a fierce agitation which has compelled the almost universal application of what is called the eight hours' system. Under such circumstances, with armies of such vigilant guardians of their own labour rights as the working men, what possible chance is there that the working man will ever be deprived of his Sunday's rest? As regards the question before the House, the working men, as a body, both here and in England, have always favoured the policy that opened up the means of rational enjoyment and recreation, as well as instruction, to them on a Sunday. A working man, if so disposed, has generally neither the opportunity nor the inclination to occupy himself in reading after the labours of the day; he is probably more disposed for entire rest than anything else; but on Sunday he has the whole day to himself, and I, for one, believe that it would be difficult for him to spend it in a more instructive, enlightened, and even religious manner than by passing some hours in a public library or museum, deriving all the benefits and advantages from a study of the great masters of English literature or in the contemplation of the most interesting works of God's creation. Our opponents would deprive him of this great boon, and seem bent on consigning him, and all of us, to the gloom and misery of a dark and benighted fanaticism which, erroneously, imagines religion to consist of forms, ceremonies, and observances accompanied by a sour-visaged affectation of dejection which finds expression in groans and howls and blatant bellowings, making both night and day hideous to all within hearing. Reference has been made to Scotland, and the great advantages of the strict observance of the Sabbath that prevails in that country. In regard to this I cannot speak of the state of things there at present, but when I lived there, many years ago, this very strictness of observance forced the people to excesses under cover of the roofs of their houses, which, if a rational freedom prevailed, would have been avoided. On a Sunday in Edinburgh you would imagine that famine and pestilence had decimated the people, all was as still as the grave, not a mouse stirring ; outwardly the town was apparently plunged in profound slumber, the streets empty, and scarcely a vehicle visible. But could the eye of the spectator only penetrate the walls of the houses scenes of drunkenness and debauchery, in far too many houses, would meet the gaze, proving that the outward observance indicated no proportionate piety on the part of the people, but was rather forced upon them against their will, and in spite of their inclination. While all the numerous churches are open three times a day, five hundred public-houses were open, going like spring wells, after church hours, and vomiting forth, every now and then, crowds of men and women, and even children, whom they have dragged with them through their mad debauch. All this was well known to my experience of Edinburgh up to the year I left it. At that time I have no hesitation in saying that Sunday was the most drunken day of the Edinburgh people, and that this was mainly brought about by their barbarous notions of Sabbath observance which shut them up to no other course by closing against the people every place of enjoyment and recreation, such as libraries, exhibitions of art, and even public gardens, while all the public-houses were left open as if purposely to drive the people into them. What we propose by opening public libraries, museums, exhibitions of art on the Sunday is to attract the masses of the people to those sources of instruction, and so wean them away from the public-house. The working man wants recreation as well as rest on the Sunday, and while he should never forget the worship of God on that day, he should not be debarred from the enjoyment of all innocent and rational sources of amusement, instruction, and recreation. The clergy may rely upon it that they will never drive the people into their churches by force. The more clearly the people discover and see the aim of the clergy in this Sabbath observance agitation the more determinedly will they set their faces against coercion of any kind in this matter. The rational way to spend the Sunday, I should imagine, would be to spend a portion of the day in the worship of God, a portion in healthy open-air exercise, and, if so disposed, a portion in visiting our public library and museum, or in reading any instructive or entertaining book at home. As matters stand at present the only places open to the people on Sundays are the churches and the public-houses, and how well the latter are patronized no one requires to be informed. This Parliament, in opening our free public library and museum on Sundays, did so in the best interests of the people, and the extraordinary numbers who have taken advantage of the boon prove conclusively the beneficence of the reform. I trust, therefore, that this House will, by an overwhelming majority, reject the motion now before it and maintain intact the reform which the people value so highly. Such a reform will go hand-in-hand with the enlightened observance of the Sabbath day while it is in harmony with the pure teachings of the Christian religion. I trust that the members of this House, as well as the people of this country, will always distinguish between the simple, cheerful beauty of the religion of Christ and the mad hysterical ravings of fanaticism; that they will not fail to see the difference between the sweet religion of the New Testament and the pine-apple rum religion of "Stiggins;" and that, while regarding with pure and holy feelings of reverence and love the grandeur and life-giving efficacy of the pure and undefiled religion of Christ, they will entertain a corresponding detestation of that miserable, hollow-hearted, semi-delirious cant which has invaded this House with the present motion, and which resembles true religion as much as "starlight resembles street mud." I again ask all enlightened friends of the people here assembled to vote with me against the insolence and intolerance of the motion before the House; that they will stamp for ever with the seal of their deepest aversion this wretched bigotry, barren as the east wind, which a nauseous intolerance would force upon us, and so secure to the people of this country enlightened advantages which will enable them to spend their Sundays like rational men, while at the same time rescuing true religion from the degradation of a blind, ignorant, blighting, and brawling fanaticism. (Loud cheers.)

[The motion was thrown out by over two to one amidst great cheering.]

Eulogy of Garibaldi.

~~ON THE~~ DEATH OF GARIBALDI.

[ON the news reaching Sydney of the death of Garibaldi, the
Italian residents advertised a public meeting for the
purpose of expressing regret at the departure of the great
patriot, and also to pass resolutions expressive of respect
and regard for his memory. The meeting was held in the
Garden Palace, Exhibition Building, and was crowded to
excess, over 12,000 people assembling to honour the great
Italian hero. Almost every public man of note, from Sir
Alfred Stephen, the Lieutenant-Governor, downwards,
attended. Dr. Marano, Italian Consul, occupied the chair,
and the first resolution was moved by Colonel Fariola de
Razzoli, Mr. Buchanan seconding it in the following
speech :—]

MR. CHAIRMAN, ~~AND~~ LADIES AND GENTLEMEN,—It
is with the utmost cordiality and the greatest
pleasure that I appear before you to do myself
the honour of seconding this motion, and also to
do what little I can to promote the high and
sacred objects that this vast assembly has in view.
~~(Loud cheers.)~~ It has often occurred to me that
there is no historical character of any age or
country who has so completely challenged the
admiration and respect, and so entirely enlisted the
sympathies and warmest affections of the vast
majority of the civilized world, to the same extent
as the illustrious man whose life and deeds we are

met here this day to commemorate and to honour.
(Cheers.) The very name of Garibaldi sent a
thrill of deep interest and warm affection through
all generous and manly hearts. (Great cheering.)
We cannot hear his name pronounced without
thinking of his noble, patriotic devotion, his in-
vincible and enduring courage, his indomitable
energy, his never-ceasing, never-tiring zeal in the
cause of his country, his splendid audacity and
matchless daring, all combining to bring about the
grand object of his life—the union and regenera-
tion of his country. (Loud cheers.) That grand
consummation could never have been achieved
without the presence and the unexampled heroism
of Garibaldi. He was the very soul of Italy.
(Great cheers.) He was an earnest impassioned
patriot and enthusiast, a great soldier, a statesman of no ordinary calibre, and as pure a philan-
thropist as ever lived. (Cheers.) He seemed to
have the power of communicating his own earnest
enthusiasm to others and leading them on, with
splendid valour, against fearful odds and formidable dangers. With an unequalled courage and
daring he dashed onwards at the head of his un-
disciplined hordes against the well-trained legions
of France and Austria, and with death-defiant
energy drove them from the field. (Loud cheers.)
Garibaldi's title to the character of a great soldier
has sometimes been questioned, but what soldier
now living could have achieved what he did—with
the same material and under the same circumstances? (Cheers.) I venture to affirm that
there is not a soldier in Europe at the present
moment who could have done the work of Garibaldi; and what is more, I don't believe there is
one who has the courage to have attempted it.
The daring and audacity of Garibaldi, accom-

panied as it was by so much splendid success,
made people think that he was an inspired man
who walked about the earth a constant terror to
the enemies of freedom. (Cheers.) It was a
remarkable quality in the character of Garibaldi
the power with which he gained the affections of
all peoples and nations. Is this enormous meeting not a striking proof of what I am saying?
(Loud cheers.) Here, in New South Wales, far
removed from Europe, this meeting is barely
announced by one or two short advertisements, no
speakers' names published, and, as if by magic,
this enormous hall is crowded to excess. What
did this but the bare mention of the name of
Garibaldi and the esteem and affection in which
it is held by the people of this country? (Much
applause.) I can scarcely imagine a more perfect
proof of the high estimation in which Garibaldi
is held by the people of Sydney than the fact of
this meeting, the largest, the most unanimous,
and the most enthusiastic ever held in Sydney.
(Cheers.) It is not my intention to speak of
Garibaldi's splendid career in South America.
Every one knows that he there performed prodi-
gies of valour that would have made the name
and reputation of a score of heroes. A sentence
of death, passed upon him by the tribunals of his
own country, forced him to retreat from the scene
and endure a considerable exile. He returned
with this sentence still applicable to him, and
landed in spite of it. There had been an attempt
upon Rome to destroy the temporal power of the
Pope, and burning to assist in this great enterprise, Garibaldi sounded his trumpet call to
arms in the shape of one of those fiery addresses
to his soldiers, which, in their spirit-stirring
energy, seemed as if they would raise a

soul under the ribs of death itself. (Cheers.)
The state of Italy at this time was deplorable.
The Pope ruled as a temporal prince at Rome, and
his government was, without exception, the most
infamous and corrupt in Europe; or if there was
a worse one, it was that of King Bomba at Naples.
(Loud and continued cheers.) The dungeons of
the Inquisition at Rome were full to overflowing
with victims guilty of no crime but love of
country. The people were weltering in ignorance;
crime and vice were rampant, while an army of
idle, profligate priests (loud cheers) lived luxuri-
ously on the open plunder of the people. The
Pope's prime minister, Cardinal Antonelli, ruled
with a hand of iron. This is the same Antonelli
who died some time ago leaving behind him the
enormous sum of nearly two millions sterling,
and now his children—mark that—the children
of a priest—are fighting for the spoil in the courts
of law in Italy. (Loud laughter and cheers.)
This was the state of affairs at Rome under the
enlightened sway of Pope Pius IX., while his
friend and brother, Bomba, at Naples, had earned
the execrations of all nations by the savage
cruelty of his rule. It was the government of this
wretch that Mr. Gladstone exposed so thoroughly
in a powerful and able pamphlet which filled
England with horror. Well, this government of
the ruffian King Bomba was described by the
Pope as a model government, while Mr. Gladstone
denounced it as "an outrage against religion,
civilization, humanity and decency." (Loud and
continued cheers.) Garibaldi, then brimful of
wrath against all this, raised an army of volun-
teers quickly, and marched upon Rome. He encountered the Pope's troops and scattered them to
the winds. (Great cheering.) The Pope himself

fled, and where do you think he went? Like a
genuine priest he threw himself into the protecting arms of King Bomba, the most detestable
wretch in Europe. (Loud cheers and laughter.)
Garibaldi, radiant with victory, was soon at his
heels and was met by the army of King Bomba.
He routed it with ease, for which the Pope
ordered a *Te Deum*, as for a victory for himself
and Bomba. A short time after Garibaldi again
encountered the army of Bomba and so signally
routed and ruined it that the Pope did not sing
any more *Te Deums*. (Great cheering.) Garibaldi
was then recalled by the republican Government
of Rome to defend it against the French. He
met the French general Oudinot, 7,000 strong,
and with 5,000 men Garibaldi attacked him with
an impetuous fiery ardour which forced him to
give way, leaving 500 prisoners in Garibaldi's
hands and as many dead on the field. (Loud and
continued cheering.) The French, however, were
soon reinforced and swarmed in upon poor Italy
in enormous numbers. And now commenced one
of the most bloody sieges on record. Garibaldi
was everywhere inspiring his troops and fighting
with the desperation of a demon. All was, however, of no use; the French general sent up
reserve after reserve, and Garibaldi saw that all
was over. Heartbroken and dejected, he retired
with those of his followers who chose to follow
his fortunes, and with his poor wife a hopeless
invalid, he retreated from Rome only to see his
wife perish in his arms and he himself forced to
leave her remains to be buried by strangers while
he struggled to escape Austrian capture. To my
mind it was a very inferior courage that enabled
Garibaldi to brave many a whirlwind of musket
bullets on many a bloody field compared to the

sublime heroism that nerved his great soul as he
bore away his dying wife from the beleaguered
city of Rome, and exposed to every conceivable
danger, stuck to her and tended her with overflowing affection till she died in his loving and
devoted arms. (Loud applause.) This episode in
his picturesque, romantic story, is deeply mournful
and pathetic, and is in the highest degree touching and tragic. It cannot be read without carrying away the sympathies and the tears of all
manly hearts. (Much cheering.) Garibaldi soon
reached neutral territory, and there prepared for
one more effort in his country's cause. His next
adventure was his splendid Sicilian campaign,
where, after a whole series of magnificent vic-
tories, he met King Victor Emanuel, hailed him as
King of Italy, and presented him with a kingdom.
Garibaldi had unlimited means during this campaign of possessing himself of wealth, but after
presenting the King of Italy with a kingdom, he
had not as much money as would carry him back
to Caprera, his island home. (Enthusiastic
cheers.) Garibaldi had several other struggles
before he saw the realization of all his holiest
aspirations and his fondest hopes in a regenerated
and united Italy, with Rome as its capital. I
cannot conclude without a slight reference to
Garibaldi's marvellous reception in London.
-(Cheers.) All England seemed to rise to receive
him. No crowned head that ever visited England,
or ever will visit England, could meet with a
tithe of the honour. The Queen of England herself, much loved and deservedly popular as she is,
(loud cheers)—could scarcely have been received
with more affection than this grand old hero. The
aristocracy vied with each other to do him honour.
Statesmen, men of science, poets and historians

crowded round him and felt honoured by a shake
of his hand.   Working-men in England and Scotland sent him addresses and affectionate invita-
tions to visit them.   Things were assuming such
a shape that the despots of the world began to
tremble and only breathed freely when Garibaldi
departed.   But was there not a deep meaning in
all this universal love and respect for Garibaldi?
Yes.   It spoke of England's love of courage, devotion, patriotism, endurance, purity, and virtue.
(Loud cheers).   The English people, and the
world, knew Garibaldi to be an honourable, manly,
upright soldier, pure in motive and high in character, not one of those cowardly wretches who
skulk in corners and secret places, plotting assassinations (loud cheering, continued, and again
and again repeated) and manufacturing infernal
machines for the cruel, cold-blooded purpose of
indiscriminate murder.   They knew Garibaldi to
be a soldier who always met his enemies, sword
in hand, in the open field.   (Great cheering.)   It
was this and many other fine traits in his great
character that captivated the English people to
the extent it did, and made us all feel a pang as
the news reached us that his pure, gentle spirit
had passed away for ever. [Ladies and gentlemen,
no one is more alive than myself to the feebleness
and inefficiency of this poor attempt of mine to do
justice to the great character of a great man.   I
feel incapable of rising to the greatness of the
theme.   I feel that any language that I, or any
man, could use would be wholly inadequate to
paint the glories and the virtues of the renowned
Garibaldi.   He was a hero and a patriot worthy
of the deepest veneration and the warmest regard
of all true men.   The name of this illustrious man
will for ever gather around it the suffrages of the

world. His noble, gallant life, his artless simplicity of character, the lofty grandeur and greatness
of his aspirations, his singleness of purpose and
unselfish devotion, all combine to stamp him as
one of nature's noblemen, whose great name,
undimmed by any paltry, insignificant title—
(great cheers)—will go down, covered with glory
as it is, to the remotest posterity, inspiring every
struggling patriot in all future ages with a never-
ceasing love for the cause of human freedom—
(loud cheers)—and nerving men, by the very
magic of its sound, to deeds of dauntless daring,
as they bear onwards the great principle for
which he fought and bled on many a gallant field.
(Enthusiastic cheers.)   Glory to the memory of
Garibaldi—(great cheers)—as the world's plaudits
encircle his great name with imperishable renown.
(Loud and long-continued cheering.)

[The resolution was enthusiastically carried.]

DEATH OF GENERAL GARFIELD.

[On the 21st of September Sir Henry Parkes, K.C.M.G., Premier of New South Wales, moved the following resolution:—" That Mr. Speaker be requested to communicate to Mrs. Garfield the profound sympathy and sorrow of the members of the Legislative Assembly of New South Wales at the untimely death of her illustrious husband." On this occasion Mr. Buchanan spoke as follows:—]

Mr. Speaker,—It was my intention, without consulting anyone, to have spoken a few earnest words on this sad event, and also to have put myself in order by moving the adjournment of the House; but the motion now before the House renders that course unnecessary. The death of the chief ruler of the United States is an event which has elicited universal sympathy and sorrow. The news of the monstrous and detestable crime which has so cruelly deprived the world of so much nobleness and goodness, sent a thrill of horror and consternation to the uttermost corners of the earth, and now that the deplorable attempt upon General Garfield's life has culminated in his most affecting and deeply mournful death, the mind and heart of the world seems troubled and agitated in the contemplation of a catastrophe so sorrowful and so appalling. General Garfield was no ordinary man; he was a man of rare excellence—earnest, devoted, and undaunted. He was born in the midst of trying and depressing poverty; his life, in its early years, being one continuous struggle with overpowering hardship; he was entangled and beset by every conceivable obstacle and difficulty. But he cut himself free from the jungle of his early perplexities and dangers, and emerged and advanced to the very front rank of scholars and statesmen; and, not resting there, he rose, by the force of his own genius and character, to the highest position which it is competent for any citizen of the United States to hold. Looking down the long roll of illustrious rulers who have swayed the destinies of that great country until the eyes are dazzled by the lustre that surrounds the name of Washington, there is not one of those great men who stands higher in nobleness of character, intellectual attainments, or high moral worth than the late lamented President. President Garfield, the soldier, scholar, and statesman, has fallen by a most cowardly and hateful act, and by the cruellest possible death. His death has elicited the sorrow of the whole world and the sympathy of mankind, while undying hatred of the deed will for ever move the human heart. When we reflect upon the character of this great man; when we see that no paltry, vain, insignificant title brought obloquy and contempt on the name of James Garfield; when we see him standing out, like all his illustrious predecessors, in the native simplicity of his own innate nobility—we cannot help being struck with the majesty and dignity of a figure so imposing. Looking at the high-souled honour and undeviating rectitude which guided him from obscurity into the blaze of a rare distinction; noticing his elevation by the voice of

8

probably the greatest nation on the face of the
earth to the highest position in its gift; observ-
ing him conducting the duties of that great office
with rare justice and wisdom, infusing into every
department of Government a tone of sterling
probity, and performing all the grand functions
of his great office with the intellectual power and
purity of thought and feeling which marked his
career from first to last—looking at all this, and
reflecting on the monstrous crime which brought
so much worth and goodness to an end, I may
almost be pardoned for altering two of Campbell's
lines, and quoting them thus —

> Hope for a season bade the world farewell,
> And justice wept when the noble Garfield fell.

I intended to propose that we suspend our business for the day as a mark of respect to the
memory of this great man, as proving our detestation of the atrocious crime which led to his
death, and as indicating our deepest sympathy
with the woes and sorrows of a great nation ; but
as the honourable gentleman at the head of the
Government has proposed the motion now under
consideration, I shall content myself by giving it
my most cordial support. It would ill become me to
speak any further on this melancholy event.   The
late illustrious President seems to have captivated
the hearts of all men.   When I think of his great
character and of the high promise which he held out
to the nations of the world in the administration of
the great office to which he was called, and also of
the base and wretched instrument by which his fall
was brought about, I cannot help quoting, and
concluding, with two of Shakespeare's lines —

> An eagle, towering in his pride of place,
> Was by a mousing owl hawked at and killed.

(Applause from all sides of the House.)

SIR HENRY PARKES AND SIR JOHN ROBERTSON: THEIR POLITICAL DECAY AND DEATH.

[THIS speech was delivered in the Parliament of New South Wales immediately on the assembling of Parliament after the dissolution on Wednesday, 3rd January, 1883.]

THE Government of Sir Henry Parkes and Sir John Robertson, probably the strongest we ever had in this country—strong, not in ability, but in the large amount of support it received—alienated almost all that support by a series of the most questionable acts, culminating in an open violation of the Constitution repeated again and again —spending large sums of the public money without the sanction of Parliament, there being no urgent necessity compelling such action, and treating it, on repeated occasions, with undisguised contempt, the crisis was brought about by their receiving a crushing defeat on the second reading of their Land Bill. On this occasion Sir Henry Parkes and Sir John Robertson recommended an appeal to the country, assuring His Excellency the Governor that everything was right as regarded supply; this, afterwards, turned out to be

very far from the truth—in any case, the Press
and public loudly condemned the appeal to the
country, as being unconstitutional and wrong
—especially as the Leader of the Opposition was
prepared at once to take their places with a land
policy which he had formulated on the second
reading of their defeated Land Bill. Wrong and
unconstitutional as the granting of this dissolution was, it took place with memorable results.
Sir Henry Parkes and three of his ministers
were thrown out by large majorities—those three
ministers were rejected for other constituencies,
some of them on three occasions; Sir Henry
Parkes himself was returned by a mere accident,
where, in an obscure constituency, the only candidate resigned in his favour on the day of his
nomination, leaving no time for further opposition, so he was returned without the chance of
opposing him. Sir John Robertson was returned
for Mudgee, in charity for his years and pitiable
position. He went crying through the district,
" Pity the sorrows of a poor old man," and
touched the hearts of the people by the intensity
and earnestness of his supplications. Every
supporter of the Government, with the exception
of some half-dozen, was rejected by the people,
so that the appeal to the country literally
destroyed the Government—rejecting three of
the ministers themselves, and leaving them with
only half-a-dozen followers. Notwithstanding all
this, Sir Henry Parkes and Sir John Robertson
still clung to office—making appointments and
dismissing public servants, just as if they were a
Government clothed with power and responsibility, instead of being the mere remnant of
what was once a Government without a vestige
of power, responsibility, or support of any kind.

In this position Sir Henry Parkes and Sir John Robertson had the hardihood and brazen insolence to meet Parliament under the pretext of providing Supply, although they had previously told His Excellency that they had Supply sufficient to cover the Dissolution. They were, however, forced, at last, to resign—the incoming Government, most righteously, declining to take Supply at their hands, which fact resulted in such an exposure of the misconduct of Sir Henry Parkes and Sir John Robertson that almost the first act of their successors was to bring in a bill of indemnity, to save public officers from the responsibility of their illegal and unconstitutional acts. When Parliament met, Sir Henry Parkes and Sir John Robertson still clung to office and its emoluments, half their colleagues having been rejected, and almost all their supporters; and it is necessary that all this should be known to a full understanding and appreciation of the following speech. The first act of the new Parliament was to elect a Speaker, and Sir George Wigram Allen was proposed for the office, to which motion an amendment was moved, that Mr. Barton be Speaker—whereupon Mr. Buchanan moved a further amendment, as follows: "That in the opinion of this House our first duty is to uphold its honour and dignity, and, in pursuance of this high purpose, and before the election of Speaker, or the transaction of any other business, this House calls upon the remnant of the Government left, as the result of the late appeal to the people, to resign at once, and so save the country from the disgrace and scandal of its existence a moment longer; and, further, that this resolution be communicated, by address, to His Excellency the Governor." On moving this amendment Mr.

Buchanan delivered the following speech. Addressing the principal clerk of the House, there being no Speaker, he said:—

Mr. Jones,—I have a further amendment to propose, and the reason I rise so early in the debate is to place that amendment before the House. (*Amendment as above here read.*) I am sure this amendment will be acceptable to many honourable members, and I further think it would be a deep and sad reflection on the character of this Assembly if we suffered the remnant of the Government that has survived the Dissolution to escape the just and well-merited censure it has so richly earned and deserved. Sir Henry Parkes and Sir John Robertson are the principal delinquents, and if the people of this country ever come to know the full extent of their misconduct, as Ministers of the Crown, no vestige of trust or confidence will ever again be reposed in those two honourable gentlemen. Their conduct in office has been inexpressibly bad. The Constitution under which we live has been, by them, totally disregarded. During the appeal to the country, which has just concluded with results so ruinous to the Government, Ministers of the Crown, from the highest to the lowest, degraded themselves into low electioneering agents. Even the Premier of the country, Sir Henry Parkes, descended from his high position and prostituted his great office into a mere electioneering spouter, and went canvassing different electorates on behalf of the minions of authority, who had no other distinction than their mean, crawling subserviency to him. Not only has he done this, but, after the very soul has been knocked out of his Government, and his power shattered to invisible atoms by the destructive and overwhelming action of the people,

he has actually had the audacity, in the present
mangled state of his Government and power, to
make important appointments in the public service.
A more unconstitutional—a more scandalously
disgraceful—and, in every sense, illegal procedure
never took place in this country before; and this
newly-elected Parliament, if it is alive to its own
dignity and honour, ought not to suffer the
monstrous proceedings of these men to pass
without impeachment, and the severest censure.
We will fail in our essential duty if we fail in
this, and will give encouragement to gross profligacy in the highest offices of State if we pass
by unnoticed the unexampled misconduct of Sir
Henry Parkes and Sir John Robertson, and when
I speak of those two honourable gentlemen I
speak of the Government. Can there be imagined
anything more indecent and unseemly than the
frightful tenacity which they exhibit in clinging
to office when all power has departed from them,
and even the respect of their own friends? Was
there ever such a spectacle seen in this world
before of men stripped of every vestige of
authority, condemned by the people to whom
they appealed, and by them reduced to utter
helplessness and impotency, still clinging to office
and its emoluments, and pretending to govern
when the whole frame of Government is struck
dead, and lies helpless before us? Surely it
is time for the people's representatives to remove
forcibly the dead body of this Government and
bury the hideous thing out of sight without any
farther delay. The excuse that these honourable
gentlemen offer for their continuing in office under
circumstances so dishonouring and so humiliating
is " That it is necessary Supply should be got."
What outrageous work is this, after assuring his

Excellency and the country that no Supply would be wanted—that they had enough to cover the Dissolution. I, for one, will resist to the death this thing miscalled a Government, which now sits before me, performing one single act of Government, and I do trust those who come after them will refuse to accept Supply at their hands. There is only one act that Sir Henry Parkes and Sir John Robertson can now perform—an act which should have been performed long ago. I mean the one honest act remaining to them, namely, instant resignation. Supply, indeed! The supply they want is supply to their own pockets, £40 per week—that is the supply Sir Henry Parkes and Sir John Robertson have trampled on the Constitution to obtain a few weeks longer, and for which they cling to office, to the scandal and disgrace of Representative Government—not only here, but, indirectly, everywhere. The conduct of Sir Henry Parkes and his fellow knight has been so gross and unworthy that I can scarcely restrain my tongue in depicting it, but I know that I cannot use any language, however harsh and severe, that will not fall infinitely short in the description of the unexampled infamy that has characterized the Government since the Dissolution. Do we not all remember how the Premier, Sir Henry Parkes, in his whining and most hypocritical tones, used to nauseate us by his oft-repeated statement, "That he would not hold office a minute longer than he enjoyed the confidence of the people. Only tell me," he used to say, "that we have no longer the confidence of the people and we will resign that moment." And now, after he has sustained such a defeat as no Minister in this world ever before suffered, he holds on to office, a spectacle for the commiseration of both

men and gods. Never before in this world did
any Government get so complete, so instantaneous,
and ignominious a destruction and total shipwreck as this Government of Sir Henry Parkes
on appealing to the people. They appeal to
the people and they are destroyed by the
people. Not only are half the Ministry, and
almost all their supporters, destroyed, but every
man infected with the slightest taint of
attachment to the two knights is plunged into
nothingness the moment the people get a chance
at him; and wonderful to relate, they still hold on
to office, and I now ask the honourable members
of this House is it their fault or mine that I am
forced to tell them that they do so from the
wretched motive of still having the chance of
drawing their salaries, which, under the circumstances, is neither more nor less than a flagrant
act of public robbery. So great is my respect for
the institutions of this country and the high offices
of State that I would not utter what I am now
saying, unless the truth was forced upon me, and
from me. What other conclusion can I come to,
looking on at what I see? and, therefore, at the
door of Sir Henry Parkes and his colleagues let
the infamy rest of having brought unparalleled
degradation on the public life and public institutions of this country. Strong and emphatic as
my language is, I know that it will find a response
in every manly and intelligent soul; and I say
that it is our bounden duty before electing a
Speaker—before doing a single legislative act—to
tear these men from the position and emoluments
which they are clinging to with such inveterate
tenacity, and hugging to their hungry souls in the
spirit, and with the principles, of burglars. Those
honourable gentlemen opposite me dissolved the

late Parliament without a shadow of justification, and on grounds the most unprincipled, and, in doing so, they outraged every known principle of the Constitution; indeed, they induced the Governor to consent to a Dissolution by stating to him that they had Supply sufficient for the public service during the time occupied by the elections, which we now know to have been not true; so, it is clear, the Dissolution was brought about by means of false pretences; and when we find Sir Henry Parkes still hanging to his office, after he has been stripped of every vestige of authority, am I not justified in denouncing him and his colleagues as clearly doing so for the purpose of keeping a few weeks longer the filthy lucre which seems to have corrupted the whole of them? I think I am justified in saying, in view of the facts of the case, that it is that consideration alone which has led them to prostitute their offices, to degrade and outrage the Constitution—to lower themselves beneath the contempt of all men, and to alienate from them even some of the creeping things who used to crawl after them with such uniform docility. What other grounds can the Government assign for the course they have taken? A Dissolution would give them a few weeks more of salary, and therefore it is resorted to without reference to the public interest. A Dissolution on their thrice wretched Land Bill that the people have been condemning for the last twenty years— the product of an idiot—it has, with all its multifarious injustice and cruel wrong, weighed upon the vital interests of this country with the withering blight of a pestilence. It has brought two large classes of the community into savage and deadly hostility, and enabled them to carry on the war against each other by legalizing every species of fraud, lying, and deception. It has offered a premium to the scoundrel in carrying on his misdeeds, and at the same time brought ruin and disaster on the honest man. It has spread dismay all round; and while inviting the people to settle on the public lands, it has sealed their doom that moment they did so by the innumerable snares and traps it has there set for them. It has been a downdrag and a curse to the country, and from its introduction up to the present moment no heavier calamity has weighed and preyed on its existence. All this was well known to the people, and has been variously expressed by them from one end of the country to the other. To appeal to the people on such a Bill as this with a thought of a favourable verdict was the madness of Sir Henry Parkes, led into it by the stronger madness of Sir John Robertson. Well, then, the appeal to the people is decided upon, and now behold Sir Henry Parkes preparing for his perilous voyage. See him standing at the helm of the State ship with Sir John Robertson's Land Bill as a 'mainsail swelling to the breeze, steering his course into the great ocean of public opinion. No sooner is he there than wild winds howl around him—the tempest rages—angry, remorseless waves sweep his decks—thunder-peals roar from above—ocean opens to receive him, and down he sinks, engulphed, without leaving so much as a solitary spar, or even a tatter of rope or bunting on the surface of the water. And thus Sir Henry Parkes ends his joyous voyage to the country. The storm that thus wrecked and ruined Sir Henry Parkes and his Government will be ever memorable in the history of this country. It will teach the lesson that flagrant misconduct in high office shall never go unpunished, that no minister can trample on the

Law and Constitution with impunity, that "corruption wins not more than honesty," and that evil-disposed and unprincipled men in office can be brought to book and covered with obloquy and contempt, as in the case of the honourable gentlemen who now sit opposite me. I now feel most anxious that this House should understand and do its duty. If what I have said is true, and there is not an honourable member of this House who dare deny a word of it, then I call upon the House to go along with me in censuring Sir Henry Parkes and Sir John Robertson for all the injury and infamy they have, as Ministers of the Crown, inflicted on this country. I call upon every independent and upright man in this House to stand by the purity of Government, and assist in bringing to punishment the men who have plunged the whole system of Representative Government into a sink of scandalous corruption. I call upon the House to visit with severe condemnation men who still cling to office when all power and support have left them ; when, in fact, they are no longer a Government, and who, notwithstanding, continue to make appointments to the public service, when they can be no longer held responsible for what they do. I ask the House to look at the flagrant misconduct of all this, and to say whether it thinks any action of any men could have brought more degradation and pollution on the great offices of State and on the public life and public institutions of the country than the action of Sir Henry Parkes and his colleagues during the last six months of his administration. In dealing with such men as Sir Henry Parkes and Sir John Robertson it becomes us, as representatives of the people, who value our own credit and character, to put our strong sense of the misconduct of these gentlemen on record, so that those who come after us may find to what extent every known principle of the Constitution which we value has been trampled upon and departed from by the two gentlemen who, for those misdeeds, are now, by the action of the people, stripped of every vestige of power, and are, to all intents and purposes, politically dead. In conclusion I may say I have tried to do my duty in thus speaking, and it is now for the people's representatives, who should be the guardians of the public honour, to do theirs.

[Mr. Buchanan's speech was admitted to be true by the manner it was received. Sometimes it was cheered, but no expressions of dissent fell from the lips of a single member.

Mr. Buchanan's amendment could not be put, there being no Speaker. He consequently expressed his intention of taking another opportunity of reintroducing the subject. The Government of Sir Henry Parkes at last resigned that very night.]

THE COMPOSITION OF MR. STUART'S GOVERNMENT CRITICIZED.

[On the resignation of the Government of Sir Henry Parkes, Mr. Stuart was called upon to form a Government, and in noticing its composition the following speech was delivered. The Address in reply to the Governor's speech having been moved and seconded, Mr. Buchanan rose and spoke as follows :—]

Mr. Speaker,—Time and the hour run through the roughest day, no man can tether either the one or the other, and so we are now in the presence of the new Government, every member of it being present, with the exception of one man, the Minister of Public Works, who has been defeated by his constituents at Newtown. The first blow, therefore, aimed at this new state of things is delivered by the intelligent electors of the great metropolitan constituency of Newtown. (Hear, hear.) I think, in an Assembly of this kind, it is every independent member's duty to express himself boldly and freely on the occasion of a crisis so important as the formation of a new Government. This is a deliberative Assembly ; we are here for the express purpose of deliberation. Our system of Government is government by debate,

government by public discussion, government by
public opinion. If we therefore fail to express ourselves upon all important occasions, we miss the
very object of our being here, and fail egregiously
in recognising the very spirit and essence of our
system of government. It is, therefore, not my
intention to be silent on this occasion. (Hear,
hear.) On the contrary, I mean to speak exactly
what I think and feel, in reference to the new
constitution of things, and I mean to do so freely
and boldly. (Laughter and cheers.) The honourable gentlemen who constitute the Government
have been before their constituents, and the most
noticeable thing in reference to their doings and
sayings there, is, that they all seem to have
agreed upon the grand purpose of singing each
other's praises. According to their own account,
no more remarkable set of men has ever before
appeared in the Government of this country.
They are all, according to their own dictum,
paragons of perfection (laughter), marvels of
superhuman capacity, and wherever they go, they
entertain the people with anthems and hallelujahs
in absurd praise of themselves. (Hear, hear.)
Well, this is all very laughable and very amusing,
and as the people have had the Ministerial account
of their own high qualities and miraculous powers,
it may not be out of place, in this House, that
something like the truth should be told bearing
upon this most interesting matter. (Hear, hear.)
I am sure the members of this House entertain
very moderate views as to the qualifications of the
gentlemen at present occupying the Treasury
Benches. (Hear, hear, and laughter.) Some of
them, I believe, are held to be totally unfit for
that high position—(hear, hear)—and I, for one,
don't hesitate to announce that as my own

opinion. But since they have been so absurdly extravagant in singing their own praises all through the country, I will have the less delicacy in entering upon a just, though lively, criticism of a set of men who herald themselves with so much vehement blowing of their own trumpets. Well, then, let us begin with the Premier, a man destitute of any notable quality—(hear, hear)— undistinguished in this House, and known as a very ordinary man, feeble and irresolute, and wearisome to listen to, obsolete in his political opinions, and without the power of adequately expressing them, which may be looked upon as an advantage under the circumstances. Well, then, this gentleman signalises his advent to power, as Premier of the country, by four distinct acts of palpable desertion of his best friends. (Hear, hear.) We all remember the other day, when we were called upon to elect a Speaker, the humiliating action adopted by the present Premier. (Cheers). Although he said that Sir George Wigram Allen, one of the candidates, was his old friend of thirty years' standing, and although he further said that Sir George Wigram Allen, during his long tenure of the high office of Speaker, had performed its duties most admirably, he illustrates the value of his friendship by refusing to vote for him. This was desertion number one. At this time, as we all know, the Premier was Leader of the Opposition—raised to that onerous position by the devotion of a large number of followers. Well, then, how did the Premier act towards them? He treated them as he had treated his friend, Sir George Wigram Allen, by refusing to vote for their nominee (Mr. Barton), and so deserted them in the most shameful manner—(loud cheers)—immediately on

the back of his equally shameful desertion of the
late Speaker. In the history of weak, feeble,
vacillating action no parallel can be found to this.
It was as weak as it was unprincipled, and brought
the undisguised contempt of the whole House on
the honourable member. Was there ever such
silly, futile action heard of in any quarter of the
globe? The honourable member, the present
Premier, refuses to vote for his old friend,
although he thinks him an admirable man for
the office, and he also refuses to vote for the
candidate put forth by his own friends of the
Opposition, although he has no fault to find with
him, and thus he nullifies himself, extinguishes
himself, renders himself nugatory, and, by this
poor, weak, unprincipled, and wretched conduct,
cancels himself as completely as the Kilkenny cats
ever did. (Laughter and cheers.) Who could
put any trust in a man of whom all this could
be said? Well, this was desertion number
two, since which time the honourable gentleman has been translated from Leader of the
Opposition to that of Premier of the country,
and the way he has distributed the offices
of his Government marks a desertion of faithful
qualified friends as lamentable as the two cases
spoken of. Men who have fought for years with
him in Opposition, and of marked ability, have
been thrown overboard, and comparative strangers
to Parliament and public life preferred to them.
But desertion number four is probably the worst
of all, and in saying this I refer to the case of
Mr. Garrett. The honourable gentleman at the
head of the Government was not above sending
for Mr. Garrett, and taking him into his councils,
at a time when he knew he would be almost the

T

next week called upon to form a Government, and having advised with the honourable member for Camden, and received the benefit of his larger knowledge, the honourable member for Camden is met with the reward of being, without the least compunction, thrown overboard. If the Premier had no intention to take the honourable member for Camden as a colleague, he had no right to consult with him, and so gain the advantage of his superior knowledge and capacity. This was dishonest action in every sense of the word, and I don't envy the country which places in the high position of its Prime Minister a man against whom all this can be truthfully said. (Cheers.) A man so base in common everyday principle, so infirm of purpose, and so weak, is a danger, as well as a disgrace, to any State, and I am sure he will not remain long in office before this is found out. Moreover—and what I am to speak of now is of very grave importance—honourable gentlemen will remember that the present Premier was a short time ago appointed to the high office of Agent-General with a salary of £2000 a year. The honourable gentleman accepted this office, but had to relinquish it for some cause or other. If that cause was that he was in the power and under the thumb of any of our Banks or monetary institutions, then I say that, if he is still in that position, I don't say he is, but if the fact be that he actually is so, then I can imagine nothing so wrong as his accepting the office of Premier. The people here have large transactions with our great Banks, and it is not seemly, decent, or proper, that our chief ruler should be in the position that any of those institutions should have it in its power to crush him at a moment's notice. It is not a very splendid position for the Premier of any country to be in, and it is by no means a comfortable thought for the people to reflect on. Considering the large transactions the people of this country have with the Banks here, the people's rulers, who conduct these transactions, should be free and independent, and in no way under influences such as I have hinted at. So much for the Premier. As to the Vice-President of the Executive Council, Sir Patrick Jennings, who sits next to him, I have nothing adverse to say. He is a courteous and affable gentleman, and the little bit of business he did for the Government the other day he did with great affability, I might even say, without exaggeration, he did it with *extreme unction.** (Great laughter.) So much so, that at the time I thought it very ominous of the speedy dissolution of the Government. (Hear, hear, and laughter.) I dare say honourable members will agree with me that the Vice-President of the Executive Council will act as a very solid and substantial piece of ballast, and tend to keep the State vessel on an even keel. I have now to treat of the honourable the Attorney-General—that pretty little piece of human pinchbeck, garnished with rubies, and tipped with kid, scented and ornamented in a fashion truly exquisite. No wonder such beings as the Postmaster-General and the Minister for Works fell prostrate before his sublime haw-haw. (Great laughter.) But seriously speaking does anyone know anything of Mr. Dalley's political opinions? Does anyone know anything of his opinions on this great Land Question? The only opinions of his we know anything of are his opinions on the Education Question, and, in reference to this question, and indeed I may say, with truth, all others, he stands in the present Administration as the representative

* Sir Patrick is a leading Roman Catholic.

of a dark fanaticism and a benighted priestcraft.
(Cheers.) The Attorney-General, in the estimation of his colleagues, it would appear, is their
trump card. They each and all of them became
absolutely nauseous in their puerile praises of their
Attorney-General while appealing for re-election.
(Hear). Well then, if the colleagues of the
Attorney-General know nothing about him, many
of the members of this House understand him
well, and I would like to ask when did the
Attorney-General ever take the slightest interest
in the affairs of this country, with the solitary
exception of the Education Question, when the
priestcraft, before which he bends and bows,
lashed him into a benighted action? Did anyone
ever see the Attorney-General seek election to this
House for the purpose of struggling, without
money and without price, in the people's cause?
Have they not rather seen him immovable until
some office of emolument brought him down from
his lofty pedestal—(loud cheers)—only to retire
when the office and emolument left him? (Hear,
hear.) For the last twenty years has not this been
the honourable gentleman's action? Did he not
constantly lie dead to every political duty until
the offer of a rich office galvanised him into life?
(Hear, hear.) Was he ever known to accompany
his friends into Opposition? No! with the dis-
appearance of office and emolument, the disap-
pearance of the Attorney-General resulted, only to
return when office and emolument returned, and
to mark his systematic adherence to this unworthy
and contemptible conduct, he did not care whether
he took office from the present Premier or from
Sir John Robertson his opponent. Nay, I believe
he would have jumped at office and emolument
even if it had been offered him by Sir Henry

Parkes, if Sir Henry had ever been foolish
enough to do so. Suppose this Government is
turned out a month hence, will the Attorney-
General accompany them into Opposition and
assist them there? Do we not all know he will
not, but will leave his colleagues to their
fate, perfectly heedless what that fate may be,
and get himself again hoisted to his pedestal, there
to wait till some turn of the political wheel again
brings some rich office to his door. (Hear, hear.)
Can anyone deny these facts? The history of Mr.
Dalley, the present Attorney-General, for the last
twenty years proves their strict truth to the very
letter. One cannot help feeling something like
bitter scorn as we see the Attorney-General affecting to sneer at Mr. Davies, not a long time ago his
colleague in another Government, and for whom
he had then nothing but fulsome and ridiculous
praises, but then his office and emoluments were
in danger, and anything to save those; and so,
even now, we see the right honourable Attorney-
General condescending to play the part of an electioneering hack, and go spouting through the city
singing the praises of illiterate, ignorant dolts and
clodhoppers, who sit with him as colleagues in this
most pitiful Government, and all to preserve his own
office and its dear emoluments. To the winds with
public life and all his colleagues, will be the ejacula-
tion of the Attorney-General, when the rising storm
of public disgust and indignation swells into a furi-
ous tempest, and scatters this incompetent Government, a miserable wreck, to the four quarters.
The Attorney-General's interest in public life and
the progress of his country will then cease—his
colleagues may sink to perdition never more to
rise, while he himself will have his eyes open to
nothing but the chance of having another grab,

no matter under what auspices, at office and its—
under the circumstances—ignominious advantages.
The Attorney-General is a man given up to strong
delusion that he, of necessity, must believe the
worst of lies, and I ask the members of this honourable House can any Government expect honour,
credit, or anything but injury, from the alliance
of such a man as this? I now come to that very
pliant, elastic, and most flexible gentleman, the
Minister of Education. I am not surprised at that
honourable gentleman's rise, such as it is, considering the quantity of gas he contains (much
laughter) ; he has gone up like a balloon, and like
a balloon he will come down, probably in the usual
state of wreck. (Hear, hear.) Childishness seems
to be his main characteristic. If there is ever any
notable piece of donkey worship to be performed,
the Minister of Education is sure to be selected as
the high priest to perform this ceremony. He
has an inexhaustible mine of insufferable frivolity
and puerility about him, and, the misfortune is,
he is always digging in it. (Loud laughter and
cheers.) Well, shallow and superficial as the
Minister of Education is, he is in a position where
he may do much mischief, and he has already
begun this mischief, as I shall instantly show.
Let honourable members never forget that the
Vice-President of the Executive Council and the
Attorney-General, as well as the Premier himself,
are mortal enemies of the Public Schools Act.
Well, while, of course, they dare not attempt to
publicly interfere with that Act, they may injure
the cause frightfully by acting upon a weak, pliant
minister, who has no earnest opinions upon the
subject at all—(hear, hear)—and this, I assert,
has been done in the case of altering the intention
to convert St. James's Denominational School into

a large and effective Public School. (Loud cheers.)
Honourable members will understand that this St.
James's School was a very large Church of England
Denominational School, situated in the very heart
of the city. With the cessation of all State aid to
Denominational Schools, which only took place
the other day, this school fell into the hands of
the Government, and the late Minister of Education, under the recommendation of the officers of
the department, and the advice of the School
Board, most wisely resolved to open it as a large
public school, and so provide for the hundreds of
scholars who had attended the Denominational
School. This was being speedily and wisely done,
when the present Government came into office,
and now we hear, to the astonishment of every
sane man, the present Minister has rashly and
ignorantly resolved that there shall be no Public
School at this spot, but that the school shall be
turned into a High School, although the great
Sydney Grammar School is right opposite. Now,
the policy of the new Minister of Education is
simply so stupid that it can be accounted for in no
way but on the supposition that pressure has been
brought to bear upon him not to open a Public
School there, as it might interfere unduly with
St. Mary's Roman Catholic School hard by. (Loud
cheers, and laughter from the Minister.) The
policy of the Minister is in no other way to be
accounted for. Here is a grand site for a great
Public School, with the scholars all ready to enter,
and the certainty that it would form another Fort
Street School, and supply an absolutely necessary
want of the locality, and do no end of public good
—the thing recommended by officers of the Government School Boards, and decided upon by the late
Minister himself, and now we find this new Minister,

with a characteristic thoughtlessness, losing this grand opportunity of establishing probably the largest and finest Public School in Sydney. I call upon honourable members to have their eyes open to this matter, and others of the same kind, all the more necessary while we have an Administration opposed to our Public School System, and ready to injure it in favour of Denominationalism, whenever opportunity offers. The presence in office of a frivolous, superficial, pliant Minister of Education, who will bend any way, is too glorious a chance for Romish priestcraft to miss. Therefore, I say, beware, and watch a danger that is imminent, and might be ruinous to the whole fabric of our Public School System. (Cheers.) The Treasurer, Mr. G. R. Dibbs, is a man of small and narrow mind, rash and inconsiderate, and pretty certain to bring distress upon his colleagues and injury to the country, but he may look upon himself as a most fortunate man in winning the prize without ever having run in the race. The honourable the Minister for Justice is in the same position. As to him, what shall I say? Well, let me charitably say with Portia in the "Merchant of Venice," " God made him, let him therefore pass for a man." The Minister for Works is absent, defeated and extinguished; it would, therefore, scarcely be fair to speak of him. The advent of the Minister for Mines proves what I have often alleged—how much our Parliaments have deteriorated. When we reflect that such a man as Sir Henry Parkes was seventeen years in this House before he reached office, what a commentary is this upon several of the offices of State filled by such men as I see before me. Nowadays, every puny whipster has office thrust upon him without reference to experience or qualification. But now I come to the Postmaster-General, and this is the most remarkable appointment of all. Did anyone ever hear of an utter stranger to public life entering the House of Commons, and never so much as opening his mouth there, being lifted into high office without anyone ever having heard the tone of his voice? I do not suppose anyone ever did or ever will hear of such a thing ; but it has happened here in the case of our Post-master-General. How it has been brought about no one can tell or even imagine; but we all believe there is something more in this than appears on the surface, if philosophy could only find it out. In consideration of his total silence during the year he has sat as a member of this House, I suppose he has been appointed to office in order that he might give practical realization to the grand old principle of a "wink being as good as a nod to a blind horse"—the Premier being the blind horse; but he tells us himself that it was because he was a carrier that he was selected. If this was sound policy, a carrier of letters rather than a carrier of wool and tallow would be the likelier man for the office. The thing puts me in mind of the man who, being asked if he could speak French, replied, "No, but I have a brother who can play upon the German flute"—the analogy here being not more remote than in the case of the Postmaster-General, appointed to that office in virtue of his being a carrier. (Loud laughter.) Suppose the Premier pushes this principle to its utmost consequences, we may then look to have a jail-warder Minister of Justice, a detective Attorney-General, and a policeman Chief Secretary. The first fruit of such an appointment is this, told by the Post-master-General himself. While addressing his

constituents, he said that he informed the clerks at
the Post Office "that he was going to be
master there;" and the Minister for Works said
he did the same thing.   The vulgar ignorance
of this at once proves incompetency, and speaks
volumes as to the absurdity of appointing carriers
and navvies to high office.   (Cheers and laughter.)
The Minister for Lands is the last member of the
Ministry I have to notice, and I say this, that the
fact of his having received a testimonial of £1,800
and a service of plate for performing duties as
a Minister of the Crown that he was paid £1,500 a
year for doing, fills all men with suspicion—doubly
does it do so when the names of the subscribers
to this extraordinary testimonial have never been
up to this hour divulged, although repeatedly
called for.   This testimonial was never given by
the people, but it is said it was given by the
squatter class; and whether or not, it calls loudly
for explanation, the more especially at this
moment when the same gentleman enters upon
our land administration at a time of great public
excitement.   I have heard it said that the Land
Minister was appointed on account of the influence
he had in this House.   I deny his influence here
or anywhere.   The man of influence here, in this
Assembly, and in all assemblies of the kind, is the
man who can put a truth vigorously, earnestly,
and vividly before the House, and who can as
vigorously and earnestly expose the falseness of
a falsehood.   The man who can do this with
eloquent power is the only influential man here,
and I care not were he as poor as Lazarus and
went about in rags, you must listen to him, so
supreme and paramount is the power of intellect
in overwhelming and destroying ignorance, however outwardly gilded or adventitiously upheld.

What would become of the present Ministers in the presence of a difficult, abstruse, complex political problem, demanding instant solution, defence, or exposure? What, I say, would your Wrights and Stuarts and Farnells do under such circumstances? Well, I will tell you what they would do. They would run for light to their oracles, Morris and Rankin, whom they have just appointed as a Royal Commission to assist them with their new Land Bill. The attitude of the Government here is supremely contemptible. The country has placed them in power to produce a Land Bill, instead of doing which they pray for time and appoint a Commission to assist them in doing what we demand should be done by themselves. The men whom I have so severely criticized have justified my utmost severity in the poor puling tone they have adopted since they became a Government. They are afraid to face the Land Bill, knowing that the moment they touch it their doom is sealed. The composition of the Government is bad, the offices are filled, in some instances, by very incompetent men, and the feeling of this House, as far as I can read it, is to cast them adrift as soon as opportunity avails. (Cheers.)

VOTE OF CENSURE.

[On the occasion of Mr. (now Sir Henry) Parkes moving an amendment on the address in reply to the Governor's speech on the opening of Parliament, Mr. Buchanan delivered a speech of great power. It was completely destroyed by the imperfect reports of the daily papers. We have only space to give the concluding sentences, which we offer as a fair sample of the whole speech, by far the finest we ever heard in our Parliament.— "Cumberland Mercury."]

THERE is another matter in connection with his Excellency the Governor's conduct in leaving his post for so long a time, that I implore the attention of the Press and the country to. At the time of his Excellency's leaving, there were three men lying under sentence of death. The cases of those men were only considered last Monday, and in every case a reprieve was granted. But can honourable gentlemen form the least estimate of the intolerable burden of cruel, racking anxiety that weighed upon the souls of those men for six long weeks, in order that the Governor might enjoy the sport of horse-racing in another colony? Who can picture the sleepless nights of agony endured by those unhappy men, with visions of the ghastly gibbet perpetually haunting them, making night hideous, and the day too horrible for endurance? What language can depict the slow consuming misery that gnawed at their

hearts as they imagined that each day brought
them nearer to their doom—a doom so frightful
and appalling, intensified in its horror by this
long, unnecessary uncertainty and suspense? If
honourable members can imagine how full of
horrors those men must have supped, stretched,
as they were, for six weeks on the rack of a cruel,
inhuman and culpable neglect, let them try to
judge of the character, and measure the weight
of the condemnation that should fall upon the
Government and on his Excellency the Governor,
the authors of this stupendous wrong. Had life
and death been more important to his Excellency
than grovelling in all the revolting·immoralities
of a miserable race-course, the fate of those men
would have been known to them six weeks ago,
and a world of dreary wretchedness lifted from
their trembling souls. But what recked he, or
the Government, what agonies of painful, anxious
thought those men suffered so long as the one
saw the races and the others drew their salaries?
If misconduct, cruel, heartless abandonment of
duty on the part of the Governor and Government, leading to intense suffering to others, even
if those others were condemned felons, was ever
perpetrated under heaven's canopy, surely it was
here. I call upon every man in this House to
come forward and attest his manhood by voting
destruction to a Government so lost to every
sense of the sacredness of the trust they hold,
so insensible to the wrongs and agonies of men
to whom they owed a solemn duty, and who
would have been relieved from intolerable distress
by its performance, and so utterly regardless of
every principle of humanity, that in the name of
that humanity, so grossly outraged, I call for
their extinction.

THE SOUDAN EXPEDITION.

[THIS Soudan business was by no means so popular in New South Wales as people at a distance might suppose—with the exception of a very few noisy and talkative people, led on by a singularly weak and vapid Press. In Sydney, the people, as a whole, derided it and laughed at it, while large numbers of the most solid and sensible portion of the population condemned it as "a rash and ignorant display of our own weakness," and foolish interference in matters which in no way concerned us or our interest in any way. In the following speech of Mr. Buchanan, delivered in Parliament, the subject was handled in his own vigorous style, and a considerable amount of truth and sound sense poured upon honourable members. Parliament was specially called together on the 17th of March for the express purpose of getting "Parliamentary sanction to the act of the Government in sending troops to the Soudan." The address in reply to the speech from the Governor having been moved and seconded, Mr. H. Clarke moved an amendment to the following effect:—"That the address be amended by the omission of the second paragraph with the view to the insertion in its place of the following paragraph: 'We, however, feel bound to state that the occasion did not warrant the despatch of troops from this country without the authority of Parliament.'" This amendment having been seconded, Mr. Buchanan rose and spoke as follows:—]

MR. SPEAKER,—It is my intention to support this amendment, although I wish it had been more emphatic, more conclusive, and a more complete and perfect expression of our dissent from proceedings on the part of the Government that I, for one, consider in every sense criminal. I refuse to listen to the shallow talk that is put forward in justification of this enormity, and which has mainly characterized the speech of the mover of the address. No one could listen to that speech without a feeling of regret. It was paltry and puerile to a degree, worthy of all that has taken place since the inception of this astounding act of sheer madness which the Government has been guilty of in sending our men out of the country to fight in a foreign war. This, sir, is an occasion the importance of which it is impossible to exaggerate. The act of the Government has imperilled the safety of this country and its people, and it has done this without the sanction of Parliament, and in defiance of every principle of constitutional law, and in total disregard of those common everyday prudential considerations that even fools respect and suffer themselves to be guided by. This very gross misconduct on the part of the Government should call forth the strongest expression of dissent as well as denunciation from this Assembly. It is most scandalous in its illegality and inherent baseness, and can be justified by no man in the possession of his senses. The whole thing resolves itself into an empty, ignorant, unprincipled piece of reckless swagger, in every way pitiful and contemptible, and very worthy of the source from which it sprung. I believe it was done at the instigation and through the caprice and thoughtless vanity of one member of the Government without consulting any of his colleagues, and inspired by the one thought of creating a loud, sensational noise, utterly regardless of the country's dearest interests. I do not believe the Premier of the country knew anything of it, nor do I believe that the Attorney-General, Mr. Dalley, who is the principal delinquent here,

condescended to even mention the matter to his
colleagues until the wretched, abortive act, displaying in so clear a light our weakness and imbecility, had been consummated. No one can
deny that what has been done is illegal and unconstitutional in every sense. The Government
have enlisted soldiers in this country to fight in a
foreign quarrel, and have sent them out of the
country for that purpose; and they have done this
without the sanction of Parliament. A grosser
treason to the best and highest interests of this
country could scarcely be imagined. And what, I
would like to ask, is the wretched, false excuse
offered for this misconduct? Serious as the
matter is, one can scarcely think of it without
laughter. The excuse is that England was in an
emergency—in extreme need. We were even
told that poor old England was at her last gasp,
stricken with paralysis, and that this mighty
armament of five hundred men from New South
Wales was required to protect and save her. This
is actually the ludicrous defence the Government
put forward for their high-handed, illegal, and
unconstitutional acts. Need I tell this House
that the excuse is a tissue of barefaced falsehoods,
and this gives a very vivid colour to the fact that,
in their senseless, thoughtless action, the Government were influenced and inspired by no higher
purpose than the creating of a noisy demonstration
by which, as is so commonly said, the country
might be advertised and talked about. The pretence
put forward by the Government in justification of
their insane procedure is false to the very heart
of it. England was in no emergency, in no want
of troops; and well did the Government know
this, as we may judge from telegrams laid upon
the table of this House since we met, but when

published in the Press, some fortnight ago, important portions of them were held back from publication so as to deceive and mislead the people as to this matter of urgency. Signally disgraceful to the Government has been all this deception, lying, and double-dealing. Why, the English Government told our Government that there was no hurry, that the troops were going into summer quarters, and that our troops would be in time enough if they were there by the autumn. Our Government struck this out in publishing the telegrams, and left the poor, ignorant people to believe that the emergency was vital, and that England was ' *in extremis.* But what a view does this give us of the little peddling, paltry purposes of the Attorney-General. Had any thought of England's interests been in his mind, he might have sent a united armament of some strength and importance from all the Colonies, because at the time I believe their rulers were insane enough for this; but our Attorney-General, Mr. Dalley, palpably wished to have a monopoly of the so-called glory in his own hands, and hurried away his handful of men before Victoria or any other Colony had a chance of participating in it. That the Attorney-General never gave a thought to the interests of this country is plain enough. A sensational, empty noise, based upon the prevailing spurious notions of what he calls loyalty, was the only thought in his small mind in landing this country, it may be, in responsibilities that, if continued for any length of time, will lead to its inevitable ruin. Under this most lamentable policy we are going, voluntarily, thousands of miles out of our way to seek trouble and disaster. No one asks us to do so.

w

We have no call to do so. Every interest of this country is opposed to such madness, and will suffer by it in every imaginable way. Just let us reflect for one moment what a dreadful calamity war is, even when forced upon us by the insolence of an invader, the only war we should ever be engaged in. Did the Attorney-General, when he embarked upon this sea of troubles, without rhyme or reason, and without a shadow of cause or excuse, reflect that this country has at present a public debt of thirty million sterling, and that when we have borrowed all the money we have got liberty from Parliament to borrow our debt will have reached fifty millions sterling, a consideration that is well calculated to "give us pause"? No doubt this enormous debt, enormous to be contracted by under a million of people, has been incurred for the construction of reproductive works, such as railways ; but suppose, along with this, we adopt a policy of ignorant, uncalled-for intermeddling with the wars of England, does the blindest man not see that those fifty millions would soon swell into proportions that would leave us hopelessly ruined and exhausted? And, at best, this war in the Soudan is not worthy of the name. A wretched scrimmage with a few barbarians, which could be extinguished by England, acting with due vigour, at any moment, is certainly a most laughable event to call forth all this illegal, unconstitutional, and extravagant folly on the part of this country. Surely England had reached the depth of her infatuation when she accepted the aid of this contingent from New South Wales. By doing this, undoubtedly without thought, England approved of a most disastrous and ruinous policy for this country. Under no circumstances should this country ever send troops

out of it to fight in foreign wars. If we understood our duty, we should know that our true
policy is to organize all our warlike power to
meet an invader; to conserve our force here at
home, and be ready for any emergency of attack
from without. This should be our policy now and
for ever. If this accursed precedent is in any
way followed, this country would be ruined and
beggared in no time were it a hundred times
greater than it is in wealth and population. And
what a wretched war we have sent our men to
fight in. England is at the present moment
attempting to enforce upon those poor Arabs a
hatefully corrupt and villainous government. Both
Lord Dufferin and General Stewart have spoken
of the detestable government of the Egyptians,
and how much the Arabs of the Soudan were
justified in rebelling and fighting against it.
If I understand the matter right, England is
fighting to reimpose this detestable Government
on the oppressed and cruelly ill-treated Arabs, and
our men have gone to assist in this debasing business. May such luck attend them as such an enterprise deserves. One of the most humiliating
features in the base, contemptible business, is to
see bishops and clergymen coming forward and
invoking the blessing of God upon this blood-
thirsty enterprise of ours, where our men have
gone forth to slay people with whom they have no
quarrel, who have done them no harm, and who
are engaged in a death-struggle for their own
rights and liberties, and against the bitterness of
unbearable oppression. Such bishops and clergymen seem to be the leaders and teachers of the
devil's worship instead of the worship of God.
Be this as it may, the question this House is
now asked to decide is, whether the Government

was justified in organizing and sending away this
contingent of troops without first having consulted
Parliament and obtained its sanction. We have
seen that the excuse of urgency and England's
helplessness is ridiculous as well as false to the
core, and the Government stands condemned for
resorting to the meanness of falsehood to justify
its illegal and infamous procedure. There is not
a shadow of justification for the act of our Government—an act, the offspring of shallowness and
childish vanity, conceived and carried out by the
reckless irresponsibility and diseased sentimen-
tality of one man in every way unfitted to form
any accurate estimate of the ultimate injury to
this country by the adoption of a policy so ruinous
and destructive. We are in no position to send
soldiers abroad, and, as I have already said, even
if we were, it would be a ruinous policy for us to
adopt. When this offer was made to the British
Government by the Attorney-General, without
consulting his colleagues, we had not a single
soldier enlisted. It was all done after the foolish
offer was so foolishly accepted. As it is, many of
the five hundred who have gone are married men,
in desperate circumstances, who have left their
wives and families to the mercy of the waves
during their absence. And this is nicknamed
patriotism, forsooth! If it were properly designated, a very different word from patriotism would
require to be used. Those men have deserted
their wives and families not to fight for liberty
and country, but to assist in imposing an iron yoke
of oppression upon unfortunate men who are doing
so. Amidst all the noisy tumult of a half-witted
excitement and hollow agitation, those things
may be lost sight of, but the true bearing of this
egregious folly will yet be seen in its true light

when the public mind is restored to something
like calmness and clearness. It is curious to
observe that no sooner had our handful of troops
left, than we heard ominous reports of war between Russia and England. Even this did not
open the blind eyes of the Government to the folly
of sending from our shores our only means of
defence against an invading enemy. Surely England's answer to us, if she had given half a thought
to the subject, when this preposterous offer of a
handful of troops was made to her, should have
been—" We are much obliged, but had you not
better keep what armaments you have for your
own defence ?" This is the answer England should
have sent, and if it had been sent it would have
saved us from the mess we are now in, and from
an expense which we cannot well bear with our
millions of debt weighing us down to the very dust
at the present moment. We have heard, and do
hear every day, a great deal about our loyalty to
the mother country. This loyalty is clearly more
in the mouth than anywhere else. We had a
grand illustration of this the other day when England ran counter to our wishes respecting the
occupation of New Guinea. Then the fiercest
denunciations were hurled at England and her
Secretary of State for the Colonies, and nothing
was heard but loud cries for separation, and I say,
advisedly, that wherever there is any self-interest
involved and endangered, on either side, the tie
that binds those Colonies to England will snap like
a silken thread. (Cries of " No " from some
honourable members.) It is all very well to call
out " No," but a short time will soon prove who is
right. The natural and certain fate of this country
is to grow into an independent nation, just as, in
human life, youth grows into manhood and indepen-

dence.   Honourable members of this House know
well that I have always advocated separation
from England as the best policy for both countries.
In advocating this policy I have always despised any
imputation on my loyalty to England in so acting.
It is true loyalty to England as well as to this
country that forces me to this action.   Anyone
with eyes in his head must see at a glance
that the true policy of this country, and all England's Colonies, is to separate from her for their
mutual interest and advantage.   England, in the
midst of European complications, is always liable
to be immersed in war with some of the great
European States, and the misery and danger to us
is that, from our political connection, which has
yielded us nothing, every enemy of England becomes an enemy of ours—and that enemy may at
any time strike a blow at us.   We have no voice
as to the justice of England's wars; England
may be hurried into a war of the rankest injustice by the folly of her rulers—we have no
say as to whether those wars should be entered
upon or not.   Yet we are involved in the same
wars, and may be struck disastrously by any, or
all, of England's enemies.   Why should we incur
such a danger as this?   England, on the other
hand, has her fleets scattered over the whole
world, protecting her distant colonies, which
lands her in enormous expense, and cripples her
power to an incalculable degree.   It is, therefore,
for the mutual benefit of England and her colonies
that I advocate separation; and I laugh to scorn
the shallow, sentimental trash that is nowadays
talked about, called by the sounding name of
"imperial federation," as if England could hold
under her rule growing countries thousands of
miles away from her, when she cannot very well

hold Ireland, lying alongside of her. Every
nation on the face of the earth is governed by
self-interest, and every earthly consideration melts
and disappears under the fierce friction of this
overpowering instinct. This country has interests
of its own widely different from those of England, and when those interests clash, disruption
and separation are the inevitable consequences.
Nature points to this as the certain issue, and
time and circumstances will assuredly work out
the result. This tendency was beautifully exemplified in the late New Guinea business, and we
will see it again, notwithstanding our hollow and
pretended loyalty, whenever England's action
imperils any interest of ours. It will then be
seen how naturally will arise the question of
separation, and, with it, the necessity of organizing
our own defences, and never dream of fighting
anywhere but against an invading foe. A celebrated writer of the present century, a relative
and namesake of my own, in a work entitled "An
inquiry into the taxation and commercial policy of
Great Britain," has this to say on the subject I
am speaking upon: "It is now generally acknow-
ledged that colonies are of no real advantage to
the mother country. The monopoly of the trade
is a positive injury to both parties; to the dependent as well as to the parent State; and the
sovereignty, however it may flatter the national
vanity, brings with it no solid benefit. The
undue importance attached by Great Britain to
her American colonies was fully proved by the
event. The wisest statesmen were impressed with
the notion that the loss of this great empire, the
brightest ornament, as it was said, of the British
Crown, would be a serious blow to the national
prosperity. How entirely has the subsequent

prosperity of England belied those vain fears. The loss of America has in no degree affected the commercial greatness of Britain; it has rather redounded to her advantage; and the only regret now is that the Canadas were not united in the same successful revolt, which would have freed the mother country from all farther care or expense concerning them, and from the injurious monopolies established, as well as from the danger of being involved in wars with other powers on their account." With those sentiments I entirely concur, and undoubtedly it is merely a question of time as to their realization in practical results, which may be precipitated sooner than many honourable gentlemen of this House imagine. Although this matter has no direct bearing on the question before the House, still as there has been so much sorry talk of loyalty in reference to this expedition to the Soudan, I have thought it my duty to speak out boldly my own views of what loyalty means. There is no question about any one's loyalty here, and it is a matter that should never be lightly called in question. There is a despicable pretended loyalty, spurious and barren, which is never out of the mouths of a certain class in this country. The loyalty I refer to is rotten and nauseous to the very heart of it—most rank and loathsome in the extravagance of its idiotic expression, destined to pass away with the fools that indulge in it, giving place to a manly, genuine independence, an independence based upon complete freedom, and inspired by a patriotism very different from the brawling, blustering, bellowing, which, the other day, filled the air with discord, and covered all concerned in it with unmixed contempt as this wretched expedition left our shores. The Attorney-General is the grand manufacturer of this sentimental loyalty and sickly patriotism, the great political Barnum of the occasion, the organizer of those wild explosions of popular folly, so frequent of late, and the grand reservoir from which flowed all that frothy jargon and imbecile rant that has been so carefully preserved to us in the columns of the daily press. It is indeed monstrous that this Attorney-General, in a fiction, in a dream of patriotism, should force his soul so to his own conceit that, by her working, a large portion of this community seemed to have lost the guidance of reason. And what has our Press of Sydney been doing throughout this crisis in our history? I answer, with one noble excepion, it has acted like a great overgrown, soft-headed baby. Time-serving, timid, feeble as the Press of Sydney has been for years past, in this supreme moment of our history, it gave us no other guidance than the hysterical ravings and screams of a half-demented school girl. The Government boast a good deal about what they call the patriotic fund, raised for the purpose of relieving the wives and children of those who may fall in battle. Judged by this test, I submit that the country is against the Government as to this matter of sending troops to the Soudan. Whatever sum has been raised, I assert that twenty men have subscribed half of it; that the people have not responded to this call at all, and that not more than three hundred of the people have subscribed, apart from the civil servants of the Government, who have been compelled to do so. I can imagine nothing so mean and contemptible in its petty tyranny as the act of the Government in sending a circular among the civil servants asking them to subscribe to this fund. Do honourable members

fail to see what this means? Does it not mean,
and even say, you must subscribe, and if you do
not you will be marked men, and ways and means
will be found to make this tell against you? In
the history of base, degrading tyranny, I know of
nothing so base or mean as the sending of this
circular among the civil servants of the Government; and notwithstanding all this whipping and
spurring and unprecedented pressure, I still say
that considerably more than half of the sum collected has been subscribed by twenty men. Let
me say a word as to the action of the Chief Justice
of this country. He never was so much out of
place as when, the other night, he stood upon a
political platform and talked politics to the people,
when he might have been called upon the very next
day to give judgment in a case arising out of the
present action of the Government. The Chief
Justice attended a stormy political meeting at
which a motion was proposed to approve of the
policy of the Government touching this matter.
There was so much dissent from the objects of the
promoters of the meeting that it was a question
whether any of their resolutions were carried,
although the Chairman declared them to be so.
Yet in this atmosphere of violent political party
feeling our Chief Justice thought it not beneath
his dignity to appear and move one of the resolutions. The high office of Chief Justice suffered,
through this action, in the estimation of all high-
minded, intelligent, thoughtful men. At this
meeting, clearly of the "Jingo" stamp, honoured
by the presence of the Chief Justice, all manner of
extravagant nauseous stuff was talked about this
Soudan enterprise. It was called "inspiration,"
"genius," "the grandest and greatest event that
has ever happened in the world;" "it has made

us a nation," "struck terror into the hearts of all
foreign powers," "paralysed the arm of Russia,"
and left the rulers of France and Germany
"sicklied o'er with the pale cast of thought."
Ineffable twaddle of this description has saturated
our poor Sydney newspapers for weeks past, and
is a fair specimen of the inflated rubbish that fell
from most of the speakers at the meeting in question. With regard to England's conduct in accepting those Australian troops, I put it down to
weakness on the part of her rulers. There seems
to be a sad want of spirit and resolute purpose on
the part of England's rulers in dealing with foreign
affairs. In one of to-day's newspapers I read a
telegram as follows:—"Earl Granville stated in
the House of Lords this afternoon that her
Majesty's Government had received information
concerning the report that the British flag had
been lowered at Victoria Cameroons, and the German flag hoisted in its place. He expressed his
conviction that, in any case, Prince Bismarck
would take such an attitude in the matter as would
prevent trouble arising out of any action on the
part of German officers." Do honourable members
of this House not feel a sense of humiliation on
reading such a telegram as this? Surely this is
not the tone that would have been sounded by any
of England's great rulers of old in the face of so
gross an insult. Let honourable members observe
that England is not expected to redress this intolerable wrong and insult to herself. No! England is to wait, humbly, on Prince Bismarck's
action! Can you imagine anything more humiliating? The deadliest insult that could be offered
to England was to lower the British flag and hoist
another in its place, and when this is actually done,
instead of England instantly resenting it with fire

and sword, and with the last drop of her blood, if
need be, the Foreign Minister of England, in the
spirit of the most abject poltroonery, coolly tells
us that, although it is true that our flag has been
lowered, yet we can do nothing, and must wait for
what redress it may please Prince Bismarck to
charitably dole out to us. This is not the style in
which the England of old was accustomed to redress her wrongs. It would be a blessing for the
old country if she would call to her counsels true
men of the old stamp, with somewhat of the nerve
and spirit of the great Cromwell in them, to
grapple with her enemies, and carry her on to the
heights of glory so familiar to her of old. Serious
and important as the subject before the House is,
it is not my intention to trouble honourable members with any further remarks upon it. While
supporting the amendment, I am by no means
satisfied with the terms of it, and, if allowable, I
will move now that the following words be added
to it—" And, further, that in the opinion of this
House, the act of the Government in sending men
from this country, without Parliamentary sanction,
to act as soldiers and fight in a foreign war against
people with whom we have no quarrel, who have
done us no harm, and who desire to do us no harm,
is unconstitutional, illegal, and a very gross
wrong ; suicidal to us as a rising and progressive
community, ruinous to the best interests of the
State, and inevitably leading to serious disaster,
financially and otherwise, while, in all probability,
culminating in national dishonour and disgrace."
I move that those words be added to the amendment as a clearer intimation of the general feeling
of the people of New South Wales as to the reckless folly of this most impolitic act of the Government. The means we have of estimating or

gauging public opinion on this question entirely favours the idea that the body of the people is earnestly opposed to it. The patriotic fund is a distinct failure, and in over a dozen districts public meetings have expressed themselves in strong terms of dissent from the Government policy. This dissent is every day increasing in force and volume, as the people begin to calmly reflect on the stupendous absurdity of this country sending armaments from its shores to fight in wars that cannot, by any straining of even the imagination, be brought to concern us in the remotest degree. To satisfy the hollow vanity of a few deplorable blockheads, this destructive 'policy is imposed upon us—a policy which we cannot continue if the necessities of war require its continuance, and which, of necessity, if pursued, must leave us beggared and bankrupt—which can gain us neither honour nor credit nor advantage of any kind, and whose only justification is a vain, presumptuous, insolent spirit of weak impotent intermeddling. No doubt the Government have a majority, and a large one, in favour of the motion ; but this does not mean much at present. The solid sense of the country is not entirely dead, and, rely upon it, the supporters of the Government, in this madness, will not be overlooked when the people get a chance at them. The supporters of the amendment, which is the side of truth and justice, have nothing to fear. They will vote with the consciousness that they are trying to shield this country from the heaviest evil that has yet fallen upon it, and the clear, intelligent vote they will give will, at least, afford them the satisfaction of knowing that they are voting for the benefit of England as well as Australia, and with the truest regard to their mutual safety and security. (Loud cheers greeted this deliverance.)

[As was expected, the Government carried the motion by 64 to 23, the sympathies of the people being largely with the minority, and this sympathy increasing every day. If such another expedition were attempted now it would be scouted by the whole people, so much has the feeling changed.]

NOTE.—Since the foregoing speech was delivered by Mr. Buchanan, Mr. Froude has published a book upon Australia, and I have no hesitation in stating that those who look to that book for authentic information on the subject will find themselves egregiously misled and misinformed. Some time ago Mr. Fronde made some disparaging remarks on the Australian Agents-General, which, being resented, Mr. Froude offered an explanation to the effect that a wrong construction had been put upon what he had said, and, further, that he had only met one of the Agents-General. Mr. Froude seems to have been in a similar position in giving judgment on the people of New South Wales. He came overland, by rail, from Melbourne, travelling by night, and he remained a very short time in Sydney, and, I believe, was never out of it. He saw two or three of our public men, and evidently derived all his information concerning the people from one of them. He says the people speak good English! no doubt, if the rankest Cockneyism can be called good English. Among the people, and even in the Parliament, the r's and h's are sadly misused. This statement is not more absurd than the other he makes, to the effect that the people are Conservatives! If so, those Conservatives have enacted, as law, the abolition of State aid to religion, manhood suffrage, vote by ballot, and triennial parliaments. Mr. Froude goes on to say that Mr. Gladstone is everywhere unpopular here! Not very long ago one of the largest and most influential meetings ever held in Sydney unanimously passed resolutions applauding to the echo Mr. Gladstone and his policy, and forwarded said resolutions to Mr. Gladstone with an address of high appreciation and respect. He says "he never saw in Australia a hungry man, or met a discontented face." He might have seen both in numbers had he only opened his eyes to look. At this very moment the Government of New South Wales have great difficulty in providing for hundreds of unemployed men, and are making work for them as best they can. Mr. Froude takes care to bespatter with extravagant eulogy only the men here who agree with him in his puerile and essentially shallow notions about what he calls "Imperial Federation," which the most rational and sensible of the Australian people treat with derision, knowing well that the ultimate fate of these great colonies is a separate and independent nationality. The people of New South Wales, as a whole, glory in the genius and power of Mr. Gladstone, and his great name is cherished among all classes with affection and respect. In this note I have pointed out a few of Mr. Froude's extravagant and ridiculous statements, and, if space permitted, they could be largely added to.—EDITOR.

MOTION OF CENSURE AGAINST THE SPEAKER.

[On Thursday, the 28th of March, 1885, Mr. Buchanan moved the following motion standing in his name:—"That the act of the Speaker of this Assembly attending a public political and party banquet given to the Ministry by their friends and supporters was inconsistent with the neutrality and impartiality of his office, and not favourable to the fair and upright conduct of the business of this House." When the House met, Mr. Buchanan gave notice of his intention to add the following words to the above motion, namely, "That the act of the Speaker of this Assembly attending and taking part in a public political and party meeting concerning a matter of a political interest so intense that the whole community were arrayed against each other in two hostile camps, was entirely inconsistent with the character of his high office and disrespectful to this House;" and, further, "That the action of the Speaker in enforcing upon this Assembly the new rules of the House of Commons, rules notoriously instituted by that body to suppress a state of absolute riot there, was an insult and a degradation to the character of this Assembly, from which it was the duty of the Speaker to take the lead in defending it." The Speaker ruled that Mr. Buchanan could not move the additional words he proposed to add to his motion. Mr. Buchanan, therefore, contented himself by moving the motion as it stood on the business paper of the House, and he did so in the following speech :—]

Mr. Speaker—It was from a high sense of public duty that I put this motion on the paper.

I desire to enter upon the discussion of it with perfect calmness. I am perfectly aware of the delicacy that attaches to such a proceeding, and I am equally aware how essentially important it is that the conduct of the Speaker of this Assembly should, on all occasions, be far above the possibility of doubt or question. When it is not so, a duty lies at the door of every member of this House, for the sake of its character and dignity, to interfere, promptly, as it falls to my lot to do on this occasion. I need not say how disagreeable and painful the performance of this duty is to me, but I do say that it would be ten times more painful if I allowed any consideration to silence me in view of an impropriety on the part of the Speaker of this Assembly, so flagrant that to pass it by unnoticed would be to reflect discredit as well as dishonour upon the character of this Assembly. The Speaker is chosen by a majority of the members of this House. At the time of his choice he may be an earnest partisan, but the moment he is raised to the dignity of occupying the chair he is lifted high above all thoughts of party—he becomes the mouthpiece not of any section or side of the House, but of the whole House, and as long as he continues to fill his high office he should be blind and insensible to all party interests or objects, showing no favour or leaning to either side of the House, but treating both sides and all sections of it with uniform impartiality. Holding this view of the genius and character of this great office, I can scarcely describe what I felt when I saw it announced that the Speaker had attended a banquet given to the Ministry by their friends and supporters. I felt astounded and shocked beyond expression when I

x

saw that the Speaker had identified himself with a notorious party-demonstration. It was an impropriety that no previous Speaker had ever indulged in, and I resolved that, if no other member of this House brought it under public notice, that I myself would not fail to do so. I mentioned the matter to several friends, among whom were members of the House, and they all denounced this act of the Speaker in much stronger terms than I am now using. I think honourable members will agree with me that the Speaker should be scrupulously exact, at all times and places, in guarding himself from any misconception of his conduct; notoriously, he ought to avoid all such positions as attending public meetings of a party character, or public events got up for the honour and glory of any party in the State. What could be more palpable than that this banquet was a party banquet, when we know it was the Government who were selected, by their friends and supporters, for this honourable recognition? In this House a large section of it meet the Government as opponents, and do their utmost by every fair and constitutional means to destroy them. The banquet was given to honour men whom we, on this side of the House, are constantly trying to discredit and destroy. We do this because we imagine that their presence on the Government benches is an injury to the best interests of the country. We are a component part of this Assembly—the Speaker presides over us as well as the Government, and we have exactly the same claim to his consideration as that enjoyed by the Government; and any Speaker who acts in conformity to the spirit and character of his office will avoid, with religious punctilio, the very thought of appearing

to lean to one side more than another. Now, I
ask this House, could a party feeling, or leaning,
be shown more conspicuously than by the Speaker
of this Assembly attending a party banquet got up
by the friends of the Ministry to do them honour?
Could a stronger party disposition be shown by anyone? At such a banquet, no doubt, the members
of the Opposition were pretty sure to be singled
out for severe and caustic criticism—their efforts
and themselves covered with contempt and ridicule.
Will anyone say that it was decent or proper for
the Speaker to be present at a meeting of this
description, listening, it may have been, to a
section of the Assembly he presides over, equally
entitled to his respect with any other section,
misrepresented, abused, and ridiculed with all the
added gusto superinduced by the freest application
of the wine cup? It is in vain for the Speaker
or his apologists to allege that the banquet in
question was not a party affair. The Ministry is
the head of a party, the offspring of party, dis-
tinctly called into existence and created by party;
and nothing conceivable could so much partake of
political party spirit, or feeling, as a demonstration
got up in honour of any Ministry. Party is the very
life of a Ministry; apart from it it would die. No
Ministry could live an hour separated from party,
any more than a human body could live separated
from the spirit. To say that this banquet to the
Ministry had nothing to do with party is about as
ridiculous as to speak of a prayer meeting that
had nothing to do with religion. A Ministry can
no more divest itself of the quality of party than
arsenic can divest itself of the quality of poison;
and it would be as absurd to speak of a public
banquet to the Ministry that had nothing to do
with party as to say "This is a dose of arsenic," but

it has nothing to do with poison." I ask honourable members would it have been proper for the leader of the Opposition to have gone to this banquet to the Ministry in honour of men whom to oust from their positions is his thought by day and night, and the business of his life ? If, therefore, it is an impossibility, from regard to common decency, that the leader of the Opposition should appear at such a banquet, how much more was it incumbent on the Speaker of this House to guard himself and his office from the faintest breath of adverse criticism, to say nothing of just and righteous condemnation which was sure to light upon him by such conduct ? This House may be divided into two parties only, and it may be divided into a dozen. It is the duty, the religious duty, of the Speaker to stand aloof from them all; to be as friendly and courteous to the one as to the other; to be entirely free from any taint of partisanship. Can anyone tell me that the Speaker is in that position when he goes and sits down with the supporters of the Government at a banquet especially arranged in their honour and for their support ? Can it be said that the Speaker of any Parliament, in so acting, has not departed from the tone of high-minded, strict impartiality that should at all times govern the conduct of such an officer ? No one who understood clearly what he was doing would go to a demonstration in honour of any Government unless he meant it to be understood that he was a supporter and partisan of that Government. If he was not favourable to the Government he had no right there. If this applies to any private citizen, with what tenfold force does it apply to a gentleman holding the high office of Speaker ? The Speaker's duty to all parties should have kept

him away from such a meeting; and it is just
because he owes a duty to all parties, in virtue of
the office he holds, that he should be scrupulously
careful to avoid giving offence to any. For my
part, I know of no course that could be adopted
by the Speaker better calculated to give very gross
offence to the opponents of the Government than
his attending a banquet got up for the especial
honour of the Ministry. The Speaker carries
great weight and influence wherever he goes, and
his presence at the Ministerial banquet went far
to support and bolster up a weak and decaying
Ministry. I say, broadly, that this was unpardonable conduct on the part of the Speaker, and I do
not envy that man who thinks otherwise. I defy
any honourable member of this House to cite a
solitary instance where any Speaker of the British
Parliament was ever guilty of similar conduct to
that I am at present commenting upon; and I am
perfectly certain that if the Speaker of the House
of Commons attended a banquet given in honour
of the Gladstone Government, or any Government,
that sharp and instant action would be taken in
the House of Commons to bring down upon
such conduct its just and proper condemnation.
If honourable members consider this matter
without prejudice, I am sure they will say with
me that the Speaker of this Assembly committed
a grave mistake in appearing at this banquet;
and if they do so, they will of course vote with
me. For my part I neither know nor care
how they will vote. I have not even asked any
one to second this motion, and I do not know
whether it will have a seconder. But if it is not
seconded it will not be for want of conviction on
the part of many honourable members, because
numbers of them have expressed to me their strong

sense of the impropriety of the Speaker's conduct. (Honourable members: "Name.") I know this House very well. It is with me at heart, but it is too cowardly to act.—Mr. Speaker: The honourable member will be encouraged in every way to proceed with his speech, but he cannot be allowed to do so until he has withdrawn the expression of gross insult to this House which has just fallen from his lips. The honourable member may, under this motion, insult the chair to his heart's content, but the chair must protect the House from insult. The honourable member must withdraw the words he has used, and must apologise to the House for their use.—Mr. Buchanan: I withdraw the words.—Mr. Speaker: Does the honourable member apologise?—Mr. Buchanan: I apologise, and I am astonished at the anxiety of Mr. Speaker. —Mr. Speaker: The honourable member will please resume his seat. The chair is very anxious to hear the honourable member until the close of his speech, and I hope the honourable member will not resort to any action which will have the effect of suspending his discourse.—Mr. Buchanan: Do not threaten me, sir, but do whatever else you like.—Mr. Speaker: The honourable member should know that I am not in the least degree likely to threaten any honourable member of this House. The honourable member having insulted the House, he must not only withdraw that insult but must tender an apology to the House. The House will agree with me that the honourable member cannot be allowed to proceed until he has taken that course.—(Honourable members: "Hear, hear.")—Mr. Buchanan: The other evening a gentleman on the Opposition benches indulged in grossly disorderly language, but the Speaker did not threaten him because he happened to be Sir

John Robertson.—Mr. Speaker: The honourable member must confine himself to the motion of which he has given notice, and it is not competent for the honourable member to indulge in any invective of the chair apart from that matter. I am sure, however, that the House is assured of the impartiality of the chair on the occasion to which the honourable member refers. — (Honourable members: " Hear, hear.")—Mr. Buchanan: In reference to the Speaker's remark that I am at liberty to insult the chair to my heart's content, I protest against this remark from the Speaker. I appeal to honourable members—have I insulted the chair since I began to speak? I have not used any language which is in the slightest degree improper. It was not my purpose to insult the chair, and whatever I have said has been said by me more in sorrow than in anger. Had it been my cue to even speak harshly of the gentleman who occupies the chair of this honourable House, the circumstances which surround the motion I am now discussing would afford me ample and just grounds for that purpose, but I have studiously avoided saying a word that could be fairly construed into an insult to the chair, and the apparent feeling displayed by the Speaker in using the words I protest against seem to give some sort of colour to the thought that the Speaker is now satisfied that the gentleman occupying the high position of Speaker of this honourable Assembly cannot attend any public, political, party banquet, or meeting, without inflicting degradation on his great office and insult upon this House. If I do not find a seconder to this motion, I, at all events, stand out as one who has done his utmost for the vindication of the honour and character of Parliament, as well as for the purity and honour of the chair. If this motion is not seconded, it will not matter much to me. I have nothing to do with that. Honourable members are the masters of their own actions. All I know is, that many of them have, privately, expressed as strong an opinion as I have in reference to the impropriety that has demanded the action I am now taking. It is now for the House to say whether this act of the Speaker's in attending a political party banquet was consistent with the dignity, honour, and impartiality that should, at all times and all places, distinguish the gentleman occupying the high and honourable position of Speaker of this House.

The motion was seconded by the honourable member for the Upper Hunter, Mr. John Mc Elhone, who was the only member who voted with the mover. Several members walked out and did not vote at all, and forty members recorded their votes against the motion. Mr. Mc Elhone was the member who was solely instrumental in procuring the Speaker's nomination for the office. But for Mr. McElhone the Speaker would not have been nominated, and, having procured his nomination, Mr. McElhone was indefatigable in his efforts to obtain victory, and may be said to have been the main cause of the victory that was secured. Mr. McElhone has always had the courage of his opinions, and the honesty to act upon them under every state of circumstances. He is one of those members, rarely met with, who vote for what they believe to be the truth apart from every other consideration, a line of conduct not often followed by all of the members of the Parliament of New South Wales. After this debate Mr. Buchanan wrote to some of the most distinguished of England's public men, asking "If they thought it right for the Speaker of any free Parliament to attend a public banquet to the Ministry of the day, or a public political meeting, and move a resolution, although among the resolutions to be moved there was one approving of the policy of the Government touching the matter as to which the meeting was convened?" The following letters received in answer from the Speaker of the House of Commons, and the then leader of the Opposition, Sir Stafford H. Northcote, take exactly Mr. Buchanan's view of the matter, and decide it entirely in his favour. Mr. Gladstone declines to answer the question, but his letter is given as interesting and curious.

"May 5th, 1885.

"SIR,

"In reply to your letter of the 27th of March, received to-day, I am directed by the Speaker to say that the Speaker of the House of Commons in this country is entirely disassociated from political parties, and he would not consider it consistent with his duty to attend either the public banquet to the Ministry of the day or the public political meeting referred to by you. The Speaker on a dissolution is free to act as other candidates for Parliament, with such restraint, however, as is imposed upon him by the fact that he remains Speaker till the new Parliament assembles.

"I am, sir, your obedient servant,
"EDWARD PONSONBY,
"Speaker's Secretary.
"To D. Buchanan, Esq., M.P."

Sir Stafford H. Northcote is not less clear and distinct in his answer.

"30, St. James's Place,
                    "May 5th, 1885.
"SIR,
       "In reply to your letter of the 27th March,
I would say that according to present practice it
would not be thought right for the Speaker of
the House of Commons to take part in a political
meeting of a party character.
   "I have the honour to be, your faithful servant,
               "STAFFORD H. NORTHCOTE.
"David Buchanan, Esq., M.P."

         "10, Downing Street,
              "Whitehall, May 14th, 1885.
"DEAR SIR,
       "Perceiving that your letter touches upon
the borders of controversy, I should be unwilling
to reply to it if the answer were to involve giving
an opinion on any matter of doubt.   But while I
can well understand that it may be matter of
argument whether an English precedent is in all
respects applicable to New South Wales, the
facts with regard to the Speakers of the House
of Commons are among us matter of notoriety.
A Speaker in no way renounces his political creed
or any of its articles, but he places the practical
application of them largely in abeyance, on the
principle, as I suppose, that he more effectively
serves all portions of the nation, including his
own party, by promoting in the chair the efficiency
of the House of Commons in general than by a
purely personal action, more directly connected
with his opinions, but lying within a narrower
and lower sphere.   The constituency of the
Speaker is no doubt entitled to call upon him, as
any other constituency is entitled to call on any
other member, in what pertains to his direct re-

lations with them; but this power is commonly exercised with much consideration and reserve. I have never known a case of a Speaker rejected at the poll when anticipating re-election to the chair. I remember in 1834 an occasion when the Speaker of the day, speaking in Committee of the whole House with reference to a matter specially touching his constituents, and much contested, said he should certainly hold himself entitled to give a vote on the merits if he thought proper. The Chairman of Committees, who is also Deputy-Speaker, exercises in a very limited degree something of the abstention observed by the Speaker; he votes freely, except when in the chair, but he does not often interfere actively in debate on contested matters, or in political action out-of-doors. The Lord Chancellor is Speaker of the House of Lords, and interferes in politics by speech and vote, and by acting in the Cabinet—but he is not armed with the large powers over debate and procedure which is entrusted to the Speaker of the House of Commons. Having said thus much, I would rather, at the same time, not take upon me to answer any question applicable to a peculiar case and combination of circumstances, which I think would be beyond my province.

"I have the honour to be, dear sir, your faithful servant,

"W. E. GLADSTONE.

"David Buchanan, Esq., &c., &c., &c."

A SCENE IN THE HOUSE.

[On a motion before the House in reference to the Bathurst Jury List, an honourable member, more distinguished for wealth than any other quality, made an uncalled-for attack on Mr. Buchanan, not in the best of taste, which called forth the following effective reply :—]

Mr. ——: I notice whenever the honourable member for the Western Gold Fields, Mr. Buchanan, speaks in this House he is pretty sure to make an attack upon the squatters. He should remember the time when the work the squatters gave him to do enabled him to keep body and soul together, and probably saved him from starvation.

Mr. Buchanan : Mr. Speaker,—The honourable gentleman who has just sat down has, with admirable taste and propriety, reminded me of the days when I was a labouring man in this country, doing work for the squatters and others. What the honourable member says is true. I did labour in the way he states, and this is a part of my history that I delight to speak of among my friends. But suppose the honourable member had been in my position, would he ever have found his way into this House? I am afraid he would have lived and died a labouring man, if he had heart or spirit enough to sustain him in that position. The

honourable member is very much at his ease in
the possession of inherited riches, which he, of
course, gained by the accident of birth.   But just
let him come out from behind the shelter of his
great wealth, and let us both be placed in a
foreign land without a friend and without a
shilling in either of our pockets. How would it
fare with the honourable gentleman under those
circumstances?   Well do I know what the result
would be — while I would, most certainly, be
struggling with difficulties, kicking obstacles out
of the way, and bending my whole mental and
physical energies to the subjugation of all opposing forces, what would the honourable gentleman
be doing?   Why, to a certainty, his poor little
heart would be sinking and dying within him, and
he would, in the depth of his heart-broken despair, inevitably crawl to my door, where I would
be shocked to see him, in rags and wretchedness,
on his knees soliciting my charity and commiseration.   The honourable gentleman may thank his
stars that I have dealt so leniently with him, and
he should also feel grateful for this effort of mine
to teach him a little wisdom and humility. (Loud
cheers from all sides.)

APPENDIX.

THOUGHTS ON THE IRISH QUESTION.

TO THE EDITOR OF THE "DAILY CHRONICLE."

Sir,—Even here, in the middle of the Red Sea, the distraction, and, as Carlyle would say, the delirium, of English statesmen and politicians on this Irish question is patent enough. In throwing out a few thoughts on the monstrous folly that seems completely to blind Mr. Gladstone and his insincere pretended followers in this matter, I would like in the first place to ask Mr. Gladstone, or any one of his supporters, what right or political privilege at present enjoyed by Englishmen or Scotchmen is denied to Irishmen? The answer to this question must be, clearly and undeniably, that no right enjoyed by either Englishmen or Scotchmen is denied to Irishmen; that they all enjoy the same and equal rights; and that, therefore, the claims of the Irish are groundless and untenable, unless they aim at declaring themselves an independent nation, which is their true aim and object, however much they may attempt to disguise or deny it. Since the Catholics were emancipated and the English Church disestablished the Irish people have had nothing to complain of that political action of the ordinary stamp could not easily remedy any more than their brethren of England and Scotland, and the agitation and turmoil that has continued in Ireland, in spite of the reforms mentioned and the disposition of England to go all reasonable lengths in this line, means, if it mean anything, complete and entire severance from England, and Irish independence, and this Bill of Mr. Gladstone's will give them this as effectually as if they had never been united or connected in any way whatever. How well the Irish leaders know this a blind man might see, but our poor peddling English rulers and their pliant followers affect not to see it, and are now engaged playing the game of the Irish national party to rare perfection. The weakness and wretched futility of English statesmen have rendered it now a very difficult matter to govern Ireland, and in the absence of the competent and determined man for that grave duty, it would be infinitely preferable to let Ireland go rather than to witness the wreck and ruin that will be the sure result of any further continuance of that feebleness and hesitating imbecility that has so long prevailed, and that has been taken so much advantage of.

A hundred times sooner let Ireland go free, and rule herself as best she may, than look on at a repetition of such rule as English statesmen have mocked with the name of government for years past. The verdict of posterity will be that England did not deserve to hold Ireland, because, through the imbecility and weakness of her rule, there was no security for either life or property, crime in a large degree went unpunished, and that, while crime was rampant and lawlessness almost universal, the poor, weak, infirm English Government, instead of striking with all its force at such a state of things, propounded pitiful measures of conciliation, degenerating into mere namby-pambyism and dangerous effeminacy—and this by way of curing the evil! The first duty of a ruler is to see that the law is respected. So did not think Mr. Gladstone on the occasion here referred to, but thought to convert the law-breakers into obedience by mistimed and contemptible measures of conciliation. One would think that a child might have known that conciliation was the last thing to be thought of while insolent rebellion was rampant, and lawlessness the main feature of almost every district in Ireland. Who can wonder that lawlessness and crime have now triumphed over weak and cowardly rulers, and that the connection between England and Ireland will soon be spoken of as a thing of the past unless a very different set of men from those who have ruled of late grasp the reins? Even at this distance from the scene I am close enough to observe most extraordinary things. For instance, Mr. Bright writes a letter to a man in Birmingham saying that some day soon he will go into the whole matter " in your Town Hall." But why not in the House of Commons, where he is sent for the purpose, and which, of all places, is the most appropriate place, and, if delivered there, might have a chance of doing some good, especially among a body of men so infirm of purpose, but not probably impervious to the splendid periods of Mr. Bright? In the letter referred to Mr. Bright makes the following extraordinary statement:—"That if Mr. Gladstone's Bill had been introduced by any other person not 20 mem-

bers outside the Irish party would be found voting
for it." This statement I believe to be true, and
it is the most severe and damning censure of the
present House of Commons that could well be
imagined. Besides all this, looking at the stupidity of the Bill, if it passed in its present shape
it would place Ireland in an inferior position to
any of our free Colonies. The Colonies can
deal with Customs duties as they like, also
police and military forces. All this, under the
Bill, Ireland is precluded from touching. Does
anyone suppose that Ireland would submit
to a degraded position of this description for
a single moment? And does this not prove
the truth of what I have already said, that the
Bill means total and entire severance and separation from England for ever. It is somewhat
amusing to ordinary people to listen to Mr. Gladstone as he talks with an apparent air of triumph,
to the effect that if his dangerous and ruinous
policy is not adopted, the only alternative is
coercion for 20 years. This is about the saddest
stuff I ever heard or read of. One would think
that it was a plain A B C proposition that coercion
and punishment, not for 20 years, but for ever,
must be enforced in all countries, so long as the
law is violated and crime is rampant. The main
and prime duty of any and all Governments
worthy of the name is to put this crime and lawlessness down, and not to stay its hand in the
fiercest coercion until it is put down. This is the
course adopted in England and everywhere where
Government exists.

It may be here asked, is there any hope to be
looked for from the other party? Not a vestige.
The Parnell party, after labouring to defeat Mr.
Gladstone at the late general election, lost faith

Y

in the Tories, and turned upon them, which, of
course, prompted Lord Salisbury to trim his sails
and steer another course; and he and his followers
are now pretending to be seriously opposed to Mr.
Gladstone's Bill. But can any honest man put
the slightest faith in them? I believe, most
sincerely, that for the sake of holding office Lord
Salisbury and his friends would go as far as Mr.
Gladstone has gone in attempting to ruin both
England and Ireland; and with such facts as we
have before us, it is impossible for any upright
man to think otherwise. At all events, Lord
Salisbury will probably soon be called upon to
display the utmost force and power that is in him,
both of honesty and statesmanship, in ruling the
kingdom. If Mr. Gladstone and his Bill are rejected by the people, the task of Lord Salisbury
begins. To a man like the great Cromwell, with
a tithe of the powers and appliances that Lord
Salisbury, as Premier of England, has at his back,
the task would be a very simple one, and easily
and permanently settled. But alas! Lord Salisbury is not a man like Cromwell; and, therefore,
instead of firm and determined rule, we may look
for timidity, feebleness, vacillation, uncertainty,
and all the ills that flow from incompetence and
cowardice. To rule Ireland after Mr. Gladstone's
failure will require a prompt, decisive, and inflexible rule, till every vestige of lawlessness is
tamed into submission. Is Lord Salisbury the
man for such a crisis as this? If not, his in-
capacity will make itself apparent at once. It is
a task for a true, able, patriotic man, sound of
head and heart, fearless and unbending, and with
a nerve that will grow in firmness with the occasion. Whoever undertakes this task, minus those
qualities, will end in failure and defeat and vanish

under a tempest of derision. There is one important matter never noticed by English statesmen, although very clearly seen by them, as Mr. Gladstone exemplified when he lately wrote his pamphlet on Vaticanism, and that is, that a Roman Catholic population, in any numbers, living under a Protestant dynasty, will never be loyal and true to that dynasty. They have sworn a superior allegiance to a foreign potentate, and as all Protestant Powers repudiate the preposterous claims put forth by that potentate, his adherents will always act in his interests when those interests clash with those of the Power they are ruled by and live under. Does anyone suppose that there would be any Irish question or trouble from Ireland if Ireland was like Scotland, Protestant? It may suit the policy of English statesmen to ignore this, but it is true notwithstanding, and they know it; but if they don't know it, the Protestants of the North know it, and know farther what they have to expect from a Popish Parliament sitting in Dublin. The Protestants of the north will never suffer such a thing while the spirit of God's truth lives in them; and if this idea is persisted in, I venture to predict that it will be the cause and occasion of as bloody a resistance as ever covered with honour and glory the brave acts of their earnest and devoted ancestors. It will not be with cowardly assassinations and wretched dynamite explosions that the brave men of the North will fight their battle, nor will the issue end in a cabbage-garden. The Protestants of Ireland are high-minded, intelligent, earnest men, and their determination when put to it is unquestionable. They will have the sympathy of Scotland and England in their struggle, and the prayers of the righteous will not be wanting in resisting what, to them, will be a cruel, dastardly, and grinding tyranny. May the appeal to the English people for ever put an end to so sad a prospect by consigning Mr. Gladstone and his measure to a long, undisturbed oblivion! Then let men arise and rule like men in the spirit of those brave ones of old, who made the name of England feared and respected in every clime and country on the face of the earth. If such men do not appear, cut the tie at once that binds Ireland to England, for there will be neither peace nor advantage on any other terms. The North will then, if left to itself, most certainly subdue and conquer the South, and then the Irish of that quarter will get something like the justice they have so long clamoured for. This will be a comfort and blessing to England as well as Ireland.

I have the honour to remain, Sir,

Yours respectfully,

DAVID BUCHANAN.

Written on board R.M.S *Bulimba* while sailing up the Red Sea, June 23.

THE DECAY OF EXECUTIVE AUTHORITY IN ENGLAND.

TO THE EDITOR OF THE "DAILY CHRONICLE."

SIR,—I do not think an apology is necessary in offering a few remarks on the above subject. It is one of vital interest and importance, and it will be my earnest endeavour to write truthfully upon it, with such light and intelligence as I can command. I have long thought that there is a marked deterioration in the public life of England as compared with what it was, say, 40 years ago. There is, undoubtedly, a distinct falling off in the intellectual character of the House of Commons, and the tone of the place is very different to what it once was, while those who occupy official positions are, comparatively, weak and inferior. What I have particularly to remark is that governments seem to be afraid to do the right thing, even when they know what that right thing is. They prefer to do the wrong thing, or to do nothing at all, by way of conciliating some section of the people whom, they imagine, it would be dangerous to offend. A Government acting upon such principles is pretty sure to bring contempt upon itself, while it encourages all sorts of insolent demands on the part of different sections of the people, and teaches the dangerous lesson that continued turmoil and agitation will wring from weak and vacillating authority almost anything. I think it will be admitted by all candid persons that the different Governments of England for many years past answer pretty well to this description. To prove the truth of such an assertion, I do not require to go back to the time of Home Secretary Walpole, who on the occasion of a riotous mob assembling in Hyde Park and seriously endangering the public peace, burst into a flood of tears as he thanked Mr. Beales, who had assured him that he (Beales) would take care that the peace was preserved. This was inimitable in its way, the Home Secretary handing over all his power and authority to the irresponsible Beales, and actually thanking him, with watery eyes, for undertaking the duty. Government was pretty well washed out on this memorable occasion; but was it not equally so the other day when a lawless, plundering, villainous rabble held possession of London for several hours, sacking shops and wrecking houses at their leisure? It will surely be admitted that

Government was at a discount on this melancholy
and disastrous occasion. No excuse or apology
will in the least degree palliate the misconduct of
the Government in thus failing to protect the
people against the violence of a dangerous mob.
It will not do to say the police were at fault. The
Government, and the Government alone, was
answerable for the mischief, and it makes one
gravely reflect what might happen under a more
formidable crisis. No one doubts for one moment
the strength and force of the power that would
scatter to the four winds any repetition of such
lawlessness ; but the danger is that the Government
of the country may be in hands so feeble and trembling as to be incapable of promptly and vigorously
applying such force, thereby allowing the lawless
and dangerous elements to gain an ascendancy
difficult to control and subdue.

Looking on at the formation of the present
Government by Lord Salisbury, I can notice
action of the most questionable character on the
part of his lordship, leading one to the belief that
the Government is not to be a bold, determined
organization, resolved to rule upon high principle,
with an immovable fidelity to justice and right.
Can anyone tell me why Mr. Matthews has been
appointed Home Secretary ? He has never been
in office before. He has not, I believe, distin-
tinguished himself in debate. No one knows
anything of any administrative power he may
possess, and—worst of all—there are several men
of tried and tested ability, with infinitely higher
claims on the party, who have been passed over to
make way for Mr. Matthews. There undoubtedly
must be some reason for this extraordinary procedure. I again ask, Can anyone inform us what
that reason is? In the absence of any informa-

tion on the subject, will you allow me to guess
at the reason? Mr. Matthews is a Roman
Catholic, and probably he has been appointed to
the high and onerous office of Home Secretary,
regardless of his qualification, as a sop to the
Roman Catholics of Ireland, and by way of conciliation. This is a mere guess of mine, but if I
have lighted on the truth in my guess it will not
be long before we will see Lord Salisbury's conciliation go the full length of Mr. Gladstone's.
It is fashionable to speak of Lord Randolph
Churchill in anything but respectful terms, but I
cannot divest myself of the feeling that, in spite
of all the blame and condemnation attached to
him, I have more confidence in him as a ruler
than any member of the Administration, not excepting Lord Salisbury himself. He is a bold,
outspoken, fearless man, and for such rare and
invaluable qualities in our public life I am prepared to swallow a host of defects. People will
alter their opinion about Lord R. Churchill ere
long. It seems, as Leader of the House, he is to
be overwhelmed with the invectives of the Opposition. Very good. If this is so, I venture to
predict that the Opposition will be paid back with
compound interest, and will not continue the game
very long.

I think the history of the late Government is a
most striking exemplification of the truth of my
assertion as to the failure of Government here.
Mr. Gladstone, while admitting that coercion was
the right course to adopt, and practising it, suddenly wheels round and tries the very opposite
course, conciliation; and he does this while
crime is rampant and lawlessness everywhere
prevalent in Ireland. A short time ago he imprisoned the Irish leaders. Now, while they are

still exactly what they were, he joins them, and unites with them in doing what he so lately imprisoned them for.   Is this government, or is it not more like the total abandonment of all government, at the dictates of lawless violence and, all but, open rebellion?   The talk of giving Ireland a Parliament and still holding her bound to England is mere shallow absurdity. Once grant a Parliament to Ireland and there is an end of the English connection, simply because you cannot grant such a Parliament without giving it the full powers of a Parliament, which would sever the tie at once.   There is a piece of puerile legerdemain in connection with this subject which prompts the assertion that Scotland and Wales are to have Home Rule too.   But, as far as any of us can see, neither Scotland nor Wales wants Home Rule, and they would be great fools if they did, and I am satisfied that Ireland would be of the same mind if the bulk of its population was not Roman Catholic.   A Roman Catholic Parliament in Dublin could, of course, serve the Church materially, and such a prospect is never overlooked by that body.   But without entering further into this part of the subject, I would just like before concluding to speculate a little as to what prospect there is in reference to the maintenance of government under the present men. They have it in their power to vindicate the character of government and gain the respect of the people for an institution which has long tottered about, in trembling weakness and futile action, despised by all rational men. They will not satisfy Ireland by any legislation short of Mr. Gladstone's. Let them, therefore, be prepared to rule under those circumstances, and to rule with determined and inflexible purpose. Let there be no weakness or time-serving compromise. If they feel unfit for their positions, in God's name give them up, and open the door for Mr. Gladstone to make ducks and drakes of both countries. Better this than any feeble indecisive parleying or tampering with the great interests of a great empire. Let them strike down lawlessness and crime in every district of Ireland, and maintain, with their very lives, if necessary, the integrity and union of the empire, never ceasing to remember the great words of a great ruler of old, "I will suffer to be rolled into my grave and buried with infamy sooner than yield an inch in this great cause." May his immortal spirit guide the councils of England now and at all times is the fervent prayer of, Sir, yours very respectfully,

DAVID BUCHANAN,

Member of the Parliament of New South Wales for the last 25 years.

London, Aug, 8.

_____

IMPERIAL FEDERATION.

TO THE EDITOR OF THE "DAILY CHRONICLE."

SIR,—Imperial Federation is a fine high-sounding sonorous phrase much used in these times by certain cliques and coteries at home and abroad. A few English enthusiasts and colonial nondescripts are mainly answerable for the very small talk that is occasionally heard on this subject. When we ask any of its advocates what it means we are at once enveloped in clouds of vague high-flown sentiment signifying nothing. The nearest approach to any practical result is given us in the

idea that the Colonies are to be drawn, by some
unrevealed means, closer to the mother country,
and this is apparently to be " the be all and end
all " of the grand conception. I do not know
that this matter is anywhere talked of so much as
in Australia, and as I know pretty well the state
of things there I would like to tell the truth about
it as far as I can. Those who interest themselves
about this question in the Australian Colonies are
generally a small clique of probably the shallowest
of our public men. It would scarcely be credited
in England the extent to which the lust for small
titles, such as C.M.G., K.C.M.G., &c., rages in
Australia. Whig and Tory, Radical and Republican, are with few exceptions all smitten with
this epidemic, while the body of the people look on
at the struggle among our public men for this
sorry distinction with open undisguised derision
and contempt. The curious thing is that our
chief Radicals and flaming Democrats are as
anxious for the small decoration as the most ex-
clusive Conservative, and this question of Imperial
Federation is seized upon by them and used as a
means of conciliating the goodwill of England,
and so furthering the grand object of their ambition—namely, the possession of this much coveted,
though small distinction. Some of those who
have already obtained the title so vigorously
hunted are destitute alike of public services or
public merit, and it is an insoluble riddle in
Australia to this hour how some of those titles
have been obtained.

In noticing the deputation that waited on Lord
Salisbury the other day on this matter of Imperial
Federation I did not know a single Australian
name but that of Mr. Service, and I venture to

affirm that there is not a public man in Victoria
or New South Wales unknown to me. I observed
that Mr. Service was designated on that occasion
as the Hon. James Service—this is an illustration
of that vulgar colonial love of title that I have
spoken of. Mr. Service should have been designated
plain Mr. Service, minus the title, and I mention
this simply to introduce a very good story on the
subject. If a colonial Minister has been three
years in office he is entitled to wear the title
Honourable before his name on application to and
leave granted by her Majesty the Queen, but this
title and privilege is granted to him only within
the colony. He cannot adopt the title unless he
applies for and receives leave to do so. Fancy a
man applying to the English authorities to be
allowed to call himself honourable! The story I
was about to tell was this: A Member of Parliament in Sydney, having so applied, was addressed
in the House as "The Honourable Member,
honourable within the colony only, and, as a
natural consequence, dishonourable everywhere
else." The chorus of laughter occasioned by such
a joke as this does not deter men from making so
contemptible and humiliating an application as
the one referred to, and serves to show how strong
is the mania among colonials for the very smallest
of titles.

There is no doubt that the Australian Colonies are
loyal and true to England beyond expression,
which the people always affectionately speak of as
home, and love with their whole hearts, but this
does not prevent them from looking closely to
their own interests, or from seeing what is detri-
mental or advantageous to them. With all their
loud and genuine professions of loyalty to the

mother country, they are sensitively alive to the slightest danger to themselves, and would, as far as I can see, sacrifice the English connection at a moment's notice if circumstances necessitated such action. Every nation on the face of the earth is governed and guided by self-interest, and under the fierce friction of this imperious instinct every consideration but that of self-preservation and self-advantage is swallowed up. Australia proved this very palpably in the late New Guinea agitation, when loud and menacing cries of separation, both in the Press and by the people in public meeting assembled, reverberated through the land. No doubt the earnest, reflecting people of England would have not the slightest objection to this separation. The Australian Colonies have been doing their very best of late to embroil England with both Germany and France, and if the language and attitude of Australia at present adopted, is persisted in, England will be landed in no end of dangerous trouble.

The colonists have an enormous territory unpeopled, and the population of the whole Australian Continent is about a million less than London; yet they keep demanding that England shall take possession of this island and that island, without a thought of the responsibility and difficulty entailed upon England by so doing. Mr. Service talks about negotiating the French out of the Hebrides and the Germans out of New Guinea, as if the Australians could make the slightest use of either place if they had it. The French, of course, have no right in the Hebrides in the face of treaties prohibiting them; but England may be relied upon to see to this without being embarrassed by the pompous and impotent threats of the Colonies. As to New Guinea, I trust that the Germans will remain there and colonise a most unpromising land —they are excellent colonists, and would be admirable and friendly neighbours of ours.

Just let us reflect for a moment. What is going on alongside of this silly agitation for what is called Imperial Federation?—no one as yet being able to tell us what Imperial Federation means. At the very heart of the Empire itself there are elements of disruption at work, which have just been stilled by the strong sense and patriotic determination of the people. Does any sane man, under such circumstances, think it prudent and politic to ask England to take upon herself increased governmental responsibilities as to countries thousands of miles away from her with opposing interests and aspirations, and growing rapidly into powerful independent nations. He must be short-sighted indeed who does not see the inevitable future of Australia. That she will rise into an independent nation in the near future is certain enough, and that such a consummation should be devoutly wished by both England and Australia should go without saying. As things are at present the connection between Australia and England is a danger to both countries. Every war that England is involved in is a danger to Australia. Australia has no voice in the declaration of those wars, and may entirely disapprove of them,·yet she is open to be struck by any, or all, of England's enemies; while England, in the midst of all manner of foreign complications, of which Australia is totally and entirely ignorant, may be, by the action of Australia, involved in foreign quarrels which would never have been thought of but for this useless connection; besides, the ex-

pense to England of defending those numerous
Australian Colonies is by no means an inconsider-
able item.   One thing is quite clear, that England
will not suffer itself to be dragooned by the
Colonies into taking possession of any further
territory, nor will she suffer dictation from them
as to the language she shall use to foreign powers.
I have seen so much inconsiderate rashness of the
Australian Colonies in talking of both France and
Germany that this alone will seriously endanger
the integrity of the tie that binds them to England, if it does not ultimately snap it.   And then
what would be the result? Things would remain
in statu quo, with this difference, that Australia
would be free from all danger from England's
enemies, and England would be relieved from no
end of trouble and embarrassment, as well as expense, in looking after those far-away possessions,
while the same extensive commerce and large correspondence would go on between the two countries
the same as ever.

I have thrown out these few thoughts to expose
the absurdity of this talk about Imperial Federation, one of the most patent anomalies of it being
that some of its most distinguished advocates have
taken the lead in the support of Mr. Gladstone's
Bill for the disruption of the home or mother
country, thus placing themselves in the singularly
absurd position of, with the one hand, attempting
to unite in one federal whole the entire empire,
and with the other trying to sever Ireland from
England.   To such absurdities do men reduce
themselves when they allow vague wild sentiment
and extravagant imaginings to usurp the place of
sound, solid reason and common sense.   Whatever
is done by England's rulers or people, I trust and

pray that the great and glorious country will ever stand out, in bold relief, the paragon of nations, the home of freedom, and the birthplace of all that is great in intellect and worth.

I have the honour to remain, Sir,
Very respectfully yours,
DAVID BUCHANAN,
Member of the Parliament of New South Wales for the last 25 years.

. London, Aug. 15.

THE END.

www.ingramcontent.com/pod-product-compliance
Lightning Source LLC
Chambersburg PA
CBHW021118270326
41929CB00009B/944